Dreamwalker

The Path of
Sacred Power

Dreamwalker

The Path of
Sacred Power

Mary
Summer Rain

Author of *Spirit Song*
and *Phoenix Rising*

**THE
DONNING COMPANY**
PUBLISHERS

Distributed by
Schiffer Publishing Ltd.
1469 Morstein Road, West Chester, PA 19380

Books by Mary Summer Rain

Spirit Song
Phoenix Rising
Dreamwalker
Phantoms Afoot
Earthway

Children's Book
Mountains, Meadows & Moonbeams

Cover art by Bern Seabourn, Oklahoma City, Oklahoma
Author photo by Dan Caldwell, Colorado Springs, Colorado

Fifth Printing

Distributed by Schiffer Publishing, Ltd.
1469 Morstein Road
West Chester, Pennsylvania 19380
Please write for a free catalog
This book may be purchased from the publisher.
Please include $2.00 postage.
Try your bookstore first.

Library of Congress Cataloging-in-Publication Data

Rain, Mary Summer.
   Dreamwalker.

   Sequel to: Phoenix rising.
   1. Spiritual life. 2. New Age movement. 3. Prophecies. 4. No-Eyes, 1892?-1984. 5. Chippewa Indians—Biography. 6. Shamans—Colorado—Biography. 7. Chippewa Indians—Religion and mythology. 8. Indians of North America—Colorado—Religion and mythology. I. Title
BP605.N48R33   1988   133.80924   88-20221
ISBN: 0-89865-622-2 (pbk.)

Printed in the United States of America

AUTHOR'S NOTE
Readers interested in contacting Mary Summer Rain directly concerning any of her titles, may write her at:
P.O. Box 6699
Woodland Park, CO 80866
Please include a stamped, self-addressed envelope.

Contents

To my precious friend, Many Heart—
For sustaining me through the Thirsty Season,
For easing me over the long, rougher Trails,
And for taking my hand and guiding me further
along the Sacred Path of the Dreamwalker.

It has been said that Dreamers are but mere Fools. Yet tell me, what damaging criteria do wise men judge the poor Fools by?

I once observed the passing procession of a revered Wise Man whom I perceived as being quite the Fool, while, hidden within the onlooking crowd gathered along the wayside, I did spy a simple commoner whose gentle eyes sparkled with the intense clarity of deep inner wisdom.

Who the Fool?

Who the Wise Man?

One speaks eloquently.

One stands mute.

But you are clever. You say you can differentiate between the two. Therefore, I caution you, take your judgment and place it before the Entity of Truth. Go seek the One who sees clearly through Men's elaborate exterior facades.

My friend, go and ask the Dreamwalker.

Author's Foreword

The Way is brightly illuminated by the eternal Beacon of Light that emits from the Eye of the Source.

We are but minute motes, seemingly inconsequential, drifting aimlessly within the Light's warm current; learning and absorbing Its nourishing Life Force—Its ancient Heritage of Spirit. And, tumbling this way and that within the starry embryonic fluid, we grow in enlightenment and discover our fumbling way back to the Source, until ultimately, we are once again within the secure Womb from whence we came.

The eventual trail of a man's life is ironic indeed. The events that ultimately materialize are oftentimes those that have not been carefully calculated, neither have they been logically anticipated. We have scores of self-expectations, some great, for our future. We meticulously plot our lives according to real life goals and, sometimes, from the colorful musings of daydreams. And we become conscious centered, one-minded in the high business of bringing those all-important goals and daydreams to a touchable fruition.

But nature has other ideas for us, and because of various quirks and twists that prove to detour the stringent path of our goals, we are frequently caught off course—sometimes far off the intended mark. This straying is not in itself a negative aspect, if one takes the intelligent time to analyze its purpose; for most detours prove to be required acquisitions needed in order to gain advancement along one's selected byway through life.

Goals and dreams are necessary in our valiant attempts to accomplish the gaining of productive and resourceful lives, but the inevitable sidetracks are an unavoidable fact that must be accepted with logic and grace. The walking of unexpected detours often bestows precious insight to hazards avoided and pitfalls circumvented. The detours frequently prove to be pathways to vital perceptions needed to continue the chosen course of life.

So day by day, and mile by mile, we tread upon the trails that are spread out before us. We make the choices, reap what vital knowledge is made available to us and, ideally, become a better individual for the physical or spiritual effort it has caused us to expend. And, as we exit the detour and gaze onto the path we have chosen, we take a last look behind us—over the detoured trail, and we ask ourselves, "What was it all for? What have I learned? What needed wisdom was granted to me?" And hopefully, we will be able to step upon our path with the light heart that comes with the awareness of one or more revealed truths. Hopefully, we will continue with the deeper comprehension that accompanies acceptance of that newfound wisdom.

There are a rare few who have traversed many a detour; in fact, they have traveled so many altered byways that they have accepted those unexpected paths as being the norm for their way through life. They have shed a personalized goal in deference to being led by the spirit, thereby observing, absorbing, and learning all the glorious facets of knowledge that truth has laid before them. And by accepting those trails with a pure and open heart and mind, these brave travelers have shed the yoke of desire and self-want. They have discarded the need for material gain and they have discarded all evidence of negative thought in order for reality to consume their clear-thinking conscious-ness and for acceptance to thrive within their tender hearts.

Perhaps one day, while you are irritated and angered because you have been detained upon a seemingly unnecessary byway, you will perchance come upon a gentle individual who is clear of eye and soft of voice. Perhaps along one of your byways, you will have the good fortune to come upon a Dreamwalker.

August

Season of the copper Moon of Thirst

Night of the Weeping Moon

Only the Fool says that Nature does not, cannot, weep.

It was August. And as the first weekend of that late summer month drew nearer, I found myself without any definite plans for the first time in a long while, as my routine weekend visit out to No-Eyes' cabin was being postponed.

During my last meeting with her, she had casually announced that she was expecting visitors to come out to her place the first weekend of August and that I would be free to spend some extra time with my family. And, even though I loved driving through the mountains to spend my days with the wise visionary who soon became someone dear to my heart, I found myself appreciating the brief hiatus that was unexpectedly granted.

I knew the old one had several friends who frequently visited her and caringly updated her supplies of staples. They'd make the long drive once a month up to her remote cabin from the southern city of Pueblo. They'd stay the entire day performing various chores for her, chopping wood and stacking it beside her fireplace, housecleaning, etc. But when she mentioned the visitors this time, her tone of voice was altered and, although she coolly maintained a facade of nonchalant indifference, I knew that her anticipated guest or guests were not the usual routine ones—these were going to be special. I knew so. I caught the sudden sparkle of excitement that flashed from her ebony eyes. And I subliminally wondered if these special people had anything to do with me.

The silent split-second musing didn't pass unnoticed. The old one bowed her head and shook the wispy grey hairs. "Summer not be *only* person No-Eyes be concerned 'bout. Why you think you be only person No-Eyes workin' with?" She raised her proud head and stepped closer to me. We were nearly nose to nose as she raised a bony finger and stabbed it in my face. "Tsk-tsk," she clucked, "Summer not be No-Eyes' *only* business. No-Eyes got others of importance to deal with. No-Eyes got *powerful* others to meet with."

I had apologized for my seemingly egotistical display of pompous self-worth. And, on my way home that late Sunday afternoon, my thoughts were centered on who her special guests might be. Could she be teaching someone else at the same time she was instructing me? Was this other student proving to be an accomplished adept? She had said that he was powerful. My feelings of inadequacy were surging full force to the surface. Maybe I wasn't performing well—up to her high expectations. Maybe I was merely a mediocre student. I had thought we were relating well with one another. I had thought we two had developed a unique sort of companionship, a sensitive understanding, a special bond. But now, all my doubts surged to the forefront, they humbled me down to believing myself to be the lowly student that I truly was. After all, I reconsidered, the aged visionary had said more than once that she was here to teach, so why would I be the only one to occupy her schoolroom? And what would make me so high and mighty to so boldly think that I was the one to be at the head of the class? Yes, I was merely a simple learner, a common seeker. Of course No-Eyes would have students who were more accomplished than I, and I felt a flush of shame warm my cheeks as I remembered her sharp words that accompanied the accusing finger—words that effectively served to cut me back down to size.

It was these same thoughts that wove in and out of my mind as I lay awake on Saturday morning. The silent house was like a dark cocoon wrapped securely around all the other sleeping occupants. The strangeness of being home hit hard, for ordinarily I'd have been up and on my way to my schoolhouse by now.

In the solitary silence, I watched the first rays of predawn greyness slice through the wooden slats of our woven bedroom blinds. I felt out of place—out of sync—being here with a free weekend, with nothing constructive planned. I was so used to being with No-Eyes, so accustomed to having something physical to do, having my mental faculties pulled and stretched to their expanded limits, and I wondered how I could possibly occupy the many upcoming empty hours without feeling restless. Then my serious ponderings were interrupted. I turned to look at Bill. He was studying me.

"Feel sort of funny, don't you," he perceived softly. "Feel strange being here—kind of like the odd man out."

I smiled as I turned into his outstretched arm. And resting my head into the crook of his arm, I laid my hand over his chest. "Yeah, I do. As a matter of fact, I was just thinking about how I could occupy this weekend."

He frowned and recoiled in hurtful dismay. "You mean to say that three kids, a dog, and a husband aren't enough to keep you busy?"

I playfully slapped his chest. "That's not what I mean and you know it! That's not what I meant at all."

He hugged me and grinned. "I know, I know," he soothed patronizingly.

Silence filled the room while the Entity of Daybreak grew in radiance and flooded through the blind's narrow spaces.

Bill's soft voice broke through the stillness. "I know what we could do this weekend," he said excitedly. "We could clean out the garage!"

I gave him an incredulous look. "You're kidding, right?"

And expertly maintaining a serious countenance, he continued, "Well...no. We've been talking about doing that for weeks now. This would be a great opportunity to get it out of the way."

I rose up on my elbow and looked him hard in the eye.

His veneer cracked. "Well," he laughed, "it was just a thought."

I grinned and snuggled back down into his warmth. "Any more brainy thoughts like that and you can just keep them to yourself."

Just then, the bedroom door exploded open and three kids and a dog pounced onto the bed. The girls were bubbling with heightened static excitement, and Rainbow was busy raining wet kisses on the two covered occupants.

"Com'on you guys! Better get going, it's getting late!" they screamed at us.

I suspiciously looked from one kid to another. And seeing their wide eyes glowing with a secret shared, I then slid my glance over to their co-partner in crime. Some heavy conniving had been transpiring behind my back and I was going to get to the bottom of it. I leered at the grown accomplice. "Getting late for what?" I asked. "Better get going where?"

The guilty party merely shrugged his shoulders. He was feigning ignorance of the whole affair.

Rainbow barked and playfully growled as she attempted to nose her way beneath the comforter.

Jenny, our oldest daughter, giggled while trying to pull the weighty animal away as I prodded Bill for more information.

He maintained ignorance, while Rainbow, frustrated at having failed to gain access to the space between the adults, busied herself with grabbing the blanket between her teeth and backing away with the covers.

The bedroom was suddenly filled with joyful bedlam. Squealing kids, growling and tugging dog, pleading mother and grinning, denying father; and above all this commotion, the doorbell was furiously ringing in the background. Rainbow's hackles stiffened threateningly at the shrill rings and she leaped off the bed, skidded around the doorway and charged headlong to bark at the front door. On her heels, the girls raced behind her. "I'll get it. I'll get it. They're here!" they shouted excitedly.

That was it! "All right," I finally growled at my wide-eyed innocent partner, "who's here? What's going *on*?"

He shrugged.

I was about to playfully tickle it out of him when a familiar voice called from the open doorway. "Hey, you two! You guys can get frisky anytime! We've got to get going!"

Our best friends were standing just inside the room. I looked in amazement at their grinning faces, then turned back to the Innocent. "Oh, sure, we're going to clean out the garage. Oh, sure, you don't know what's going on."

The kids and the dog were back in full force trying to pull us up. "Julie and Bob got a new RV!" they cried. "Come an' see it!"

And after all the excitement wound down, I finally got my answers. Bill had conspired with our friends; we were to join them on a weekend camping trip into the high country. They had secretly planned it all out to the last detail. Figuring I'd be somewhat at a loss not being with No-Eyes, they had thoughtfully and lovingly made sure I'd be well occupied, and now it appeared we were late getting on the road.

The new RV turned out to be a camper's marvel. I had been used to dome tents, portable cookstoves, sleeping mats, washing in streams, and outhouses (sometimes), but this was a real motor home. It was something that was far beyond our own means of ever obtaining.

The girls acted like they'd lived all their days in the dark backwoods as they peered here and poked about there, curious heads disappearing in and out of cubbyholes and cupboards trying to discover all the amazing miracles that the shiny new-smelling vehicle had. And their silent hopes and dreams were satisfied when Bob assured them that he and Julie would indeed include them on their next camping adventure—as long as they were good while mom and dad were out this time.

Of course, our friends knew that that stipulation wasn't needed, as our girls were always trusted to behave whenever they were left alone in charge of the house. And these days, having three responsible daughters who you thoroughly trusted alone—for an entire weekend—was one miraculous accomplishment. It was a blessing we never forgot to count.

So when all the hidden nooks and crannies of the vehicle were discovered and announced, when all the mysterious marvels were unveiled, we reviewed our final instructions to the girls and kissed and hugged them all around before pulling out from the driveway.

Our destination was no carefully guarded secret. We were headed west toward the Tarryall Reservoir; only we wouldn't be going the full distance, we'd be making the turnoff into the Happy Meadows camp area where fishing was popular in the course of the swift Platte River. The spot wasn't remote; neither was it unknown to other campers. And, because of our delayed start, there was a probable chance that the few overnight spots would already be occupied.

It wouldn't take us more than forty minutes to reach Happy Meadows, so while Bill sat up front recounting the laughable old Army days with Bob, Julie and I sat at the dinette table. She had just picked up the most recent issue of *New Shelter* magazine and was about to enlighten me on a new earth-bermed design when she caught me glancing about the shiny vehicle interior. Her magazine remained shielding her face; only the deep sea-green eyes peered above the pages. "I'm sorry," she crooned softly. Her unexpected voice broke my train of thought and I turned to her. "What? What'd you say?" The magazine lowered. She leaned forward on her elbows. "I said I'm sorry."

I grimaced. "What for?"

"You make me feel guilty buying this monstrosity," she confessed, while letting her gaze momentarily roam around the interior.

"Guilty? Why would I make you feel that? I think it's great you two got something like this. Why, now you can take lots of trips on weekends just like we do. It'll be great fun."

Her expression remained unchanged as she took a second to gaze out the window before facing me once again. "I caught you looking things over."

"So?" I defended. "I've never been inside one of these before. I was just thinking how like a real home it is. I was thinking about how much motel money you could save traveling about the country in one of these." Then a thought struck me and I was aghast. "You don't think I'm jealous! Do you think that?"

She grinned. "I wouldn't know you very well if I thought that. Of course I don't think you're jealous, but Bob bought this just for pleasure and I know how you guys could really use something like this the way you go gallivanting all up and down the passes all over the state in all kinds of bad weather trying to help people who ask for your assistance." Her head hung slightly. "It kinda makes me feel like you're the ones who should've gotten the RV."

I waved my hand at her. "Don't be silly, this thing is just a little beyond us; besides, if we had that kind of resources we'd have gotten a new Blazer ages ago."

She brightened. "That's just what I'm getting at. This is what you guys need because of all the traveling you do. No-Eyes has you going up one mountain and down the others and usually you can't even get home without having some sort of major breakdown. You guys really...."

"Jule," I cut in, "will you quit it! That's just the way it is. You and Bob have wanted a nice RV for a long time and now that you have one—enjoy it! Honestly, why you'd want to mess up your happiness with contrived psychological barriers is beyond me."

"Yes, but...."

"No buts about it. End of story."

"But the way you were looking around, well, it sorta broke my heart to know how...."

"We're here!" came the driver's announcement as the huge vehicle slowed for the turn.

I reached out for Julie's hand and softly admonished. "Please, no more of this silly talk. Enjoy the extra pleasures you've been granted. Enjoy your fortunate blessings—you've both deserved them."

My stubborn friend was about to make a last-ditch protest.

I raised a cautioning finger to my lips. "Look," I exclaimed, leaning to the window, "there's a few spaces left!" And, with that, I had slammed the lid on the entire ridiculous subject, for we immediately got busy docking our ship and making her secure.

When we alighted, the rushing sounds of the Platte River welcomed us to her shore. The newcomers strolled the short distance to streamside. The waters were shallow there and you could see through the clearness to the sandy bottom. Large boulders protruded here and there, making ideal perches for water-loving sunbathers. I was anxious to get on with the fun.

It didn't take the men long to dig in. They soon had gathered up all their cumbersome fishing paraphernalia and were eagerly headed back along the dirt road where Bill had a favorite spot to angle off a wide boulder into a deep, dark hole.

Julie and I watched them amble toward the infamous area. I chuckled as she commented, "they're probably bursting with visions of record-weight Rainbow fighting furiously for life at the end of their lines." Then she noticed my mirth. "That's funny?"

"Yeah," I revealed, "last time we brought the kids here for a weekend, all he had on the end of the line was an ugly Sucker or two."

Julie's eyes widened as she made a revolting grimace. "Don't tell me you actually ate them!"

"What would you have done if Bob had been the proud dad who returned to the tent grinning like a Cheshire cat holding up his fine catch and your kids were squealing with delight at their very clever father?"

"Ugg!"

I smiled in resignation. "One does what one must."

While the clever anglers plotted their complex strategies for catching the big one, we headed back to the camper. Julie had seen some people having a hilarious time riding oversized tubes down the twisting river, and thought it'd be a great way to have a little fun.

She disappeared into the well-equipped bathroom to change into a bathing suit. From behind the mirrored door, she babbled nonstop. "This is gonna be great, huh? Just think, a weekend of fun in the sun. We'll eat fresh fish—as long as they're not any of those damned ugly Suckers. We'll build a big campfire after dark and roast marshmallows and—oh yeah, I forgot—you don't eat sweets 'cause they're acid. Well...we've got a few bottles of great wine in the fridge. We'll break those open and listen to the nightsounds of the river and we'll all get nice and rosy and mellowed out. That sound good, Mary?"

I had been sitting at the dinette, legs stretched out on the soft cushions. I had been engrossed in the article she had previously attempted to tell me about. Without breaking my concentration, I answered her, "Sounds fine to me, Jule. I could use a good mellow-out right about now."

The hidden voice chattered on. "Hey, you know those inner tubes we saw going down the river?"

"Uhuh."

"Well," she babbled on, "I think Bob's got a couple of those stashed somewhere around here. We'll have to rummage around for 'em, but I thought we could give it a go. What'd ya say?"

"Say what?"

The bathroom door flung open and a tousled blonde head peeked out. "Hey, aren't you listening?"

I guiltily looked up from the magazine. "I'm sorry, I was, but then this article kind of swept me off in another direction."

Julie sighed. "I was thinking about the rubber rafts. I said Bob's got some around here somewhere and if we can find them, we can shoot the rapids." She exited the bathroom and strode the length of the camper. Arms outstretched, my svelte friend emulated an experienced model. "Well? How'd you like it? Bob's nuts about it."

And I could see why. The little thing left nothing to the imagination. I had washed handkerchiefs bigger than her new suit. I grinned. "Very nice, quite a little number you found." I couldn't resist a friendly jab. "Where'd you find it, in the Barbie Doll department?"

Hands on hips, she brushed off the remark. "Honestly, sometimes you're such a prude." Then she twirled. "Tell me really, do you like it?"

I closed the magazine and grinned. "Yes, I do. I think you look terrific in it."

Her proud smile altered with impish mischievousness. "Good!" she squealed, "because I've got one almost like it for you!" And she reached into the bathroom to pull out the extra hankie for me. "Ta-da!" she sang, holding the stringy pieces aloft for my review.

I stared at the Day-glo color. "Your kind-hearted thoughtfulness never ceases to amaze me, but I don't wear orange and I most certainly don't wear string bikinis."

She threw the Barbie Doll suit onto the table. "Well, guess I always knew you'd say that. Tell you what, I'll scrounge around for those inner tubes while you're changing. Then we'll . . . ."

"I'm not changing," I informed quickly.

"You mean you forgot to bring along a suit?"

"Don't own one," I replied matter-of-factly.

"Why ever not?" came the shocked question.

I simply grinned.

Julie smirked. "Oh, yeah, I forgot, you and the mountain streams go au naturel. Well, you can't do that here. Obviously we're going to have to rig up some sort of suit for you."

"No, we don't."

"Now what?" she replied in exasperation.

"You know I don't wear suits. That stuff's okay for you, but I'm not comfortable in them."

She slumped her perfect "ten" figure down across the table from me. A manicured finger shook in admonishment. "You look just as good as I do. *Now* who's making up contrived psychological excuses not to have a good time? Why, that's the most ridiculous excuse I've ever heard."

I simply shrugged. I wasn't about to parade around in a suit— string or otherwise—and my friend knew she'd never succeed in getting me into one either.

She let a long exaggerated sigh escape from her bow mouth. "Well, I suppose you don't plan on going down the river either."

My head went slowly from side to side.

"Thought so," came the dejected reply. Then she dug into her purse and, pulling out a cigarette, she lit it and drew quickly on it, allowing herself to calm down.

I watched her as she'd study the scenery through the window and glance back at me. I observed her calming process.

"Look," she began softly. "I've been behaving like a certified idiot. I guess I was caught up in the initial surprise for you. And then seeing the guys so excited about their fishing, and then the rafters having so much fun, I guess I just got a little too carried away."

And, as was usual between close friends, we understood each other's needs. We each knew that "fun" didn't necessarily have to include others in order to be fully enjoyed. We respected one another's individuality and, with that realized, we began anew to delve into reaping what enjoyments we could out of the beautifully glorious day.

After searching through the many storage cupboards, we finally discovered the secret hiding place where Bob had stashed the inner tubes and, after helping Julie pump one up, I assisted in dragging it to the shore. My friend found a deep spot and crawled aboard while I wished her well and headed for the sun-touched boulder that appeared like a warm island amid the surging clear water.

I rolled up my jeans and grinned as Julie's wild laughing screams reached me from where she had been carried off downstream. Another volley of rafters swept past me, riders all laughing and squealing; they could barely hold onto their rotating ships while attempting to wave to me. I laughed and waved back.

It was good, this day. It was good medicine. All the smiling faces around gave my heart great joy. The people were laughing, the sun was smiling and the stream was giggling and I, too, was completely content as I tenaciously stepped through the swift waters and made my way toward the smooth boulder that awaited me.

Sunlight danced on the liquid surface. It glinted sparkles into my eyes, and I sighed at the deep serenity of nature's soft mood, while I reclined back onto my island of stone that offered itself as a humble place of respite. And I thanked the stone for the coolness that began radiating from it under the weight of my shadow.

Voices of the laughing rafters faded from earshot now, and as I looked up into the arching branches of the cottonwoods that swayed gracefully along the shores, gentle whisperings became audible on the delicate wings of the wind—nature was nudging me, her breath ever so hypnotic to the receiving senses. I closed my eyes and gently stepped within the golden entity where there, I walked upon the enchanted sacred ground of my journeying spirit.

Voices, distant sounds, muted sounds echoing all around. The blazing copper sun dulled into a tarnished cinnamon moon. Ashen clouds drifted sadly beneath the russet rays. A great melancholy overtook the mood of nature and, in her unknown grief, tears rained down upon the land.

Chilling droplets from the weeping entity tumbled, glistening down upon me. One, two tears; three, four; until a torrent fell upon my warm and tender soul, sending an uncontrollable shudder throughout my entire being.

"What's the matter with her?" asked one of the faraway voices.

"Nothing a quick dunk in a cold river won't cure," replied the second.

My eyes shot open. My three weekend companions were having a great time splashing icy stream water on me, and within the split-second it took to assess the situation, I realized by the lowered position of the setting sun I'd been a long while walking upon my Sacred Ground.

Within a flash, I'd rolled off the rock and began flinging back the water. Soon all four of us were involved in a very serious game of dunk whomever you could get your hands on. After we all came down with aching stitches in our sides from laughing so hard, we made a truce and dragged our soaking selves out of the water to collapse on the grassy shore. Tempting smells from our neighbors' cookfire wafted through the air.

"God, that smells good," I groaned, sniffing the delicious scents.

Bill grinned. "Just wait until you get a good whiff of *our* dinner."

"Yeah," Bob added, "if you hadn't been way out in limbo somewhere, you would've seen what we brought back for the cooks."

I excitedly sat up. "Oh no! I missed the grand entrance. What'd you catch?" I anxiously asked Bob.

His puckish smile widened. "You tell her, Bill," he urged.

I looked to Bill. He held up his palms. "No, that's all right, you snagged the first one, you get the honors."

I looked eagerly from one noble face to the other. Then, when I caught Julie's exaggerated expression of rolling eyes and general aura of disgust, I knew. "Oh no! Not Suckers!"

Julie gagged. "The ugliest damned Suckers I've ever laid eyes on."

I grimaced. "Anyone think to bring the peanut butter an' jelly sandwiches?"

"Com'on," Julie warned, "it's getting too chilly and we've got to get out of these soaked duds. We'll dry off then fix up them Suckers so they'll taste nearly good enough to actually swallow."

As we walked back to the camper, Bill and Bob trailed behind. Their muffled snickers piqued my curiosity. I felt there were more surprises in the offing. Julie had been right about the need for us to change, though. The late afternoon sun had quickly transformed into an early evening chill as so often comes quickly in the mountains.

Julie had changed with lightning speed and, by the time I stepped into the buttery glow of the RV, she had vacated the bathroom for my use. "You did bring a change of clothes, didn't you?" she asked with a grin.

I held up an extra pair of jeans and a sweater before striding into the private room. Beyond the closed door I heard whisperings and giggles. Now what delights were they plotting? Well, I'd know soon enough.

Julie, covered in her "Kiss the Cook" apron, had already filleted the fish by the time I was presentable again. And while the men used the changing room, the women busily prepared supper in the convenient kitchen area.

Finally I made the grand announcement that the Suckers were ready and, the big question was—were we? But all the succulent fixin's were spread on the table, and I had to admit that it all looked mouth-watering. I suppose that after a day in the sun and water, anything would've looked tasty. We all hungrily dug in.

After cutting off a small piece of the white meat and furtively putting it in my mouth, my eyes widened. "What'd you do to these ugly things?" I asked the grinning cook. "This is delicious!"

Silence.

I set my fork down and stared from one stifled face to the next. They were turning crimson in their feeble attempts to withhold their laughter. I looked down at the remains of my fish. "You *rats!* This isn't Sucker, it's Trout! You caught *Trout!*"

It appeared that this was to be my day for surprises. And I felt incredibly warm inside when I looked into the smiling faces of my three best friends.

That evening it was chilly enough for the need of jackets. We sat around the campfire, stream rushing beside us, and passed around the wine that brought the promised mellowing. Our conversation drifted in and out of a multitude of subjects until I brought up my journey on the rock.

"Everything was so full of joy and gaiety," I recalled, "then when I began slipping away, everything altered drastically."

"It usually does," Julie reminded.

"I know, but this wasn't just a simple alteration, it was a total change, a complete reversal of mood."

Bob drew on his cigarette. The tip glowed brightly for a moment. "Maybe we could go deeper into the precise meaning if we had more to go by. Did you get any other clues?"

Bill asked me what I felt when nature had taken her sudden turn.

I stared into the sparkling fire that snapped and crackled sending little embers up into the surrounding darkness. "A great heaviness," I said softly. "I felt an incredible sadness."

"Sadness from within or without?" Bill pried.

"From without," I answered. "It was definitely from without because it wasn't centered—it was all around, just like all of nature was weeping."

My companions looked to one another in pensive silence. An owl hooted somewhere far up within the dense mountainside.

Bob broke the stillness. "Do you think it had anything to do with the returning Phoenix—its signs?" He had been referring to the coming Phoenix Days.

I shook my head. "No, it didn't have anything to do with those, I'm certain of that much."

"How can you be so sure?" he respectfully asked.

"Feelings, just by the feelings I got."

He mulled that over, but required more input. "Well...how would your feelings differentiate a source? I mean what exact sensations tell you what's what?"

An intelligent inquiry.

I took a sip of wine and answered. "It's no deep mystery. Really, it's very basic. A psychic sensation that stems from *precognitive* insight instills no specific emotion, it's simply a knowing of a future happening. Follow me?"

Bob nodded that he did.

"But a psychic sensation that comes from *premonition* insight instills definite emotional responses such as a vital urgency of time or sharp fear."

Julie interjected, "So since you had no immediate emotional response like fear, you deduce that the sad mood didn't have anything to do with the destructive Phoenix Days."

"Right."

She continued. "Then what's it mean? What does it have to do with?"

I frowned and shrugged.

"You mean you don't know? What good are these feelings then if you're in the dark about their meanings?"

Bill poured another round from the imported bottle. "Then they serve as signs along the way. They're telling us to be aware, to be on the lookout for something approaching. And when the warnings begin to become stronger—entering reality—then we get a clearer picture of their actual intent."

She nodded that she understood. "Sort of like road signs that warn the driver of curves or steep inclines ahead."

"Yes, that's something like it," he confirmed.

Yet even though she claimed she understood—she didn't. "But what does this altered mood of nature's forewarn then?"

I tried again. "Jule, just because nature wept doesn't mean this actually represents a natural disaster."

She was intently listening. Her concentration was serious as I attempted a clearer explanation.

"It's a strong possibility that the things that materialized during my journey were purely symbolic and had nothing at all to do with nature. It could indicate a sadness of some type that will cross my path. Or it could mean that I'll be touched by the sadness of a friend's grief. It just depends on time—time will bear out the eventual souce of the advance warning."

"That's downright spooky," she crooned.

"No it's not. That's just reality—how things work."

She drained her glass. "Still . . . seems to me to be a pretty lousy way to work it. You could at least be given more direct clues."

I chuckled at her personal desire for shortcuts. "It works just perfectly, Jule, it keeps you on your toes, it keeps you aware—always aware."

The fire was dying and the gentle wind was gaining in strength. We threw handfuls of dirt on the embers and took our party inside where a few rounds of cards were played out before the fresh mountain air got to us and began producing its magic. After fighting off the nods and yawns, we gave up and retired for the night.

The beds were nothing like the camping mats I was accustomed to; they were luxuriously soft. My partner wasted no time falling victim to night's soothing calls. The rushing river had effectively lulled everyone into a deep slumber while I remained wide awake staring up at the hard ceiling of the RV. One hour passed, two crawled by. I tossed and turned in my solitude. I was restless and irritated. Something unknown pricked at my senses and, not being able to withstand the tension, I quietly pulled on my clothes, crept out of the camper, and stepped into the chilly, clear night.

The other campers were now dark, not a soul was moving about. I was alone with the mountain night as my only companion. Pulling my woven serape tighter around me, I decided to go for a walk. I'd follow the river. My deerskin moccasins made silent footfalls through the soft wild grasses, my exit went unnoticed. And, pleased that I hadn't disturbed any of the sleepers or aroused any of the dogs that people had brought, I approached the stream and stared down into its surging waters. Mountain streams and rivers always fascinated me—their churning waters eternally racing downstream. They were a study in continual motion—nature's most animated facet of her majestic personality.

Where have you been, water spirit? What wonderful secrets have you to tell? Where are you bound for? Who has listened to you along the way? Who have you shared your mysteries with? Did they understand?

I threaded my way through the maze of willows alongside the damp bank when I came to a sandy clearing and sat in the silvery moonlight. I threw a rock into the roaring waters—no receiving sound of its splash could be heard above the constant din. And, pulling up my knees, I rested my head down on them and closed my eyes.

There it was again. Nature was altering once more.

Without bothering to look at the physical evidence, I could feel the subtle nuance of changes that shifted in the breeze. The quality of the river's voice had become more weighted. The sand beneath me cooled as ghostly clouds gathered around the face of the Moon Man. Heavy sighs hushed from the rustling cottonwoods and the surrounding air became thickened—all clear evidence of nature's extreme melancholia.

I raised my head to the somber night sky. No wondrous twinkling stars winked down at me, for the dark funereal shroud had been draped over their brilliant canopy. And, returning my attention to the river, I deciphered its nebulous cries of despair. Nature's bond within me was strong. My heart sank with the deep sorrow I was absorbing and, although I wasn't cognizant of the precise cause of her downtrodden mood, I felt confident it had definite personal ramifications.

I needed to touch the water spirit. I inched over to the edge, removed my moccasins and dangled my bare feet in the iciness. Once numbness set in, I could effectively withdraw the emotional aspect from the waters. Soon a warm surge crept up my legs until my entire being was totally united with that of nature's. Once this mystical bond of communion was complete, I could fully comprehend the finer elements of the transfusion that was taking place.

A weighted grief overtook me. It was an overall deep sadness of nature's that had a direct bearing on the present-day state of the minds of men. It was then I understood why nature was crying, why the moon appeared to be weeping. And I assured the anguished entity that I would do all I could to help enlighten men to her tender sensitivities. I would go out of my way to warn them of their apathetic follies and their subsequent devastating aftermaths.

I walked barefoot back to the silent camper and, being as quiet as a mouse, I carried my bedding out beside the river where the rushing waters could lull me to sleep. After considerable moving around on the unyielding earth, I finally got reasonably comfortable enough to drift off.

Wavering visions soon floated in fragmented bits and pieces. The shimmering images passed before me in disconnected association, always changing their intensity and form. Tears fell from the round copper moon. Trees thirsted. Rivers cried their wailing laments to the bordering shores. Cottonwoods bent in their grief. The wind wept. And a low moaning could be heard from among the aspen stands.

The view telescoped. I was sitting beside a young man who was moaning softly. He was oblivious to my presence. And, taking advantage of his state of unknown companionship, I took the time to study the man.

He had an athletic build, like one who frequently lifted weights. His thick dark hair was almost a shiny blue-black. Deep bronze skin glistened in the moonlight. And when he raised his head to face me, piercing eyes met mine. They were such a light blue, they appeared to be silver—almost mercurial.

"Who are you?" I whispered.

"I am just a Water Bearer," he replied in an unexpected voice that was as soft as a summer cloud.

Our surround of scenery altered. We had previously been wrapped within a riverside panorama, and now it cryptically changed into No-Eyes' cabin interior. I subliminally took in the homey atmosphere while a sudden shock wave rippled through me. Quickly I avoided the eerie metamorphosis and concentrated on the strange young man who, to my surprise, now had an old man's face superimposed over his own. I maintained the conversation without alluding to the new double-exposure that had materialized.

"What do they call you?"

"Many names have I," came the evasive answer.

"Why did you say you're a Water Bearer?"

"Because that is what I am. I give drink to the thirsty."

I cocked my head in curiosity. "Who thirsts?"

His enchanting eyes blinked. His manner of speech was slow—deliberate, well chosen. He glanced out the windows that flickered with orange firelight reflections. "*They* thirst."

Who was "they"? I wondered. But I didn't wish to press the subject, for he clearly was being purposely elusive. I chose another line. "Why were you moaning?"

"Because they thirst. . .so many thirst," he mused.

"Do they know they thirst?"

"No. That is what saddens me so."

Finally I felt I was gaining some ground. I moved over in front of him and sat on the familiar braided rug. I looked into his solemn face as the dancing flames illuminated his chiseled features.

The scenery faded again. Now we were within No-Eyes' woods and the specter of the old man that had shadowed the Water Bearer's countenance vanished just as mysteriously as it had appeared. An awkward silence hung between us. I mentally fumbled to maintain our verbal connection.

"Do you know who I am?" I asked.

"Do you?" came the somewhat expected reply.

"Yes, now I know because someone showed me. Do you know who I am?" I repeated.

He idly picked up a stick and ran his palm along it. "I know you thirst. That is clear. I know you walk a lonely trail—a trail that is often parched."

"But I don't thirst," I countered. "Someone gave me many drinks and now I no longer thirst." The man raised his sapphire eyes to mine. He glared intently. The colors of the opalescent orbs swirled like living quicksilver.

"You still have the thirst."

At the sound of his soft voice, the background shifted. Beyond him and as far as my peripheral vision could see without taking my eyes from his, russet and bronze reflections speared out from a rising scarlet sun to reflect upon vermilion canyon walls. I made concentrated efforts to ignore the disturbance of the distracting changing scenes, for the man remained constant and, apparently, so did I.

A golden sepia hue washed over us, making the entire surround appear like something created by an old tintype and mystically made real.

"Indians know," he said out of the blue.

"Know what?" I whispered back.

"Secrets. They know about the thirst."

"This same thirst you say I still have?"

He simply nodded.

"Can I quench this thirst?" I asked, centering my attention on the pearly eyes in order to avoid being distracted by the intensity of the background hue that altered whenever the man spoke.

"Did you not hear my words? *Indians* know. *You* know in your *heart* what I speak of."

"But can I quench this thirst?"

"That depends," he uttered as the atmosphere flared from mellow bronze to bright copper.

"On what does this depend?"

"On you this depends. You must be ready."

The sheer canyon walls faded away. They melted down like hot wax. The new background came up and intensified into deep, verdant woodlands. The Water Bearer now held a stone that he palmed with a special reverence. A coyote pack howled and yipped from somewhere in the distance, causing the man to glance up in the direction of the harrowing sound.

"Omens," he proclaimed.

"Omens of what?" I asked, looking furtively into the deep jade shadows of the forest.

"Things. Things most powerful."

A shiver rippled down my spine. "What kind of powerful things?"

The gentle soft-spoken man reached out and, uncurling his hand, offered me the stone. I gratefully took it. Magic radiated in my palm.

Showing perfect white teeth, he smiled warmly. "Magical things," he replied.

"Magic?" I looked down at the common pebble that now had an iridescent glow—almost a vibrating lifeforce.

"Yes. Many faces magic has."

Suddenly, the man's features were softened by the cast of orange reflections that flickered from No-Eyes' blazing fireplace. We were within her cabin again. We were alone, for when I checked around over the familiar surround, the old one was nowhere to be seen. And, turning my attention back to my dignified companion, I finally voiced my confusion about the changing backdrops.

"Why does the scenery keep altering?"

He casually looked about the cozy room. "Does it?"

"Yes. Do you know this room?" I tested anxiously.

"It is like home," came the gentle reply that disheartened me.

"Home? Home! Do you *know* No-Eyes? Was she your *teacher? Is* she your teacher?"

"I know many. Many have been my teacher. This No-Eyes, I know of her, yes." His glassy eyes wandered about the room in a state of reminiscent melancholy. A warm serenity glowed from his sensitive face.

And my heart thundered at what this could possibly mean.

Cottonwoods swayed in the cool breeze. Their golden leaves fluttered down around us. They wafted in the soft breeze to alight on the shining surface of a narrow stream. The season had also changed this time. The Water Bearer paid no notice.

"Listen to the cries," he uttered.

I strained my senses. A muted mourning sound was heard. "Who's crying?" I softly asked.

"Many. Those haunted places moan and cry out."

My scalp crawled.

"What haunted places?"

His deep eyes met mine with an intensity I have no words for. "You will see...maybe. Someday you will perhaps recognize those things that lie upon your path. Someday you will perhaps go and see the pain of the wretched haunted."

"Go where?"

"Haunted places," came the eerie reply. "Places where those who are but shadows walk in anguish. Places where phantoms are afoot."

Starry night. Crisp mountain air. Roaring campfire blazing warmly before us. Hidden creatures scurrying in the darkness of the underbrush.

"The scenery changed again," I advised.

He glanced about. "So it has."

"Isn't that strange? Don't you think that fact is just a little odd?"

"What is strange? Odd?"

"Scenery that constantly alters is strange. It's odd that the background keeps altering. Things just don't happen like that."

A perceptive smile tipped the corners of his mouth. "In dreams it does. In visions it does. It does in reality," came the undaunted reply.

"In reality!"

My sudden outburst didn't disturb his genuine serenity. His composed demeanor remained constant. "You're thirsty," he reminded with those peculiar eyes fixed hard on mine.

"No, I'm not," I persisted.

"You thirst for clarity between *the* Reality and that which you *perceive* as reality. You thirst for the *understanding* of those things which you presently interpret as the impossible—the incredulous, the myths."

"I'm not thirsty," I adamantly maintained.

He grinned ever so slightly. "Stubborn you are. But still, you thirst. Yet...if you say that you do not, then you thirst even more so. It cannot be otherwise."

Sun setting low beyond the western slope. We were now sitting on a high mountain ridge looking down on an autumn valley of brilliant aspens in their seasonal prime.

"Know that you thirst. That is the first step to its quenching."

"What is 'it'?"

"That which you thirst for—the truth to reality—the reality to truth."

I thought on that. "Is there anyone who does not have this thirst?"

"No, but there are those who have little thirst remaining. There are those who have quested for fulfillment and have gained their full measure—yet still, their vessels are not completely full. They are as full as that which they are capable of retaining."

"Are you one of those?"

"Perhaps."

"If you're a Water Bearer, then you must be a teacher who satisfies those who know they thirst and come to you for the refreshment they need."

The man smiled.

"Then I'm right!" I beamed.

He turned to me. "Perhaps."

I sighed with the swift deflation. "But won't you at least tell me if I'm right?"

The man's arm outstretched and slowly moved to the precipice. He eerily pointed to the wide chasm separating the high mountain ridges. He glanced down into the sheer breathtaking depths far below.

"My little friend," he whispered, "your mind is ready, but there is one yet to come who will search deep into your heart to make certain the time is right."

The Water Bearer stared at me, then his wizened eyes scanned the expanse of mountains. "From out there, from everywhere and from nowhere he will come. He will come for you when you least expect him. And if he deems you ready, all your many questions will be answered, because then, then you will be told to go and ask the Dreamwalker."

The Dreamwalker . . . Dreamwalker . . . Dreamwalker.

The word echoed within the canyons of my mind as I awoke to the cold of my riverside bedroom. I was chilled to the bone, yet I stood and wrapped the heavy woolen blankets around me while stumbling over to the rushing waters that still carried the heart-wrenching sounds.

I looked up at the clouded sky and watched as they drifted away from the bright moon that wept a tear for those who still wandered—for those who still thirsted.

And, sweeping down the mountainside on the far side of the stream, the wind stealthily approached. It swept across the rippling watercourse to touch my face and it whispered in a hushed softness.

Yes, I would go and do what was needed. I would seek the one I thirsted for. I had hearkened to nature's wise words. Her spoken wisdom was accepted within my heart—I would seek the quenching wisdom of the Dreamwalker.

Just because Nature does not speak the human tongue—does not form verbal words—does not mean It lacks a communicable language of Its own.

Man is merely ignorant, deaf to Nature's exquisite language, Her ancient Wisdom of the Ages.

The Slumbering Sentinel

Think you know a Wise Man, a Holy Man, a Visionary when you see him?

Think you have expectations as to his outward appearance? His demeanor?

My friend, think again.

The second day of our camping outing was spent shooting the white waters of the river and taking long, meaningful walks into the surrounding forests. Our conversations were sometimes light and other times they were quite deep.

Our friends had a near-total comprehension of the complex technicalities of the truths, and we'd frequently find ourselves heavily involved in in-depth discussions relating to the many finer aspects of them. Yet, I never did mention the fact that I hadn't slept all night within the warm, comfortable camper. I hadn't mentioned my midnight walk or the subsequent dream with the strange young man with the mesmerizing opalescent eyes. That part I would reserve until Bill and I were once again alone.

That Sunday evening, after Bob and Julie had dropped us off at the house and the girls were all in bed, I was about to approach the subject when Bill introduced it by asking me why I hadn't slept in the RV.

"I figured you knew," I said, handing him a freshly steeped cup of mullein tea.

His brow raised. "I went to put my arm around you and you weren't there. So I figured you went for a walk or were curled up out there under the stars somewhere." He took a sip of the steaming liquid, then frowned. "I wish you'd tell me when you're planning on doing that, though."

"I never know ahead of time," I half apologized. "I follow the promptings of my spirit."

"I know that, but I get concerned when you're suddenly not there when I'm expecting you to be. It gets to be sort of nerve-wracking dealing with your sudden disappearances."

"I know, but it was meant that I be outside last night. Nature was still weeping."

"Did you ever find out why?" he asked, hoping the enigma had been resolved at last.

"Yes. It had to do with humanity's lack of awareness toward nature, their follies and destructive ways."

He frowned again. "That's peculiar. I would've thought it'd have a more personal meaning. You seemed to think it did at the time."

"I wasn't done explaining," I added. "After I finished my walk and went to sleep, I had a real vivid dream." And I recounted the entire sequence of the dreamscape's events.

He was deeply pensive. "Have you analyzed it yet?"

"Parts. I've got the general mood of interpretation."

"So?" he urged. "What's it mean?"

"Well," I began, "first of all, the Water Bearer is obviously a highly advanced teacher of some kind."

"Physical?" he asked.

I momentarily hesitated before responding. "Yes. I think he's a physical person because of the way we two were always the constant factor of the dream. We were the main anchoring components that never altered the whole time." His one brow lifted questioningly. "Even though his eyes were not eyes of reality?"

"'Even then." I was convinced the Water Bearer represented a real-life person.

He wasn't so sure. "Even when his face became superimposed with an older person?"

I thought on that. "Yes. That'd indicate a dual purpose—a tandem force."

"Light or dark? Or both?"

"Light. Definitely a force of light."

He eyed me intently before continuing. "Have you determined the purpose of the altering backgrounds? Don't sequential changes like that signify changes for you? Your physical future surroundings?"

"Not necessarily, but in this instance, I do think it means the scenery in my future. I just have the distinct feeling that that man is going to cross my path in the future."

Silence hung between us until Bill had more to question. "What are your thoughts about the scene in front of No-Eyes' fireplace? What do you feel about that?"

Now it was my turn to do the frowning. "I'm not sure really, but I know by his deep reaction to her room, that he definitely knew her. He'd been there before—many times before."

"As a student, do you think?"

"I'm certain of it."

"A present-day student?"

I shook my head. "No. He's much too advanced to still be in the learning stage. That process was obviously over for him long ago. He had that special air about him that exuded high wisdom. His demeanor was controlled and easy...refined and well composed. His humility was profound. There wasn't a pretentious bone in his body."

I paused a moment with the vivid recall of it. "Those extraordinary eyes evidenced his attainment of high wisdom—his expanded enlightenment. It was as if he was far above any negativity touching him."

"Then you feel you're going to meet him one day," he stated with assurance.

I nodded.

Silence.

"What's the matter?" I asked, concerned about the extent of the sudden lull.

"I'm just wondering what this Water Bearer could teach you that No-Eyes can't. Doesn't quite make sense, knowing how knowledgeable she is. Why would you need to learn from anyone else?"

"I don't actually know that I do. I'm just going by my feelings. Don't forget that No-Eyes always said that different teachers shed different perspectives on the same subjects. She said that although the truths remain unalterable and constant, they can be viewed from several angles of perspective in order to gain a more rounded comprehension. Maybe I need something like that." He agreed that that could be a viable possibility. Then he moved on to the real meat of the matter.

"So...what's a Dreamwalker?"

I shrugged. "You mean *who's* a Dreamwalker."

He sighed. "Now you're sounding like No-Eyes."

I grinned. "Guess that's to be expected by now. Anyway," I added, "I don't know the answer to that one. I've never heard her mention the term before."

"Do you think she knows this mysterious new entity?"

Again I grinned. "It appears that the old one knows everybody who's anybody in the world of visionaries. I'm sure she does."

"Then why hasn't she ever spoken about a Dreamwalker in your discussions? Why hasn't she ever taught you about them or explained their purpose—what they do?"

"That's hard to say for sure. I imagine there's still a world of unknowns she hasn't taught me about yet." I became thoughtful at that idea. "Yeah, I bet there's all kinds of subjects we haven't delved into. Reality is so expansive. I guess my lessons have been very narrow compared to what they could be." I sighed. "Maybe I'm still in kindergarten and the Dreamwalker is university material."

My life companion reached over and squeezed my hand. "Honey, if you were still in kindergarten, you never would've had that dream in the first place." His comforting seriousness turned to well-intentioned playfulness. "If you were in kindergarten at all, No-Eyes wouldn't have even acknowledged you in her woods that first day—you wouldn't have even been led there. The old one wouldn't spend time with someone who was still sifting through the sandbox level."

I grinned wide as his words flashed visions before my mind, and I thought on the meaning behind them.

"Well?" he pushed. "Am I right or not? It's logical, isn't it?"

"I guess so," I half-heartedly agreed.

He brightened. "Know what else I think?"

"What?" I smiled at his sparkling steel-blue eyes.

"I think this handsome Water Bearer of yours is the forerunner of the Dreamwalker—his advance man, so to speak. I bet you've got some real interesting surprises ahead."

A sheepish smile curved up the corners of my mouth. "Nah, I'm not ready for the real advanced stuff like that. I need a lot more time with No-Eyes before I get passed up through that many grade levels. I may have graduated out of sandbox," I teased back, "but I'm a far cry from being tutored by a Dreamwalker teacher."

And with that concluding statement, we went to bed, yet little did either of us realize that evening how wrong both our ideas would ultimately prove to be, for it would appear that, while I was out having a weekend of fun, my clever teacher had been busily mapping out serious preparation for a new level of my instruction—one that would be expertly engineered by none other than a bona fide Dreamwalker.

As anxious as I was for the forthcoming weekend with No-Eyes to come into being, I was somewhat amazed at the speed with which my week flew by. I had begun compiling and organizing my natural healing notes on the extensive information given by the old one—there were literally reams and reams of it—and I had dishevelled scraps and bits scattered everywhere. I was beginning to form a mental outline for the lengthy book based on all her wondrous material that explained humanity's unique physical and spiritual bond with the earth. I had already tentatively entitled it *Earthway* and was kept busy consolidating and organizing the subject matter. It was proving to be an overwhelming project . . . a nightmarish task of monumental proportions.

So, without realizing it, I had worked all week until around two in the mornings, and now I had to be up early the following day because it would again be Saturday—a Saturday with my beloved friend.

I left the various stacks of papers and notes on the kitchen table and blew out the kerosene lamp. I desperately needed some solid sleep. No-Eyes would never tolerate a drowsy student. And, luckily, sleep came quickly. It was sound, and, thankfully, refreshing.

My eyes opened to the darkness of Saturday morning's early hour. A hard knot was firmly tied within the confines of my stomach and my sensitive psyche pricked at the surface of my consciousness. Something from within me was frantically attempting to gain access to the forefront of my mind and, for the life of me, I couldn't pull it out into the open.

I stared into the engulfing darkness of the room. Bill's rhythmic breathing appeared smooth and undisturbed. And I wondered what it was that kept trying so desperately to tell me something—what did I need to know? Usually these nebulous signals signified a forewarning and, if any kind of excursion with the truck was scheduled, we'd postpone it until another time when things felt more secure—more solidly safe to travel. But this day I was only going up to No-Eyes' place and I didn't feel that my warning signs had anything whatsoever to do with that routine mountain drive.

I tossed several times in a concentrated effort to shake off the irritating sensations, and after the unsuccessful attempts, I silently gathered up my clothes and slipped from the room. My sleeping companion stirred, turned, and with an indistinct grumble, was swept back into his private oblivion.

Tip-toeing through the house with a flashlight in hand, I checked in on the slumbering girls. All was well. The bright beam of narrow light revealed Rainbow comfortably curled up on the bottom of Sarah's bed. The animal's eyes glowed in the sudden brightness and her tail began drumming on the child's legs. I whispered for her to be quiet as she padded softly behind me back through the dark rooms and into the bathroom to keep me company while I got ready. Finally I lovingly rubbed behind her ears and told her to go back to bed. She sadly hung her head a little, turned dejectedly, and silently crept back to Sarah's room. It was still dark when I backed the old Chevy out the drive.

A murky greyness was beginning to wash over the eastern skyline. It spread like smoke rising from the mountain's jagged horizon. Here and there along the way, a thick rolling mist hung in the lower valleys of the road. It menacingly swirled before the headlights. It eerily rose to shroud the wayside pines that towered like watching gargoyles.

My hair pricked. The stubborn sensations were still with me. I slowed. The section of twisting highway was coming up and I didn't want to take any foolish chances in the ashen mist.

I rolled the window down and stuck my hand out. With fingers splayed wide, I could catch the droplets of cold moisture that wavered hauntingly about the pickup. Nothing ominous there. Nothing bringing portents of negativity existed in the atmosphere. Yet still, I remained nervously on edge.

At No-Eyes' turnoff, the vehicle made its sharp snaking climb and once I was in the near vicinity of her woodlands, I felt released from the irritation that had relentlessly plagued my psyche since I awoke. And, being grateful for the welcomed relief, I parked the truck and raced to the cabin that was barely visible through the murkiness of the low-hanging clouds.

She was waiting on her porch, matching bundles held lovingly in arms. She was grinning. "We gonna go greet this misty day."

I glanced down at the two ancient sheaths. "Then you knew I'd be here sooner than usual. You didn't happen to wake me early, did you?" I asked suspiciously.

The old one shuffled past me. "Nope. Just figured Summer be eager, that all."

I had been standing on her steps while she descended past me and began disappearing into the roiling mist.

She halted suddenly and looked back. One of the bundles shot out at me from beneath her shawl. "You comin' or you gonna stand there like some holey knot in wood?" she barked.

I hurried to her side and took the offered bundle. "These clouds are really hanging low today, huh, No-Eyes."

Without breaking the meter of her advancing pace, she nonchalantly scanned the spooky surroundings. "Yup. They huggin' good on the mountains all right."

"Think they'll burn off soon?" I asked, swirling the moisture around with my free arm.

"Maybe," came the short response.

"It's supposed to be warm today," I informed. "They said it's going to be sunny all weekend."

"Nope. They wrong," she quipped.

"No-Eyes? I was wondering...."

"Summer's mouth gonna stop flappin' soon?"

Silence.

The old one seemed irritated with my casual small talk. More like she was mentally preoccupied. I pulled up beside her and accompanied her in silence. I sensed a nervousness in her.

The predawn light was beginning to brighten. It created an almost blinding nebula as we crested the rise of her hill. From here on, the casual talk would've naturally been avoided if it hadn't already been cut short. We set the delicate sheaths on the dampened earth, removed the old pipes and went about the blessed business of performing our sacred Sunrise Benediction Rite. And, even though my concentration and reverence was total, I felt the obscure interference of eyes of a hidden observer with us on that solitary hilltop.

When we were through and the pipes were once again shielded from any outside influencing vibrations, we descended the knoll that remained blanketed in the heavy spectral garb of nature.

Without turning, the old one slid her keen eyes to me. "What the matter? Summer maybe scared? Mountain mist scare Summer?"

The feeling pricked along my spine. "No. I usually love it when the clouds roll through the mountains like this."

"Usually?" she caught.

"Well, yes . . . ," I stammered. "But No-Eyes, someone's intruded into the Rite. Somebody's been watching us!"

She casually glanced around, wise eyes narrowed to scrutinize the hoary forest. "Humph! No-Eyes must be gettin' old, I not see no body out there. You sure you didn't stay up watchin' some dumb spooky movie last night?"

That was downright silly. "I don't watch that stupid stuff. I worked late last night on organizing *Earthway*." I suddenly halted and grabbed at her thin arm. "There! There it is again. Can't you feel it? No-Eyes, somebody's *watching* us!"

A weighted sigh escaped from between her pressed lips. "Nobody out there," she insisted, testing the damp air. Then she shrugged and conceded, "Maybe somebody *observin'* though. Yup," she decided firmly, "maybe somebody doin' that observin' stuff 'round here."

I followed close beside her as the bulk of the cabin loomed into view. "Aren't you concerned? Who would be observing you?"

"Blah! Observers no can harm No-Eyes." Then her voice dropped its light, confident tone. "Besides," she growled ominously, "maybe it not be *No-Eyes* who somebody be observin'."

My eyes widened at her intent. I froze in mid-step. Her sinister words struck cold, like an icy hand placed hard on your shoulder at the heart-stopping moment of a chiller movie.

I snuck anxious glances around me and peered hard into the unearthly pallor of my surroundings. The murky outlines of the wavering pines towered in every direction. The wind whispered imagined horrors into my mind and my hair prickled while the fragile heart within my chest hammered like a pile-driver gone berserk.

The thumping sound of footsteps on the cabin porch shattered my harrowing fantasies and brought me to my senses. It was then that I realized how exposed I was, standing alone out in the open—with those unknown eyes on me. And before the viselike grip of fear had a devil of a chance to clamp me between its sharp fangs, I hollered to my disappearing friend.

"Hey, No-Eyes! Wait for me!" And I scampered headlong toward the comforting security blanket of my warm schoolroom.

In my haste to gain swift access to the small fortress, I charged the steps and rammed straight into the visionary.

The disgusted woman stared hard at her foolish student. "Some hell demon chasin' Summer? Huh?" She then raised her sights to peer through the mist into the spectral background behind me. Her ebony eyes suddenly widened to flare at some perceived horror.

I whipped around, terrified to see what was stealthily approaching behind me and, before I had time to distinguish anything manifesting, she tapped my shoulder.

"AGG!" I jumped.

"What Summer expect to see out there?" Without waiting for my idiotic reply, she sighed heavily and turned to vanish through the doorway.

And not giving a fig to what foolishness the old one thought me guilty of, I scurried hard on her heels not wishing to take another glance behind me for fear of what hideous terrors I might spy creeping out of the clinging curtain that swirled and beckoned.

Once I was enveloped by the warm glow of the cabin, a soothing serenity washed over me. How utterly juvenile I'd behaved. My previous gross immaturity hung guiltily over me, and I was deeply embarrassed by my unchecked display of fear.

Mortified, I placed the medicine pipe in its wooden box and pulled my serape up over my head. I sheepishly snuck a glance into the kitchen where No-Eyes was puttering around with some of her jars, and I inwardly steeled myself for the forthcoming tongue-lashing. There was no doubt that I was well deserving of one. Through my own backsliding moment of ineptitude, I had shamefully earned myself a royal reprimand.

"Summer want to peek out No-Eyes' window?" came the soft question from the kitchen.

"No," I mumbled under my breath, not being able to look her square in the eye.

"Eh?" she replied, placing a wrinkled hand behind an ear. "What Summer say?"

My head jerked up to boldly eye her. "No! I said I *don't* want to look out the window."

She nodded. "Oh." A mirthful curl tipped the corner of her thin lips. "No-Eyes just thought maybe Summer wanted to see them bad monsters movin' 'round outside in that scary mist."

It was now or never to speak of it. I moved toward the darkened kitchen, pulled out one of the pine branch chairs and sat at the table.

The visionary went about her work, seemingly oblivious to my close presence.

I looked up at her back. "So . . . now are you going to ignore me completely?"

Puttering about, she answered without bothering to turn. "Why No-Eyes do somethin' dumb like that?" Then she hesitated a moment, "unless Summer think that what No-Eyes should do . . . unless Summer think she *deserve* to be ignored."

I remained humble but firm. "No, I don't think I deserve that," I said as I studied my fingers. "I know how badly I acted out there and I want to talk about it."

Muttering and sputtering under her breath, the visionary inhaled deeply. "Now where did I put that dumb powder?"

I sighed. "No-Eyes, did you hear me?"

"Yup."

"Well? I want to talk about it." I squinted into the shadowy room that was barely reflecting the light from the fireplace.

"What are you looking for anyways?" I got up to see if I could help.

"Ahhh, here you are, you little bugger!" she exclaimed with satisfied relief while reaching to the uppermost shelf for an oddly shaped apothecary jar.

I sat down again. "What is that stuff?"

"Mmmm," she buzzed with a peculiar smile. "This gonna make some fine drink for Summer." She leaned over the table and winked. "*Special* drink."

I knew that cunning look and I also knew that portentous tone. I wasn't sure I liked either one; in fact, I was certain I didn't care for it. Obviously she had plans that opposed my own.

"No-Eyes," I respectfully reminded for the third time, "I want to talk about what happened with me out there."

She stopped dipping her fingers in the jar. "What so."

"Not 'what so.' We can't just brush it off like it never happened. I can't go on with anything else here until we've gone into it."

"Not *want* to go on, you mean," she uttered her revision of my statement.

"Yes, you're right. I can't and I also don't *want* to proceed without clearing this up first."

"Humph!" The measured ingredient was now in the cup and I waited while she hung a kettle of water on the fireplace hook. She shuffled back into the kitchen and sat across from me. "Now what Summer be so upset 'bout? Summer be angry 'cause No-Eyes make joke 'bout Summer bein' scared?"

"No. You had every justification for your humor. I just want to know *what* scared me so."

"Mmmm," she smiled, closing her eyes in a long blink. "What Summer think make her so scared?"

"Something different. Something powerful."

Eyes glinted through narrowed lids. "Summer been in presence of powerful somethings before. What make this so different?"

"I don't know. Maybe because that mist was so dense and I couldn't see into it, maybe that caused some kind of disorientation or something. Do you know what I'm getting at?"

"Yup. No-Eyes know all right, but that not have nothing to do with what cause this great new fear. It not like Summer to be so full of fear in mountains."

"I know, that's what's so confounding."

I listened to the pine pitch snap in the licking flames of the fireplace. "No-Eyes," I whispered, "you know, don't you. Tell me what scared me. You know how often I've been out in the mountain mists. You know how many times I loved walking through it at night, what happened out there? *Who* was there?"

My wise mentor looked away. "No-Eyes know, but Summer gotta find that stuff out for herself. I not always gonna be here to hand answers out when you in the dark 'bout some new thing. Summer gotta learn to find own answers. It be time for that now."

"But I don't know *how* to find the answers to difficult things like this. That's why I need more time with you because you can show me. How do I find answers when I don't know where to look for them?"

"Summer remember what No-Eyes say 'bout what be inside all problems?"

"You said that problems contain all the pieces of the whole. You said that problems were merely a tangle that could be unravelled, that the solution was always found within the problem itself."

She nodded, eyes twinkling.

Mine weren't twinkling, they were clouded with confusion. "No-Eyes, that still doesn't help me now."

Her head tilted as if she were listening for or to something I couldn't hear. Then she directed her full attention back to me. Her voice was controlled and soft—it reeked of wisdom. "Summer," she began, "No-Eyes teach Summer most all stuff 'bout truth, 'bout what be real. But that not be 'nough. This *knowing* stuff only be right *beginning*. It be pathway to *greater* stuff, stuff *more* powerful even."

"What kind of stuff, No-Eyes?"

The ebony pools widened and swirled. "*Visionary* stuff," she whispered secretively. "Stuff of *Dreamwalkers*."

My heart stopped, then lunged ahead. So that was it, I thought as my old friend left me to consider her words. And while she was retrieving the hot kettle, my mind played tricks on me. It told me that I was ready to be tutored by a Dreamwalker. It cruelly teased me by hinting that now was the season for my last journey into enlightenment. I desperately tried to rein in the presumptuous thoughts that arrogantly taunted my inadequate self-image. But why had she mentioned the Dreamwalker at all then?

My fragile heart drummed with the soaring implication that perhaps my thoughts weren't toying with me after all. Perhaps the wise one thought I was advanced enough for this final step. But no, how could this be? I was simply no more than a lowly student. And as I watched No-Eyes pour the steaming water into my awaiting cup, I realized my mind didn't know what it thought.

"We gonna fix that now," she confided, bringing the brew to the table. "When that cools a tiny bit, Summer gonna drink it all down real quick." I stared down into the amber-colored liquid. I knew better than to ask what the active ingredient was. I had an idea and I didn't want it verified. After I would down the contents, precious little time would be left for conscious communication between us. I decided to squeeze some in before the concoction cooled.

"Nature wept over the weekend, No-Eyes."

"No-Eyes know that."

"I had a special dream, too."

"No-Eyes know."

"Did you send it?"

"Nope. No-Eyes no have right to send that one."

"Was the Water Bearer one of your students?"

Orange reflections flickered across the log walls. The fire had found new life as it gaily danced and snapped, creating an atmosphere of tender seriousness as I looked deep into the visionary's black pools.

The time for roundabout questions and answers had come full circle. Now there was nothing left but straight talk, talk straight from the heart.

"He been here. He been No-Eyes' student long ago, long before No-Eyes find Summer in woods out there. But he walked on. He walked onto other journey path. Now he be all done."

"He's not advancing more?"

"That not what No-Eyes say. He be all done walkin' on searchin' path. He reach end. Now he be there to reach others who come 'long."

"What's his real name?"

"Names be sacred stuff. Summer know that. Maybe if Summer meet the Water Bearer some day, he maybe tell that. Depends."

"On what does this depend?"

"If he think you ready to know stuff."

"What stuff?"

She inclined her head to the cup. "Maybe that be ready now. You see."

I reluctantly slipped a finger down into the liquid. My heart sank. It wasn't hot anymore. I solemnly looked up at the woman and pushed for one last question.

"Who's the Dreamwalker?"

"Drink now," came the order that had entoned finality.

And I did. I drank the last drop, set the cup down and thoughtfully studied my hands.

No-Eyes regarded my reaction. A chuckle broke the stillness of the moment. "Why Summer lookin' so hard at fingers? You expectin' to see them change?"

"I'm not in expectation, No-Eyes."

The old one leaned forward to crane her head across the worn wooden table. "Tell No-Eyes what Summer be in then."

"I'm in between." I edged out of the fragile chair and stretched out on the kitchen floor. A slight light-headedness was weaving through my mind and, if the sensation increased, which I figured it would, I didn't want to fall off my chair.

I heard my teacher step softly into the living room where I heard her whispering to herself. The reflections from the fire flared in brightness. They glowed as they glanced off the hand-hewn beams of the kitchen ceiling. I stared at their staccato movements while No-Eyes finished replenishing the blaze and then shuffled back to her chair.

"Summer?" came the soft voice.

"I'm here."

"What you in now?" she whispered.

"Acceptance."

A few long minutes passed. I closed my eyes against the whirling room.

"Summer?"

"I'm still here," I answered drowsily.

"No-Eyes not gonna be going with you. Summer knew that, huh," her voice echoed from a distance.

"Yeah, I . . . knew, No-Eyes. I . . . . k-n-e-wwww."

"Summer? Can you hear me?"

Silence.

The wise one rested back in her chair. A tenseness tightened the thin lips. Now all she could do was wait.

"Summer?" called the faraway voice.

"Here," I replied from the cabin's yard. "I'm here." I squinted through the ghostly vapors in a vain effort to spot the caller. "Who's there?"

New sounds were carried on the floating waves of the grey fog. Shuffling sounds were nearing as footfalls swished through the damp grasses. And when I turned to them, a bulky form was slowly looming larger, clearer. At each advancing step, the outline became more distinctly solid.

"Who's there?" I called out again.

"Summer?" the voice croaked.

"Yes, I'm here, but who are you?" Strangely, I felt no fear, for I was in acceptance.

Then the man was before me. He simply stepped out of the churning mist. He smiled with a gentle nod of greeting. "Now I finally get to meet up with Summer Rain."

"Finally?"

"Yes, finally. I've been waiting quite some time for you, you know." I was in the dark. "No. I didn't know."

He pursed his full lips. "Well . . . no matter. I suppose that's how it must be."

"How *what* must be?"

Though the fog passed between us, the undeniable sparkle in his jolly eyes could not pass unnoticed. "Why, the *Way*, girl. There are *rules* for one's passage along the Way!"

"What way?"

His laugh was an unrestrained outburst. "My, my, my, you certainly *are* a live one. I was told you're full of questions. Now *I* get a taste of your exuberance, your . . . thirst."

As he spoke the last word, he had leaned nearer to me and raised a heavy brow.

"Thirst?" I said. "I have many more questions, but first, who are you and why are you here? How do you know me? What is the purpose of our meeting?"

Again, his robust laughter was amplified through the eerie surround. "Good God, child! Take some time to breathe between your inquisitiveness. You sound like a Gatling gun."

I felt somewhat reprimanded. "I'm sorry, but you have the distinct advantage, don't you think? You know me, but I don't know you."

He duly apologized for his apparent rudeness. "And right you are too, little Summer Rain. How right you are. But you see, I have many names. Which one would you like to know me by?"

His question was a clever trick. It reminded me of a serious caution No-Eyes had once drilled into me. I paused before answering. I withheld my reply until I had sized up this stranger who hailed from out of the vaporous netherworld.

He was in his late sixties, my height, but stocky. His full-blood Indian lineage gave him all the interesting classic features. Dark skin tone, intense eyes, high cheekbones, full lips, and an aura of pride that bespoke a noble heritage. His vibration was good. And he possessed very strong medicine.

I smiled at him. "All of them," I replied. "I want to hear *all* the names you go by, then I'll decide which one I want to *know* you by."

A pudgy ring-bedecked finger pointed at me. "Very good. That was good!"

"Well? I'm waiting," I grinned into the brown, weather-worn face.

"Let me tell you about yourself," he said as he began pacing before me. "You're quite..."

"No," I demanded, cutting him off. "Tell me your names first."

He nodded. "You're not an easy one to sidetrack. Again I say, very good." He guided me toward No-Eyes' hill. "Summer, I see you've already geared up your awareness, so believe me when I say that I'll try no more cleverness on you. This is a serious journey today and we must be open and honest."

Our pace was slow and easy as he talked.

I listened to every word, every inflection in his raspy voice. If any deception would occur, it would evidence itself through the voice or, if the speaker was an experienced deceiver, the flaring aura would clearly expose him. I was watchful as he continued.

"So now you are not in trust," he had cleverly observed.

"I'm in awareness, and you have yet to tell me your names."

"And I shall, I shall."

He bent to pick up a small, soddened twig which he held as we walked. "I have been known as Little Hawk, Jonathon Beemonet, the Weaver and Daniel Hilling. I have had the additional names of Cortegra and Plato. Do you wish me to continue? There's many, many more."

I grinned and parleyed. "And I have been known as Summer Rain, Sequanu and She-Who-Sees, who was formerly Walks-in-Woods."

"So!" he smiled wide. "You do not wish to know them all after all."

"Just those names you're known by in *this* life will do, thank you."

"Ah, well...that does save us considerable time." He broke the branches off the twig until only the main stem remained. "You see, little one? Now we get down to what is important. We have managed to strip away the superfluous. We become specific."

I indicated that I understood the unexpected lesson.

"In this life I am known as Wise Man, Joe Red Sky, Shaman and . . . That Injun."

I tossed the names over in my mind. "That Injun?"

"Well, that's how certain white folks refer to me."

"That's not very nice," I sympathized.

His pearly teeth gleamed as he made light of the fact. "Hey, that's their karma, not mine."

"Still. . . ."

"That's all right, Summer, names like that only expose people's ignorance and lack of enlightenment. It simply shows how lacking they are along the path of awareness. These things must be accepted."

I reached out my hand for the stick.

He gave it over with a shadow of curious interest on his face.

And, dividing the main stem into portions which I called by his names, I pointed to the tip which had no name.

"And what is this known by?" I questioned.

"Well, I'll be!" he exclaimed with genuine surprise.

"That's not what it's called," I smiled.

He shook his head. "I brought you here on No-Eyes' hillcrest to show you what it was that you sensed before. I need you to understand that which you desire to comprehend."

My finger patiently tapped the tip of the stick. "The *name*."

"Tell you what," he grinned. "I promise you'll have your answer when we're done, but not just yet."

I studied his features. I scanned the gently wavering aura. "All right, agreed," I bargained.

"Good. Now, about your fright this morning, we're here so you can discover for yourself what its source was."

The area surrounding the hill looked much the same as it did when No-Eyes and I were there earlier, only this time, the eerie sensations were completely different. They were still there—only stronger. It didn't take the high mentality of a visionary to figure it out.

"I already know what the source was, but I don't know the *why* yet." I faced the old man. "*You* were the source. *You* were the observer this morning."

"That is so, but do I instill fear in you now?"

I glanced around into the dismal fog. I looked up to where the treetops were weaving shapeless shadows. Then I lowered my eyes to fix upon his. They locked and seemed to meld.

"No, not now. But the *why* of my fear was from your power that I now know is great *and* good. I was sensing your strength and I feared that it might possibly be living within a negative source...a dark force."

His broad hand rested on my shoulder. "How did you come by this marvelous assumption of yours?"

"It's not an assumption," I declared confidently, "it's a correct conclusion."

His bushy brow rose. "Is it?"

"Yes," I strongly reaffirmed.

"Very well. It is good you do not question the final decisions of self. It is good you have gained a solid faith in that which you conclude."

"Then I was right."

"Are you seeking verification to solidify your conclusion?"

"No. I just wanted you to admit *why* you were observing us this morning."

"And for what reason do you require this admission?"

I paused to examine my reasoning. "Because your answer will tell me what I want to know—your answer will reveal the last name that you are known by. Do you intend to tell me the reason behind your observation?"

Now it was his turn to hesitate. He grinned. "Perhaps later."

"You're hedging."

"No, I'm simply being honest. Perhaps I will tell you later."

My eyes twinkled. "Or perhaps you won't have to."

His palms upturned. "Summer Rain, is it that I am so utterly transparent or that you are so astute?"

"I think neither, Joe Red Sky. I think it's because we have met here, along the pathway of the Way."

He nodded. "Then indeed, you have no need for me to speak my other name, for you already have knowledge of it."

"Yes. You are known by the dual name of Water Bearer and Dreamwalker."

Red Sky turned and began descending the hill. He motioned for me to walk beside him. "I'm curious," he mused. "Why is it that you combine the two terms?"

"Because they are one and the same. For some people who thirst, the Water Bearer gives drink to quench the thirst of knowledge, and for others who have already been quenched, the Dreamwalker gives further enlightenment through deeper understanding. But they are still both one and the same entity who appears different depending upon each individual's needs."

"Like in your dream?" he hinted.

"Yes." Of course he knew of the dream, for he was clearly one of the Dreamwalkers. "Are there many Dreamwalkers?" I asked.

"Not so many any more," he replied sadly. "Few want to expend the time and energy that it takes to walk the Way."

"That makes my heart sad. Perhaps that will change."

He glanced at me, then returned his attention to our trail. "It would be a good thing if more seekers became totally enlightened—if they walked the *entire* trail." His eyes slid to me when he emphasized the word "entire." It seemed as though he was directing it to me personally and I subliminally wondered if I would *make* the entire trail. Then I listened to his continued thoughts.

"Maybe someone will help things along so that more will feel the call within their spirits. If the truth be known, though, too few want to shoulder the burdens that are a Dreamwalker's. There are many faces they must wear . . . it all depends upon what crosses their paths."

I wondered at just what he was evasively getting at and, before I could inquire, he changed the subject.

"Summer Rain, what is it that you want from life? What is it that you're seeking?"

"I want people to wake up out of their stupors and become aware of themselves and their real surroundings—what's *within* them too . . . the God Spirit. I seek truth and a working understanding of it."

He thought on that before going on to the physical wants. "And what are your material wants?"

I chuckled at that one. "I have no material wants . . . well, I do have a material *need,* though."

His brow raised.

"We need a new vehicle."

He thought that was funny and didn't attempt to conceal his amusement over it.

I quickly clarified my statement. "Don't get me wrong, though. If it's not in the cards for us to swing it, then I'm certainly not going to be depressed over it. This old truck of ours is nearing its third lap around the odometer, and she'll last as long as we need her. We get along."

"Perhaps things will change."

I shrugged. "That'd be nice, but we're used to making do."

We had reached the cabin. Red Sky touched my hand. "You will do. You will do well, little Summer Rain. You will do okay."

I smiled with the warm comfort that radiated to my hand. I closed my eyes to better feel the warmth. The heady scent of woodsmoke wafted lazily through the air and I was suddenly engulfed by a wave of new warmth—a physical one.

"Okay, Summer," the words repeated with an echo.

"Red Sky?"

"You okay now, Summer," soothed the familiar voice, "you did okay!"

I opened my eyes to see the old woman kneeling over me. "Com'on, get up. We gonna sit at table and talk now. I got more tea. It gonna wake up Summer's cloudy head."

I leaned on my frail teacher while she slowly assisted me back to the table. It was still dark within the room. I looked around in the firelight before my eyes rested on the murky windows. "Ugg. It's still gloomy out there."

"Yup. That how No-Eyes say it gonna be today. Here," she offered, giving the steaming cup a shove in my direction. "This be ready now. It gonna shake cobwebs outta brain."

Numbly I drank the refreshing brew, and little by little, my senses sharpened. And when I felt normal once again, I looked to No-Eyes. She was beaming. I couldn't help but smile back. "Well?" I asked. "How'd I do?"

Pink gums showed. "How Summer think she do?" came the standard response.

"Is your grin any indication? Well," I admitted, "I liked the Dreamwalker. I liked him a lot."

"What you like so much 'bout him?"

"Well," I smiled wide, "for one thing, he didn't holler at me."

"Humph! Wait 'til he have more time with you. He gonna holler plenty then! Besides," she added, "Summer gonna meet some *other* one next time. Some other one gonna take Summer on journey 'long way."

I brightened. "Who? Who's going to take me?"

"I not tell that stuff. Summer see one day."

"When?"

"Don't be so Eager Beaver. Maybe Summer gonna need little bit more time with No-Eyes. Maybe Dreamwalker think Summer not be quite ready yet."

I was deep in thought.

"Now what?" she inquired of her pensive student.

"I never found out *why* Red Sky was observing us. He promised he'd tell me when we were through with our business."

She sighed heavily. "He not say that. He say 'perhaps.'"

The visionary was right. "That's right. And then I had an idea why, and he confirmed it. The reason was never really voiced at all." I leaned over the table. "No-Eyes," I said, "was he observing *me* out there this morning?"

"Yup."

"Was he observing me to see if I was ready for the Dreamwalker's words? His lessons?"

"Yup," she beamed in a childlike delight.

"And I passed inspection?"

"Yup. Why Summer sound so surprised?"

I was actually in shock. "I never would've believed it."

The old woman patted my hand. She understood my deep feelings. "It be time to head back now. No-Eyes gonna go get Summer's blanket wrap."

I bolted from the chair. "No, that's all right. You don't have to wait on me, I'll get it."

And I strode past the fireplace to retrieve my serape from where I had tossed it on the worn couch. I had subliminally gazed to her overstuffed chair in the dusky corner, when my breath caught sharply. I froze. For there, sound asleep, was an old man. I swung around to face No-Eyes.

She grinned. "Don't mind No-Eyes' old friend. He be tired. He been sleepin' whole time." She nudged me toward the door. "Yup," she said, glancing at the disheveled sleeper, "poor ol' Joe, he be gettin' on, you know."

Incredulously, I looked back and forth between my friend and the sleeper.

No-Eyes kept pushing at my shoulders. "Go on now," she urged, rushing me through the doorway. "You no need to come here tomorow. You only gonna come on Saturdays 'til No-Eyes say different."

And, standing on her porch, with the chilling haze eddying around us, No-Eyes held out her arms for me. The feel of her frail body only intensified the contrasting strength of wisdom she held within her incredible mind. We remained close for several precious moments before she finally pulled away. And raising her hand to smooth my hair, she lowered her stern exterior.

"No-Eyes be so proud of Summer today. This be day No-Eyes been waitin' for, day when Summer pass final inspection by Water Bearer. He speak to Summer to see if she be ready for Dreamwalker—and he say 'yes.'"

She had teased me before when she had hinted that perhaps I required more time with her. I avoided her reference to that. The deep tenderness of her pride was too fragile to shatter with silly banter. I took her frail hands.

"Thank you, No-Eyes. I couldn't have done it without all the knowledge you've shared with me. I couldn't have done it without your understanding patience with an often unruly and impetuous student."

Then, before we parted company, I wanted to clarify one last nagging enigma. "No-Eyes, that old man in there, he reminds me of . . . ."

"Go now, No-Eyes got much to do." She fluttered her hands in my face to shoo me away.

I descended her steps and tried once more for my answer. "But can't you just tell . . . ."

The door was closed.

As I made my way back to the truck, the swirling vapors no longer held any ominous portents for me. There were no more threatening terrors lurking within its dismal arms.

I started the tired engine and leaned forward to rest my arms up on the steering wheel. The wipers beat a tunnel of vision and I stared up at the shrouded cabin.

I smiled. "That's all right, old one, your secrets are safe with me. Goodbye, sleeping Joe Red Sky, your medicine is powerful—it's good . . . so good."

And I edged the truck out through the roiling mist to leave the two old wise ones alone within the protective warmth of their shared wisdom and companionship. The Visionary and the Dreamwalker could rest well now, their work was done.

The False Wiseman, raising his head, expects recognition and high praise, even adoration and a multitude of followers.

The True Wiseman, bowing his head, expects naught.

A Thirsty Spirit

Spiritual advancement is the Floodgate of truth's comprehension. One will not attain total understanding of specific Conceptual Ideas until, spiritually, he has reached that Theory's level of Inner Acceptance and Recognition.

The first Saturday in August will always have the prime distinction of being the beginning of my journey onto the path of the Way. It was the crossing of the threshold into the realm of Dreamwalkers where dimensional shifts were not considered impossible quirks of nature, but were rather accepted as the norm of reality. It was a nebulous place deep within the psyche, hence it was nowhere and everywhere, corporeal yet intangible, eternally immutable yet continually transitional. It was a place where all diametrical extremes were feasible. It was a place of clarity where one ventured to sail along the fragile fibers of time.

The Sunday morning following that memorable day with No-Eyes and the sleeping Joe Red Sky, Bill and I went out for breakfast at a local restaurant. Lately, the restaurant seemed like a second home, for if Bill and I weren't there for breakfast, I was there in my usual corner booth writing up notes for the books I'd promised the visionary I'd do.

On this specific morning, we were not occupying my unofficial "office," but were seated at one of the window booths where, outside, Pikes Peak could be seen rising up behind the town. It was one of those radiantly clear mornings when the sky was painted a deep robin's-egg blue and, from horizon to horizon, not a wisp of a cloud was visible. It was going to be another perfect Rocky Mountain day.

After we had finished our meal, we stayed on to talk about what had transpired the day before at the cabin. All I had told Bill the night before was that I wouldn't be going up to the old one's place on Sundays for a while and that I'd explain it all in the morning. He accepted the simple statement, knowing he'd hear all of it when I was ready to talk it through. And now I was ready.

I began with a solemnness. I began at the beginning—with the embarrassing part. "Yesterday when I was with No-Eyes, after our daybreak rite...nature scared me."

A corner of his mouth twitched with disbelief. "You're kidding, right?"

My stone-faced expression told him that this was no joke.

"But you're never scared out there," he said, glancing out the window at the famous peak. He was incredulous with the absurd idea that I could ever be frightened by the nature that I loved being within. "Why, you've stayed out there for several consecutive nights all by yourself and now you say nature scared you? And even when you were with No-Eyes?"

My stare remained unchanged and he realized I wasn't going to alter my statement.

"What the hell scared you?" He shifted his position and lit a cigarette. "Don't tell me she was up to some of her menacing tricks again. I don't like it when she just up and creates things for you to confront. I don't like it at...."

"She didn't," I softly interrupted. "She didn't create anything this time."

He held his response until the waitress had finished refilling our coffee cups. "If she didn't have anything to do with it then where did this fear come from?" he snapped, agitatedly.

I motioned a caution for him to calm down as the restaurant was full of people we knew. "I didn't say she had *nothing* to do with it, I just said she didn't *create* it."

He sighed in outward exasperation. "Well, I certainly hope you're going to tell me that the reason for this fear was a damned good one—that you learned some invaluable gem of enlightenment from it."

I smiled. I beamed. "Wait 'til you *hear!*" I quietly bubbled with excitement. And I recounted the entire bizarre story of how shamefully embarrassed I had been with my sudden fear, the special brew No-Eyes gave me, my resulting journey, and finally my utter shock at seeing the curious dishevelled old man sleeping in the shadowed corner.

He mulled it over. "That definitely had a direct connection to your dream last weekend. It's all tied in together, the pieces fit very neatly."

"No-Eyes' pieces always fit," I emphasized with a note of resignation. "That young man with the strange translucent eyes is a major player too. No-Eyes even went as far as openly admitting that he had been a student of hers but that he'd gone on."

"On to what?" he asked.

"Well, from the way she worded it, I believe he's actually advanced to the level of a Dreamwalker."

His mind groped for clarity amid the cloudy facts. "I thought the old guy, this Joe Red Sky, was the Dreamwalker."

"He was," I brightened as the excitement grew. "Joe Red Sky *and* the young man in my dream are Dreamwalkers."

My confused partner held up his hands. "Now wait a minute. I thought we'd concluded that your dream person was a Water Bearer, he said that, didn't he?"

"Yes, but...."

"So if he's this Water Bearer," he reasoned, "how can he also be a Dreamwalker?" He shook his head. "I don't think you got all your facts straight on this one. Somewhere along the line I think some serious confusion developed."

I rested back against the booth. "I hardly think my wise teacher would've let me walk away yesterday if my head was cluttered with confusing facts."

His brow raised. "Maybe she slipped up. She is getting up there, you know."

My mouth dropped at the audacity of his insinuation.

"I'm just kidding," he teased before becoming serious again. "So, I guess I was wrong when I figured who this dream man was." He paused a minute. "And so were you."

I frowned in puzzlement.

"Remember you said you were far from being ready to learn from a higher teacher? Remember your reference to you being 'just a lowly student?'"

I did recall my words. "I *am* just a lowly student, honey. I'll always be one, no matter who I study with."

He shrugged with a wry grin. "Well, then, I suppose No-Eyes has a different picture of her lowly student. I'd say that between the two of you, she's got the advantage of knowing better. She's been the judge all along. People rarely see themselves clearly, the way they really are. If she decrees you're ready and if this Joe Red Sky passed the same judgment, then I guess you're ready—evidently you're not as lowly as you believe yourself to be. Got it?"

I grinned sheepishly. "Yeah, I got it all right. I got an awful sudden case of nerves."

"Nah," he soothed, "that's just your false 'lowly' part talking. Listen, you can do it if No-Eyes has confidence that you can. Have a little faith in her verdict. Has her judgment ever faltered before?"

"No," I uttered, defeated.

"Well, there you are." His eyes twinkled. "Tell you what, when the time comes for you to accompany this Dreamwalker, just relax and be yourself. Don't try to second-guess what answers he's expecting from you; besides, he'd know you were doing that anyway—just be your usual honest, outspoken self."

That sounded good and it eased my mind—except for the last part. "I couldn't be outspoken in front of someone so enlightened," I blurted, "why, that'd show a blatant disrespect!"

Bill's shoulders slumped. "Honey," he explained sympathetically, "if this guy's as sharp as I think he's going to be, he'll see right through you. He'll see that you're putting up a shield to control the true feelings that you're concealing. He's not going to want to relate to a phony shield, he's going to want to communicate with the *real* you."

I didn't have to think through his reasoning. The facts were obviously clear. I was going to have to completely expose my true emotions when I was with my new teacher. That thought made me uncomfortable.

"Now what's the matter?" he sighed.

"I can be awfully outspoken," I cringed.

He smiled wide. "And that's usually whenever you're outraged by an injustice or by someone's crude unawareness." He tried to make me see that my occasional caustic remarks were always justified. "You've never said anything that somebody didn't bring on all by themselves."

"Yes, I know, but maybe it's time I learned to control that aspect of myself. Maybe I shouldn't be doing that anymore."

His lips pursed. "Well, then, if that's the case, I advise you to continue being yourself until you're cautioned otherwise. Let the teacher teach!"

Oh, he made it all sound so simple, so pat. But it wasn't as cut-and-dried as he thought. *He* didn't have to endure humiliating reprimands. *He* didn't have to strain his psyche to the limits and sustain it for lengthy periods of time. *He* didn't have to expend his energies on the complex mechanics of certain journeys. Nor did he have his reasoning mind bemuddled with high philosophical logic and then have to untangle it all so that it resulted in a crisp understanding, a clarity of total comprehension. Oh, this wasn't going to be any Saturday picnic, of that I was most certain.

"Well," I concluded, noticing the patrons waiting for tables, "we'd better head on home."

He motioned for me to remain seated. "One last question. When's this Dreamwalker going to arrive on the scene?"

"She didn't say, but if I understand all this correctly, I think I'm going to meet the Water Bearer first. He'll be the same man as the Dreamwalker, but he'll be initially operating in the Water Bearer capacity. That way he'll still be testing me."

"But she never actually said when?"

"No, but I don't think it'll be for a while yet, I've still got quite a few rough edges and I think she's going to want to smooth them down before she lets me loose."

He winked as we got up. "Your rough edges are great, they give you a distinctive character—nobody's ever sure what you'll say next!"

He was teasing, but he was also right. I did have a fault of being a little too honest with people and it put them on guard. I didn't like pretentions and I never liked haughtiness in people—I usually embarrassed both. At least folks knew I spoke my mind and they couldn't get away with anything in front of me. It served to separate the straightforward individuals from the pretentious ones and I ended up with open, honest friends. That wasn't all bad either. Yes, I liked that. All my friends were devoid of ulterior motives—they were good-hearted people and one can't ask for anything more treasured than that. If my outspokenness brought me true friendships then I guess it wasn't such a negative characteristic after all.

During the ensuing week, subliminal thoughts of the Dreamwalker speared through my mind. What would he teach me? And would I comprehend? What journeys would we attempt? And would I succeed? I wondered if we'd travel through the Corridor of Time. I was visited by deflating self-doubts and foreboding visions of failure. The hovering specter of inadequacy haunted the self-darkened shadows of my mind until I finally took firm command and allowed the gentleness of acceptance to bring in the light and chase the imagined shadows away. When the appointed time arrived, I would shed all remnants of expectation and calmly accept whatever was to be—I would simply speak, act and react naturally—I'd be myself. However things would eventually turn out, good or otherwise, at least I'd be able to say that, through it all, I was myself. Fail or succeed, I could still be proud that I had done my absolute best to prove that No-Eyes' judgment of my readiness was not in error.

And so it was that, despite the week-long struggle with the nagging doubts and their eventual turnaround, Saturday morning had dawned bright and clear. It was already too late to accompany No-Eyes in our daybreak greeting; she would've finished that hours ago. So

I leisurely got ready and left the quiet house.

Motor homes and campers were on the road before me. I had to stop behind a stalled RV that seemed longer than a mobile home. If this had been any other Saturday, my patience would've long since drained away, but on this particular day I felt no sense of time urgency to get to my schoolroom. There was almost a tangible laid-back feeling in the air that gave me the distinct impression that, as far as No-Eyes was concerned, it was all right for me to get there whenever I got there.

A colorful montage of vehicles halted behind me and together we made quite an extensive convoy before the crippled motor home finally sputtered and coughed its way back to health and was once again ambulatory.

Before the slow-moving caravan rolled another mile, I left the snaking procession behind and turned onto another highway that took me into the northern country. Now I wasn't as hemmed in as before, yet neither did I have the road to myself. An Eldorado blasted its horn behind me and pulled out to overtake the old pickup—Texas plates.

It amazed me how the tourists were forever in such a rush to get to their destination. Maybe they feared the main attraction would vanish before they arrived and got a chance to see it and pose for endless frames of photographs before it. Seemed to me, though, that they were speeding right past the most beautiful aspect of the entire state, that of the magnificent scenery. Well, no matter, it was hardly any concern of mine, and I doubled my attention on the surrounding vista as if to make up for the disrespectful lack of others.

The rich emerald pines that lined the roadway swayed with the soft breath of the gentle breeze. Their rhythmic movements reminded me of the smooth rise and fall of seawater swells. The delicate powder-blue branch tips of the Colorado blue spruces gave a pleasing blend of color in this living sea of life. And above all the distinctive blues and vibrant greens, the deep intensity of the fathomless turquoise sky bestowed a touch of Merlin's magic—a touch that canopied my land of nature with shimmering, mystical enchantment.

I turned off the highway onto the steep dirt road that led into the vastness of the Pike National Forest. The happy sunrays reached down through the stately evergreens to reflect the sparkling glints of mica that were imbedded in the road. They were like the jewels found set into the craggy walls of a gemstone mine.

Upward I climbed, the highway left far below now, and as the narrow dirt ribbon of road leveled off, I turned again, only this time onto a weed-choked path that had been marked by the weekly passing traces of my own tire trailings.

Deeper and deeper I went into the virgin woodlands that the

lumber companies wouldn't ever be able to touch. Finally the old truck dipped its hood down and descended into a small valley where I pulled it up next to an aged lodgepole and stopped. Looking up through the dusty windshield, I took a peaceful moment to scan the grassy rise that was crowned by my frontier schoolhouse.

Birds loudly chirped and cawed. The comical black kaibab squirrels chattered to one another as they scampered up and down the rough tree trunks. And the arm of Apollo, strong upon the dilapidated rooftop, warned that my allotted time to tarry had come to a close.

I sighed heavily as I got out of the pickup and began my ascent through the prickly mountain grasses. A warm contentedness filled my heart, it was a growing thing that expanded until I thought the throbbing vessel would surely burst with happiness. I broke out in a run with the hopes of dissipating some of the contained energy. The crude steps were taken two at a time before I flung open the rough pine door and plunged into the cool recess of the cabin.

The solemn darkness of the interior stopped me just inside the door. My eyes needed to adjust from the brilliance of the August sun. My labored breathing made an ominous sound that shattered the living silence. Dust motes floated in the diffused sunlight, creating a surrealistic surround as my vision became acclimated. And, standing across the room, looking out the window, was a man. His back was to me.

"Do you always charge in here like that?" he asked, turning slowly to face me.

I squinted my eyes to frantically search the corners of the tiny dwelling.

"She's not here," came the emotionless statement.

"Where'd she go?" I snapped in my nervousness.

"Away for the day."

The man was about my height and looked as though he was no stranger to weights. He was perhaps thirty-eight or so and had a thick shock of blue-black hair that covered the back of his collar. Deep smile lines creviced either side of his mouth making his dark skin appear leathery, as if he'd spent most of his life in the sun. A flowered western shirt tucked neatly into faded, boot-cut jeans was cinched by an engraved belt that was boldly centered by a large turquoise buckle. Scuffed and dusty cowboy boots gave clear evidence of many trails traversed on foot. His weathered hands were wide, their tanned cinnamon color contrasting sharply against the bright silver that encased turquoise ring stones. And his smile exposed large, even white teeth. He looked uncomfortably familiar.

He smiled. "Well?" he said, turning his palms up.

"Well what?" I asked, not knowing what I was supposed to answer.

His wide smile reduced to a friendly grin as he stepped closer. "Well?" he repeated, pointing to the door. "Do you always enter this place like that?"

"Oh, I . . . ah," I stammered like an idiot, glancing back at the door, then to the stranger. "Well, sometimes, sometimes I do."

I thought I had perceived a shadow of amusement cross his face before he again turned his back to me and strode to the window to gaze out at the mountains. I remained frozen in place by the door in the event I'd need a speedy exit, although I sensed no threatening vibrations.

When the young man next turned to me, the light caught his face just right. His eyes were transformed into multi-faceted prisms. Then they were momentarily translucent. I gasped.

"Is something wrong, Summer?" he asked in a wise tone that belied the innocence of his question. He had shrewdly perceived my startled recognition.

Now I was convinced who this imposing stranger was. Now I understood why the old one was "away for the day," and my heart thundered so hard I was sure he could hear it. Mind racing, I couldn't believe the time for my new teacher was at hand. I felt my legs turning to jelly. I was literally trembling with a terminal case of stage fright. I tried to control the shakiness of my voice—it miserably betrayed me—it cracked anyway.

"I know who you are," I began nervously.

"You do, do you," he grinned.

"Yes, I do. You're the Dreamwalker who's come to teach me."

Confident black eyes pierced mine. "Do I look like a Dreamwalker to you?"

"I have no expectations as to appearances, but to my feelings, yes, you feel like a Dreamwalker who is in the character of the Water Bearer."

"Oh, really?" he said, stepping nearer. "That's quite a powerfully high station for one to achieve. Are you certain of this?"

The man's deliberate mannerisms and the way he answered my questions with more questions were typical characteristics of an enlightened teacher.

I smiled. "Absolutely."

He lowered his head, eyes peering up at me. "Could be a trick."

"I believe all No-Eyes' tricks have been played out. Time's too short for any more foxy games." My head tilted slightly. "Don't you agree, Dreamwalker?"

His eyes sparkled with amusement. "I do agree. I'm here now in the initial capacity of the Water Bearer, as you so astutely reasoned out. And, since it would be most ridiculous for you to continually call me that, and because I already know your name, I think it wise to be on a first-name basis."

I grinned as he extended his hand.

"To most, I'm known as Brian Many Heart. To some I seem to have the unsavory reputation as being a wayward good-for-nothing who does odd jobs. To those who know better, I'm known otherwise. Pleased to meet you, Summer Rain."

"Call me Summer, No-Eyes does. Or just Mary if you prefer," I said, shaking his hand.

"I think we'll stick with Summer if that's all right with you."

I shrugged. "Okay by me."

An uncomfortable moment of silence fell between us. He immediately moved to dissipate its awkwardness by extending his arm with a sweeping motion. "Let's sit at the table and talk for a while."

I followed him to the sunlit room and settled into one of the pine chairs while Many Heart dug down in a styrofoam bucket. He chuckled as he held up two cans of ice-cold Pepsi and, popping the tabs, he set one in front of me. I watched as he gulped a long thirsty swig. "Ahh," he sighed with satisfaction, "that's good."

I looked suspiciously at the cold drink in front of me. I was thirsty and the can was beading with tempting droplets of moisture. Was this a clever device to see if I'd drink? Did he know I was a confirmed Pepsiholic? No-Eyes and I never drank anything but herb teas and an occasional chicory coffee. My mind churned as I eyed the cold, fizzing can of "juice."

My companion appeared entirely oblivious to my dilemma. He calmly extracted a cigarette from his breast pocket and lit it like he'd been doing it for years. "So," he began, "don't you like the pop? I'd offer you another kind, but that's the only brand I buy."

I didn't sense any contrivance within his voice or expression. "This is fine. In fact, it's the only kind I buy too." And I took a sip.

"No kidding," he exclaimed.

This time the contrivance showed and I looked up at him. "But then you knew that, didn't you?"

His head dropped in exaggerated shame. "Yea," he admitted with a sheepish grin. "I knew that. I also know you smoke, so feel free if you like." He placed a small ashtray down on the table, then turned his chair backwards, straddled it and rested his arms across the highback.

"How'd you know?" I asked. "About the Pepsi, I mean?"

His wrist flicked. "Does it matter how I knew?"

"I guess not really." And I had the sudden realization that this handsome man sitting across from me most likely knew a great deal about me. Ordinarily that would've set me on edge, but I found myself to be experiencing a very relaxed attitude and I knew it was he who was creating the comfortable ease.

"You know what's funny?" he reflected. "People think individuals like us don't and shouldn't drink things like pop. They think we shouldn't be smoking either. Don't you think that's a rather strange assumption?"

Was he drawing me into a ruse? Was the spider talking to the unsuspecting fly? Then Bill's words shattered my doubts. I certainly couldn't waste valuable time questioning every comment the Dream-walker made. I couldn't continually be thinking like some untrusting paranoid. I'd have to respond naturally—be myself. I flew into the web. "I think that's a ridiculously ignorant way to think."

The web was imaginary.

"So do I. They have this snow-white image of enlightened people. They have this crazy impression that we only drink pure vegetable and fruit juices, avoid coffee and pop like the plague and abhor smoking." He grinned. "I suppose they even think we never need to use the bathroom either."

I blushed at his exaggeration.

Many Heart laughed. "It's true! I suppose they view enlightened people as being some sort of half-human demigod."

"I don't know about the demigod part, but I have known folks who view my smoking as a sign of unattained awareness or some lesser degree of enlightenment. They have some antiquated idea that the smoke inhibits psychic functioning or performance."

He shook his head. "Those are the very ones who are exposing their own lack of knowledge on the subject. Guess they're not aware that physiological conditions have no bearing on the mechanics of the spirit. Guess they don't realize that an enlightened individual can control his bio-systems." The young man was amused at the thought, yet there was also just a hint of disgust.

"They just don't know about those things," I soothed. "Besides, does it really matter?"

His dark eyes softened. "Of course not." Then the amusing subject made a sharp turn when he asked a serious question. "Why are you here, Summer?"

That question had been asked of me many months ago by the old one. At the time, my initial reply was way off base, but a lot of water had surged under the bridge since then, now I knew where he was going with it.

"I'm here to succeed in doing what my spirit came here to accomplish."

His expression gave no indication as to what he had thought of my answer. "Do you thirst?"

"I thirst a great deal."

"For what do you thirst?"

"The end. I thirst for it all to end."

He took no moments to mull over my quick response. He knew I had left something out. The question came swiftly. "What of the *means* to that end?"

I felt I should blush with shame when I voiced that answer, but knowing it wasn't for selfish gain, I wasn't embarrassed. I threw caution to the wind as I raised my head proudly, eyes fixed on his, and said, "I thirst for money."

"Yes, for many years this has been a great thirst for you. I'm happy to see you have the freedom to admit it. There is no underlying guilt here."

"Many Heart," I said softly, "we've worked nine-to-five's all our lives just to make ends meet and keep food on the table. We've known about our mission for ten years and we've never had the monies to buy our mountain land." I sighed. "It's not as if we wanted a whole mountainside with a million-dollar house on it. We just wanted some remote property with a stream and a log cabin large enough for the five of us to have a little privacy. We wanted a couple horses and that's it. Our purpose was always stalled by meager finances."

"And this 'end'? What do you perceive this as being?"

"The Mountain Brotherhood where we can help people."

"That can be accomplished anywhere *you* are."

"Not exactly. We were told ten years ago that we'd be directed to secure mountain land where our *full-time* efforts could be utilized toward enlightening others. Presently, because my husband has to work all day and I have other obligations, the Mountain Brotherhood cannot be what it was meant to be. It cannot be fully realized until we're *living* on that land. Many Heart, we're still struggling. We still thirst for that money which will free us to be unencumbered to devote our total time to those who seek our help."

"Very well said, but what of other things—material things?"

"We neither need nor want material possessions other than a log home on our land."

His brow raised. "Nothing material?"

I grinned. "I guess you mean a vehicle." I glanced toward the window. "That old truck parked down there is very, very tired. Yeah," I admitted, "we'll need a new four-wheel."

"What about new furniture?"

I laughed. "You're joking, right? What's furniture but something folks brag about and show off? No, Many Heart, our furniture will do just fine."

"New clothes?"

"Exterior dressing which conceals or belies that which is within."

Silence.

"Electronic equipment?"

This was getting almost funny. "When there may be months without electricity?"

"A generator?"

"We've got one."

"Food supply?"

"Working on that."

Silence.

The man downed the last of his drink. "Then your thirst for this money is indeed honorably justified as it is selfless. Your thirst for the end is equally so, as that end will be the final fulfillment of your spirit's purpose here. Even so," he added, "you have yet another thirst which overshadows the other two. Are you aware of what this is?"

I was. "I need a deeper understanding of things."

"What are *things?* 'Things' is an obscure word that is limitless in scope. What are these *things* which require your comprehension?"

"Injustices. People's intense negative attitudes like bigotry and prejudice. Religion. Blind hypocrisy and skepticism. Jealousy. Hate. Egotism, materialism and . . . ."

"Whoa, Summer!" he cut off. "I read you loud and clear." His eyes indicated my hands. They were clasped in a knuckle-whitening knot. "Your thirst is great, but there is plenty of clear water in the bottom of your well. We will bring it to the surface so that you will be quenched with its enlightening refreshment."

I was both visibly relieved and encouraged by his words. "Will you do this, Many Heart? Will you really end this thirst?"

Eyes twinkled. "I cannot say. I can raise the water level, but it is you who must do the drinking and be satisfied. I can point the Way, but it is you who must choose to walk upon the pathway."

"Will you raise the level of the water and point the way?"

"I will, Summer."

Drumming sounds of happiness reverberated within my chest and I smiled wide. "Then I will drink of the water and I will walk the pathway."

Ra had reached the zenith of his journey and the small kitchen was cast in deep shadows. Outside, all of nature was bathed in the cleansing warm rays. Brian Many Heart picked up my Pepsi. "Let's get some fresh air and sunshine. We can sit on the steps."

The porch was warm and bright. We sat on the top step. Many

Heart settled in the center while I sat to one side and leaned back against the rail post.

"She's got a great spot here," he said with a soft hint of envy.

"Where's home for you?" I inquired.

"The deep woods and the copper canyons are home. The burning desert and the grassy rangeland are home." He patted the weathered wood of the porch. "Even this was home once."

"I meant where do you go when you head for home?"

"I just told you."

Evidently this man had no base to call home. I felt a sudden wave of sympathy rise within my heart.

"You have to learn to control that," he solemnly informed.

"Feelings are hard to put a lid on."

He studied the tilting tree tops. The wind hushed through thin outstretched branches. "I'm not talking about general feelings and emotions. I'm talking about your unrestrained empathy. If you don't learn to temper that. . .you'll let it destroy you."

"But I can't help it."

"Yes you can," he gently insisted.

I firmly disagreed. "I'm sorry, Many Heart, but I can't. The feelings just rise up in me."

"It can be harnessed. You can rein it in whenever you want. It requires an effort, but you are capable of this."

He just didn't understand. "I think maybe you don't understand true empathy," I foolishly countered.

His gaze went from me to the blueness of the sky. Then he shifted his position slightly and allowed his eyes to bore into mine. "Summer, tell me that I do not understand true empathy when I used to become enraged at injustices and prejudices. When I saw a poor family I wanted to give them all I possessed—meager as those possessions were. When I saw an old person who had no one, who was all alone in the world, my eyes burned with withheld tears and I wanted to go up to that old lonely person and hug them. And when I saw hunger and pain—I cried. Tell me, Summer, that I do not understand true empathy."

The blood drained from my heart, it was on the ground. "I'm sorry, Many Heart. You're an empath too."

"*Was*, Summer. . .I *was*. I controlled it, for it was holding me back—it was killing me and I realized how utterly useless I was to those who needed me."

Silence.

I listened to the merry language of the winged people who were playfully fluttering between the bottlebrush branches. I watched them gracefully glide from tree to tree. How carefree they were, I thought.

"They too have their daily problems," he said, nodding toward the winged people amid the evergreens. "Territorial maintenance, maternal duties, and worries over fledglings. Predatory fears, paternal protection, and scrounging for sustenance. Each species of people are not without real hardships. So within our immediate circle of species we do what must be done in order to effect helpfulness, otherwise we are nothing but heartless robots."

"Kind of like being the dead wood of humanity," I added.

"Even dead wood achieves helpfulness by supplying rich nutrients of nourishment for rebirth and regeneration. It still maintains its usefulness by sustaining the living organisms. Dead wood, even in death, lives."

His point was clear enough, but I had not referred to nature. "I meant the *human* dead wood of humanity," I respectfully clarified.

"Even so, Summer, human dead wood represents human failures which, in turn, feed the overblown egos of others more fortunate. The human dead wood serve as the decayed base by which successful humans continue to thrive on by feeding their egos until they look upon the dead wood in disgust and turn their prideful heads away. Yes, even human dead wood sustains human life—the negative aspect of life. How can successful men measure the extent of their exalted station or great wealth unless by comparison to the pitiful poverty and miserable failures of the so-called downtrodden dead wood?"

His explanation was so simple, yet when I went deeper into it, I realized that he had made a very profound philosophical statement—just the sort of clear reasoning I thirsted for.

"I see what you mean," I said. "That's exactly the type of understanding I'm seeking. I want to be able to comprehend the whys of negative attitudes and emotions so that through this enlightened perspective, I'll be qualified to help people."

"I know," he said softly.

At the foot of No-Eyes' hill I heard the rushing waters of the tributary below us. Its song was a joyful one that freely sang out for the pleasure of all nature. "The water spirit is happy today," I commented, leading into something I wanted to talk about.

Many Heart raised his face to the scented breeze that carried the nature being's aria. "Yes, she is glad. She sings her psalm of adoration to the Great Spirit." He fell silent again so he could enjoy the sweet sounds. Or perhaps he was waiting for me to get on with what I had wanted to say.

I spoke quietly. "I've been depressed a lot, Many Heart."

"This is not uncommon for people. Those who claim they are

never despondent are either liars or insane."

"I'm a struggling writer."

"Yes, I know of this effort of yours."

"Well," I confessed, "hearing the streamsong like this, I just wanted to say that I've taken great comfort in its singing. When I'd feel especially bad about all my publishing rejections, I'd drive up into the mountains and sit beside the surging waters. Sometimes the light spray would playfully bathe my face as if it were attempting to wash away my sorrows." I watched the spired tree tops sway against their brilliant turquoise backdrop. "I'd stare down into the rushing watercourse and realize that I had to continue on just like the creek did. If I didn't, all my hopes would dry up in a drought of perseverance. All my years of effort would have been for nothing and I would've failed."

"No success yet? No bites?"

I grimaced. "Bites, yes. But nothing firm. It's always the eventual cold rejection slips."

"What is it that you write?"

"Oh...novels mostly. Fiction."

He shook his head. "You are attempting to eat soup with a fork. You said 'mostly'; what else have you done?"

"Dozens of poems, a humor book, many, many children's self-image books, nature articles, and a philosophy book." I snuck a furtive side glance at my new friend and wondered what wisdom I'd hear about my writing follies.

Many Heart rubbed his chin. "That's interesting," he mused. "What was this humor book about?"

I cringed. "It's about people and their everyday irritations of life. You know, like the vending machines that eat your coins and then spit out the wrong thing or nothing at all. I wrote about a harried afternoon at the laundromat and one about how Carrie the Cart Crasher met her match one day in the grocery store."

He was smiling. "Who'd she meet up with?"

I blushed with the silliness. "Max the Market Masher."

His laughter echoed into the mountains. "Did you do many of these little quips at life?"

"Yeah, quite a few. In fact, I had a friend who was an artist. She drew the most hilarious cartoons to go along with my texts. It really was good."

"So?"

"So after five or six rejections, I filed *Screams* away."

"Screams?"

I shook my head. "Yeah, kind of dumb, huh. That's what I had entitled the book because the text and cartoons were about all the little irritating pet-peeves that make people want to pull out their hair and scream."

"Well," he smiled wide and patting my knee for encouragement, "I think that's great. Maybe someday it'll go."

"I don't think so . . . I don't have the cartoons anymore." I sighed. "I suppose I could find another cartoonist." I paused as I reconsidered the option. "Well, I don't think it's right now anyway. Maybe I'll just keep it on file for the future."

"That's your prerogative. What about this philosophy book, though? I'd like to hear about that."

I toyed with my fingernails. "That's not worth discussing—it's been totally rejected—it's dead."

"I think it's worth discussing."

And even though I disagreed, I realized there was probably a good reason for hashing it over. "It was a book that ate up over five hundred pages of my typing paper. It was filled with profound wisdom and forewarnings for mankind." My tone dropped. "It was dictated by our advisors from the other side." I looked away to hide my mistiness. "And nobody was aware enough to recognize its valuable worth, nobody was enlightened enough to accept it."

The young man purposely avoided the emotion I tried to conceal. "And how long did you try to sell this book?"

I chuckled in disgust. "Four years. For four years I'd excitedly send it to a publisher and then endure the nerve-wracking wait for an answer. I'd wait for months and months to get a decision from just one publishing house. After so many disappointments, I filed that one away too."

"What made that book so important?"

"It would've saved a lot of lives if people had heeded the forewarnings. It would've enlightened a heck of a lot of people and it would've been the beginning of the Mountain Brotherhood—the culmination of what we came here to do." I watched a mountain blue bird wing its way into the sun-splashed woodlands. "But the last publisher I sent to, the one publisher who we held so much hope for, changed his mind at the last minute—he too rejected it."

"Summer," he whispered, "that's all over now."

"Easy for *you* to say," I nearly sneered. "*You* haven't suffered through all the demeaning form letters. You haven't been up one day, endured the months of waiting and then been shot down into the pits of despair the next. It's made me feel like a damned manic depressive!"

The corner of his mouth lifted slightly. "You're no manic depressive. If you were, No-Eyes wouldn't have touched you with a ten-foot walking stick." He contained his mirth before going on. "She only accepts those she knows have a firm, stable grasp on reality."

"Oh, I know," I admitted with a show of exasperation, "but it just made me feel so low all the time. I was always in and out of such blackness."

"And you aren't anymore?"

I picked up a pebble-sized piece of granite off the step and rolled it about in my hand. "No, because I've put all the writings away since meeting the old one. Anyway, she claims that when we're through, I'll have success in the literary department." I hesitated a minute. "Don't see how, though. I don't see what's the big difference between my former philosophy book and what No-Eyes has in her mind for my writings. Truths are truths."

"You're right, Summer. Truths are truths. They can't be altered to fit the mood, the individual or the situation, but sometimes truth's *source* has everything to do with the ultimate success or failure of its revelation."

He reached out his hand for the pebble, and when I passed it to him, he held it up between his fingers so that the sunlight played on its quartz facets. "Just a common, nondescript segment of good ol' Rocky Mountain granite. It's what you see every day. It's what you walk on each day. It's nothing but an ordinary piece of our ground here. But," he cautioned with a wise twinkle in his eye, "but lift this common pebble up out of its camouflaged surroundings, wash it off, hold it up so that it catches the living light, and now you hold a real gem that flashes and sparkles. Same pebble, nothing altered, just brought alive with life."

The parable was beautiful. "And No-Eyes is this 'living life' that will be my *source* of truth." I grinned with the simple mechanics.

"In essence, yes. But the literary success will be finalized by the *tandem* efforts of her living life and your tender writing style."

I playfully smirked. "I don't have a writing style. I just write what I feel."

He handed the tiny stone back. "Exactly."

And I listened to the lithe water spirit's sweet song. Incessantly lilting, she was forever powerfully alive with the magic of eternal perseverance. My senses honed to a saber-edged clarity as I deeply inhaled the high mountain air that was heady with the aromatic spice of healthy evergreens. My eyes grazed over the jagged spines of the distant mountain ranges. And, high above all the intense beauty, the sleepy sun drowsily ambled along its wedgewood trail.

At this precise moment in time, I loved life. I loved all the shimmering and shining and singing aspects of nature. I loved myself for being so vitally alive within nature's intoxicating vitality. I loved the easy-going relationship with my new teacher and I loved the renewed excitement that the feeling of regained hope gave to my heart.

I looked to Many Heart. He had been observing me. My happiness smiled. "What're you looking at?"

"Only the lovely blossom," he replied cryptically.

My brows raised in question. "Blossom?"

"Yes, my curious friend," he grinned, "the blossom of hope that grows from the bitter roots of long-suffered endurance in the soil of pain."

And so it was that, on one radiant day in August when the water spirit sang and the mountains shimmered under the lazy sun, I took my first fledgling step upon the path of the Way. There were no harrowing frights nor bizarre journeys. There were no ambiguous verbal circle dances nor phantasmic guests. No frosty glares or chilled silences passed between us. The Water Bearer had conducted his discerning test on the curious newcomer with a judicious mind and compassionate heart. The initiate had accepted the test with simple openness. And the two had found a warm companionship. The bond was quickly set.

The real light of comprehension was about to illuminate the pathway. It would make the rest of the journey along the Way brilliant with the highest form of enlightenment. And now the novitiate was about to clearly see and wisely perceive through the penetrating eyes and discriminating mind of the Dreamwalker.

Like a stagnant pond is Wisdom retained. It breathes no life. It dies a slow and lingering death within the Self.

Like a mountain freshet is Wisdom shared. It endlessly pours forth clear and pure. It lives on as It breathes life and refreshment into all it touches.

Through the Jade Shadows

There are Things never spoken about.
There are Things so Sacred They never pass over lips.
Powerful Things.

—No-Eyes

When I had begun telling Bill about my visit out to the cabin, as soon as I mentioned the fact that No-Eyes wasn't there, he gave me one of his knowing sly looks. "Bet somebody else was, though," he cleverly intimated.

And when I asked him how he knew, he just said that he'd had a strong feeling that my new lessons were going to commence a lot sooner than I had anticipated. He had reasoned that No-Eyes would want to leave my "rough edges" just as they were so that the perceptive Dreamwalker would have the opportunity to analyze them. "Some rough edges are a good thing," he considered thoughtfully. "Like I said before, yours seem to suit you."

We touched on the disturbing fact that people in general shared the widespread misconception of perceiving aware individuals as being categorized and cubbyholed into neat little packages of perfection. We discussed my confession that finances was the main stumbling block that kept us from advancing on to our promised geographical location, and we reviewed Many Heart's thoughts about my future writings. Bill had a few things to say about the latter subject.

"This idea of the 'source' of truths making the difference between rejection and acceptance makes a lot of sense. When you think about it," he reflected, "people aren't actually ready for books coming from the other side. Someday, maybe, but the general awareness hasn't risen that high yet."

I agreed. "Many Heart seemed to think that if I wrote about the times No-Eyes and I spent together, people would then relate to her living words and also to our sensitive relationship."

Bill, eyes softened, peered over at me. "You don't want to do that, do you."

I shook my head. "Our days together are so special, so tender and private. Sometimes when I recall my writing promise to her, I wish I'd decided something different. Just the thought of having people read about our days, especially the more personal and sensitive conversations, makes me feel like I'm going to be desecrating sacred ground."

"I know," he comforted, patting my hand. "But don't you also feel a little bit scared too?"

I looked up at him. "Scared?"

"Maybe 'scared' isn't exactly the right word for what I mean, maybe be 'exposed' would be a more precise one. Are you having trepidations about exposing your sensitivities, your reprimands, or your beliefs?"

"We already talked that aspect through, remember? We decided that writing about No-Eyes would expose both of us and that we weren't bothering with the unaware skeptics, remember?"

His lower lip rolled out and his brows raised in a doubting expression. "Talking about bravery is a lot different from doing it. I just want you to be prepared for the worst in the event that people don't understand the real importance of the book." His doubtful expression hardened into one of determination. "Nobody's going to hurt you, though. No matter what becomes of your No-Eyes book, I won't let anyone hurt you."

I smiled. "Nobody's going to hurt me, honey. Any negative comments just show me how unaware someone is. That won't bother me."

"Easy to say now, just hope you remember that if and when the time comes."

The idea of a book about my dear old friend painfully pulled at my heart each time I thought about it. I was again melancholy. "I don't know, Bill. I just don't know if I should actually do it. For years and years she's lived so alone up there, treasuring her solitude with nature, teaching those who have been led to her, it just seems like a terrible invasion to expose her." I hesitated. "She's like a rare jewel. She's fragile."

He held my hand. "Does she want you to write the story?"

"You know she does."

"Then look at it as leaving her a wonderful legacy. View it as making her into a legend that will bring thousands into enlightenment. See it for what you can *do* for her. You'll have the great opportunity to bring out the tenderness you two are sharing together so that when people read about it, they'll laugh, they'll cry, and No-Eyes will live forever through your words. Her life will not have been lived in vain. Her solitude will not have made her obscure among humanity, but rather known to all."

I made a weak smile at his efforts. "I think *I'm* the one who's being left the wonderful legacy."

"Probably so, but don't you realize the *good* her story will do?"

Full of resignation, I nodded. "Of course, but I don't believe I'll ever shake the feeling that the exposure will rob a little bit of the sacredness I now feel about our special relationship."

"Wait until the time comes, you'll feel differently."

Perhaps I would, then again, maybe I wouldn't.

Another question pestered Bill, and even though he felt we should drop the entire subject, he asked just the same. "When your book is ready, did Many Heart suggest who to send it to?"

I nearly groaned. "Yes."

"Well? Who?"

"He said it'll be accepted in just a few weeks after we send it to the publisher who we counted on last time."

"Are you sure?" he blurted in disbelief. "Hey, we don't need any more disappointments."

I sighed. "That's what he said, all right. He said that there were a few departmental changes and that we'd have an affirmative decision in just a few weeks this time."

My partner wasn't too thrilled with the idea. "I don't know," he hedged. "After four years wasted with the last book, I sure don't want to waste another four, time's just too short."

It seemed that after years and years of perseverance, we weren't any more enthused or hopeful by Many Heart's suggestion than if we were to handle it on our own. Ten years was a long time to hold hands with faith, but then again, we couldn't deny the blossom of hope that was growing stronger within our hearts. The "end" *had* to be near, for our endurance was wearing very, very thin.

The following Friday evening, four of our friends stopped by. Doug was an attorney who worked out of Denver and his wife, Shirley, was a nurse at one of the large metropolitan hospitals in Colorado Springs. They unexpectedly appeared at the door with another couple, Mike and Anne. Mike did construction work and Anne was a researcher.

It would appear that their occupations had no common denominator, but their personal interests did. All four had met at a seminar on the subject of advanced mental capabilities which covered the complexities of the mind's paranormal functioning. And we had met them shortly after we came to Colorado.

Mike came through the door holding up a bottle of our favorite wine and that alone signaled a long evening that was going to be spent in deep discussion of alternative realities and high spiritual philosophy. These sessions could go on far into the wee morning hours, and since I was scheduled to be at the cabin the following morning, we had to cut if off at a reasonable hour, even though Anne's new research work was particularly engrossing. And before they left, she extended an invitation for us to visit the clinic for a tour.

On Saturday morning I was up and on the road early enough to avoid the crowded highway condition I encountered the weekend before. It was another captivating Rocky Mountain day and, even though I had missed out on our daybreak blessing, I mentally gave my thanks for all the resplendent bounties nature freely provided.

I was in a feather-light mood and as I smiled with the happiness that the scenery filled my heart with, I decided to try to convince Many Heart that it'd be good if we went for a woodswalk today. Being out in No-Eyes' deep forest among all the thriving life gave such an uplifting feeling of close belonging, it gave a feeling that served to intensify the words of my lessons.

When I pulled up under the lacy shadows of the high lodgepole, I noticed that the cabin door was opened. Many Heart was most likely airing out his smoke. Even though the old one occasionally puffed on a pipe, out of simple respect, the young man would naturally want to keep her place fresh.

This time I contained my energetic excitement and I climbed the hill in a slow and dignified manner that was more in keeping with the serious station of a high learner. The steps weren't taken two at a time, but were rather ascended slowly, softly. And, standing in momentary hesitation before the yawning doorway, I peered inside.

The house was dark and the weighted stillness was shattered by a hoarse cackle. "What you sneakin' 'round for?" she barked at me from within the shadowed recess. Then, suddenly appearing in my face, the old one wagged a crooked finger and shook her head. "We gonna get going now. We got lotta stuff to talk 'bout this day." And the frail woman tightened her shawl around her thin shoulders, snatched her walking stick from behind the door and agitatedly thumped down the wooden steps.

I bit my lower lip and peeked around the doorway in hopes that. . . .

"He not be here today," she sputtered impatiently. "Get down here before Summer waste whole day!"

I was disappointed that my new teacher was not there, and even though I loved the old one and was happy to be with her again, my subdued energies were all too detectable when I caught up with her.

We descended through the sweet sage of the hillside without speaking and, upon reaching the grassy bottom, she halted to sniff the pine-scented air. Chin jutting up, eyes squinting, her head turned slowly to lower even with mine. "Summer seem disappointed to see old woman today."

That assumption hurt as it stabbed at my heart. "No! I'm not. I love you!"

"Humph," she grumbled. "No-Eyes think Summer miss seein' that young man. No-Eyes not be handsome like Brian Many Heart be." Her eyes twinkled with the amusing thought.

My mouth dropped as my cheeks warmed. "That's a *terrible* thing to say! You're *wrong* to make such a preposterous presumption."

"Oh?" she sang, peering at me. "Then why Summer be blushing? Truth showing hot on Summer's cheeks." The old one snickered and hobbled away into the woodland shadows. She left me standing in the sun that beat down on my face, firing up the already heated cheeks.

I watched her slow and confident advance into the forest and, looking up into the deep cobalt sky, I caught the tail end of the falcon's slicing dive into the high evergreens. It was as if he had signaled me to pursue my thoughts—go ahead with the confrontation—and it was the falcon's added urging that made me determined not to let her get away with what she had so boldly said.

When I finally caught up with her, she had covered a good distance of the narrow footpath. I knew she was aware of my presence but she gave no outward indication of it. I sidled up beside her. "That comment wasn't fair, you know."

Silence.

"Even if I did blush, it certainly wasn't because of any guilt. People blush for other reasons, you know."

Silence.

"Are you even listening to me?" I snapped in exasperation.

"Yup, No-Eyes be listening."

"Well?"

"What so, this 'well'? Summer say why she *not* blush. No-Eyes waitin' to hear *why* Summer blush at No-Eyes' words."

"I blushed because I was embarrassed with your startling supposition. No-Eyes, you embarrassed me."

"No-Eyes be sorry. Just checking, that all," she admitted so matter-of-factly.

"Checking for what? To see if I was love-struck by the first good-looking man I had to relate with?" The very idea was incredible and I didn't hold back my opinion. "You ought to know me better than that. You ought to know I'm no schoolgirl who falls for a handsome face. Besides," I teased, "I don't go for baby-faced prettyboys—I rather like the rugged, weathered look." I had been grinning, but then my soft playfulness hardened into deadpan at the sight of the woman's wide smirk.

"Many Heart be rugged lookin'. He got a plenty weathered face."

I sighed. "Well, even if he does, I'm still not the type to fall in love with my teacher. I think this entire discussion is just ridiculous."

"Me too," came the quick chuckle. "No-Eyes just having little bit of fun with Summer, that all."

"No-Eyes," I sternly informed, "it's not called 'fun' when the other person isn't laughing—then it's called 'teasing.'"

"What so. No-Eyes tease Summer little bit then. Why Summer be so concerned 'bout what it called anyway?"

"Because you taught me to be. You taught me to be precise."

"Yup, that be so. Summer gonna need that with Many Heart, too," she firmly reminded.

Our ribbon of woodland path was a filigree of lacy shadows as the sunlight pranced within the high evergreens. It was cool under the natural canopy of greenery where nature lovingly shaded the many colorful mosses and lichens that grew upon rocks, ground and trees.

The old one's walking stick crunched rhythmically down on the trail's stony granite bed as we went deeper into the secluded mountainside. A porcupine huddled up in a ponderosa pine, clung precariously to his guard post and watched the two pass below him. I smiled at the humorous sight of the prickly creature's downy head peering down at us.

"There's a porcupine up in the tree on your right," I informed my companion. "I think he's keeping a close eye on us."

"No-Eyes hear him even before Summer see him. Yup, he keepin' sharp eye out just like Many Heart gonna do with Summer."

"Is our entire day going to be spent talking about Many Heart and how he's going to be watching everything I do?"

"Yup. This gonna be last time Summer gonna be with old wrinkled teacher before she finish learning with handsome one. I not gonna see Summer again 'til maybe when snow begin, maybe not 'til November even." The woman stopped strolling. She mysteriously inclined her head to me, stray wispy white hairs caught the sunlight that framed an aura around her head. She narrowed her lids before flaring them wide open to expose the silvery mercury that swirled over the dark surface of her liquid ebony pools. "Maybe when No-Eyes next see Summer," she whispered, "Summer gonna be somebody new inside." She poked my shoulder, then my head. Her voice was barely audible. "Maybe this new somebody inside gonna be a new

Dreamwalker."

The wise one closed her eyes and smiled with satisfaction as she turned her head to the woods. The crooked stick beat out the sound that indicated we would now walk on—my lesson for the day had officially commenced.

As we proceeded in silence, I listened to the thriving life of the forest. My senses sharpened with clarity and my mind became fully loaded with explosive questions I needed to fire off.

"That what today be for," came the sudden statement. "This day be for all Summer's questions. It be last day for No-Eyes to give answers."

I wasn't certain where I should begin. I led off with an obvious beginning question. "Can you tell me how I did last week? I know you can tell me that, but are you permitted to tell me that? I'd really like to know."

"Mmm," came the hesitant guttural sound of pondering. "No-Eyes be allowed to say that stuff."

"Well?" I pushed anxiously. "How'd I do?"

Tap, tap went the stick. "How Summer think she do?"

I should've anticipated that reply. "I think I did all right. I was straight with him and we seemed to be able to relax with one another. At first I guess I was a little uptight, but then I loosened up and just related naturally. He's very easy going and that helped a lot."

"Easy going?"

"Yes, you know, not presumptuous or hard in his character. He was a real everyday, down-home type that was easy to talk with."

"Humph! He got many strict hard stuff in him. He only being nice to Summer. Maybe Summer gonna bring out his strict stuff." She sighed. "Then again, maybe Summer never see it. Depends."

"Well," I admitted, "even if he does get stern with me, that's okay too." I softened with seriousness. "No-Eyes, I have to succeed with this important step. I have to be able to see it through and come out the other side feeling good about myself. I have to have a good journey."

"Or what?" she asked.

I was straight with her. "Or I don't know what. All I do know is that I'm determined to succeed."

The old one chuckled. "Tsk-tsk," she began with a slow shake of the head. "Determination not be what give success along *this* pathway. That stuff got nothing to do with it. Summer can leave that determination stuff at home this time."

We had been ascending a slight grade the last quarter-mile or so and I wanted my friend to take a break. "Let's rest a while," I said, offering to guide her over to some boulders.

No-Eyes gratefully accepted my help. We sat on the sun-warmed rocks. A harmless snake slithered out from his invaded territory and into the glistening emerald kinnikinnic that crept along the damp forest floor.

"We're sorry, young one," I said, offering our joint apologies, "we won't be here long. Thank you for giving up your place of rest."

No-Eyes simply nodded in agreement.

I returned to the subject of my upcoming journey. "If firm determination won't do me any good, what will I need?"

The visionary lifted her wrinkled face to the sun that flooded through to encircle the small clearing in a glow of gold. "Think, Summer. Think."

The rays were heating my hair. I looked up into the trees while my fingers deftly combed through the long mass. I reached into my jeans for the rawhide strip and tied the hair back with it. I watched the branches stir in the light breeze. "I'll need understanding," I said. "I'll need to comprehend concepts before I can do things."

The old one's expression remained unchanged as she lowered her head from the hot sun. "No. Understanding or total comprehension is not required either. Yes, Summer, you will need *some* of those but only a little."

This confused me. "But how will I be able to accomplish certain things if I have no clear understanding of how they're done?"

"Explain to me how Summer's truck engine works."

Silence.

"You see? Only a bit of comprehension allows you to do the operation—the driving. Summer puts gas in and knows the rules for safe driving, but Summer does not fully comprehend how it all works. On your journey, Summer, you will not have to know how to *build* that which you comprehend enough to operate. The fine mechanics will not be necessary to understand, for some things will be impossible to understand anyway." Then she cryptically added, "There be many, many corridors."

The point was clear.

"Does Many Heart comprehend these finer mechanics?"

The wise one closed her eyes. "There be things never spoken 'bout. There be things so sacred they never pass over lips." She whispered the last. "Powerful things."

The intenseity of her profound words created a shiver down my spine. The silence remained weighted with the dynamic mood of the moment. And when it lifted, I broke the stillness. "If word of mouth, from teacher to student is not utilized, does one gain knowledge of these powerful things through enlightenment? Does it then become a personal 'knowing' when one is ready?"

"Sometimes that is how it comes. Sometimes it comes never."

She rose from the boulder and straightened her creaking back. "If and when it comes to you, Summer, you will never find words to accurately describe the comprehension of the mechanics. Do not even try. It will make you go 'round and 'round 'til you go crazy with all your simple words that do not work—they will say nothing."

"I'll remember that, No-Eyes. I hope the time comes when the need for that memory will be useful."

"Mmm," she mumbled as she turned her back to me and began walking again. "We shall see."

When I was beside her, I was about to speak when a leathery brown hand gently raised. It demanded hushed silence. I watched in statue-stillness while the old woman slowly reached into her tattered pocket, extracted something and, in slow motion, lifted her arm high.

I dared not even blink while holding my breath, for out of nowhere came a grey-winged person. The Clark's nutcracker quickly flew to the outstretched morsel, snatched it up and quickly sped away to disappear in the shadowed woodlands.

No-Eyes smiled to herself and walked on. She was so incredible the way she related to all her neighboring creatures. I'm sure that very offering had been enacted a hundred times over during her many years living by the woods. The nature beings were as used to her presence just as naturally as an echoing thunderstorm or the changing of the seasons. Indeed, she had become a most invited guest within their private domain.

"What so, Summer!" she said, picking up on my sudden down-turn of mood.

"I feel envious of your free relationship with the people here. I was wishing how much I'd love to be able to do what you just did."

"Summer can do that."

I chuckled. "Not quite, No-Eyes, not quite. I don't get out into the mountains enough. I'm not a daily familiar sight to them."

"Time gonna come for that soon 'nough. Summer see."

I truly hoped that it wouldn't take too long in coming; nevertheless, now wasn't the time to dwell on the gaining of such tender interrelation-ships and I brought us back to my former dilemma of singling out what I needed in order to succeed on my journey to the Way.

We had been strolling the section of the forest's path where the tall evergreens crowded in on either side as if eagerly listening. Their breath hushed in strained efforts to hear our words.

"Faith," I said. "I'm going to need faith in what Many Heart speaks and I'm going to have to have faith in myself in order to succeed." I anxiously waited for confirmation while the trees whispered among themselves. They seemed to be shaking their heads in disagreement.

"Nope. Better do better than that. Faith. Summer already got plenty of that stuff. No-Eyes see that Summer already got faith in Many Heart's words. Summer already got faith in self, too. Summer gotta think deeper here."

The pines nodded and waved their spices through the wafting air. I inhaled deeply of their pure and honest simplicity. "Honesty!" I blurted out in my excitement. "I'll need complete honesty!"

"Humph," she mumbled, "Summer already got that." The old one didn't leave it at that, though, for she added, "maybe Summer got too much honesty even."

I frowned with an almost hurtful expression. "Then I *do* speak out too often, don't I? I *am* too straightforward."

Wispy brows rose above saucer eyes as she tightened her thin lips. "No-Eyes not say that—Summer say that."

"But it's true, isn't it? I know it. I just knew I'd get shot down because of that. Aware and enlightened people aren't supposed to go around putting other people in their place. They're not supposed to be...."

"Shhh!" came the sharp sound. "What so! What this s'posed stuff anyway? No-Eyes thought Summer *had* no 's'posed' this and 'cubby-holed' that 'bout enlightened peoples. Huh, Summer? Huh? What 'bout that?"

I was mortified that I had categorized myself. I spoke softly with guilt heavy in my voice. "You're right. I was wrong to think like that. I just thought that since one rarely encounters an outspoken aware person, that I was wrong to maintain that characteristic. I thought that...."

"Summer," she comforted affectionately, "enlightened peoples *do* have certain characteristics. They got humility and acceptance. They got faith and love. Some got great power while some got a little bit. They got universal knowledge. But they can be rich or poor. They can be garbage man or doctor." She slid her narrowed eyes to me. "They can be silent or outspoken."

Silence.

"Besides," she continued, "No-Eyes not say Summer need to put basket over mouth. That stuff okay for Summer 'cause you not misuse it. See?"

"Yes," I said hesitantly. "Then what did you mean when you said that maybe I had too much honesty?"

"No-Eyes see Summer need to bury that part of honesty that worry Summer."

"You mean since my outspokenness bothers me, I need to see that it really isn't a negative aspect that requires changing."

The walking stick pounded the gravel. "That what I just say! What so! I gonna say stuff over an' over here? Summer gonna echo all stuff No-Eyes say?"

Her outburst was unexpected and uncalled for; however, I retained my patience. "I just wanted to clarify what you meant. I didn't mean to repeat your words."

"Humph," she calmed. "Summer better not do that stuff with Many Heart."

I sighed. "You sure are making him out to be some kind of ogre. What is he, some sort of Jekyll and Hyde?"

"Who?" she asked, squinting up into my face.

"He was a fictitious character in a story. He could alter his personality's polarity. Never mind," I shrugged, "it's only make-believe anyway."

Her nose came to mine as the black opals bored hard. "We not *ever* deal with *make*-believe, Summer! This not be some *game* here!" Her eyes closed as her back relaxed. The woman turned back to the trail and leaned into the stick for support while she shuffled forward.

I had been severely reprimanded for my innocent comparison. Yet an aware individual doesn't make comparisons between truth and fiction—there just aren't any to make—reality often *seemed* like make-believe, but it most definitely wasn't, for the difference could be strongly felt within the heart and especially within the spirit.

I rushed to her side. "I'm sorry I say such stupid things sometimes. I realize I shouldn't have made such a dumb comparison. I promise I'll be more aware next time." This day wasn't going very well. I seemed to be saying and thinking all the wrong things.

"Better be more aware next time. Dreamwalker not gonna tolerate such unawareness. He gonna expect more thought behind Summer's words."

She was making my new teacher out to be a real live troll and I was beginning to worry. "Will he get very angry if I should slip up?"

The meter of her gait paused a second before continuing. "Dreamwalkers *got* no anger. Summer be upset with self, that all. That be 'nough."

"But you're circling, No-Eyes," I pushed. "You're saying all along how I'd better do this or I'd better not do that because of what Many Heart will do. Then you say he doesn't get angry. Which is it?"

Walking on, she coldly stated, "I not say he gonna do no thing. Summer's head say that. No-Eyes only warn Summer how to behave, that all."

"You make it *sound* like he was going to do something," I persisted.

"Nope," came the quick chirp. "Many Heart only gonna lead. If Summer be bad student then it be *Summer* who do something— Summer gonna retrace steps back to beginning of journey—not ever finish it."

I was speechless. There was nothing to say. The devastating thought of such an abrupt end of my journey caught fast in my throat. It hurt. I raised my misty eyes to the high branches that were now still—painted greenery against a stained sky of glass—nature stood still as it held its breath with the intense drama that was being played out at its feet.

I blinked back the emotion, heaved a few deep breaths and caught up with No-Eyes. "I can't help it," I spouted, pulling at her arm, "I just can't watch every single word I say. I have to be *me*! When I'm with Many Heart I have to be totally honest and straightforward. If I say some wrong things then that's just too damned bad! But the way I see it, I'll fail anyways if I'm *not* completely honest. So if I'm bad, I'm bad. I can't hide the real me for his sake, for the journey's sake or for the sake of anyone or anything!"

Silence passed through the woodlands. The trees wavered. Nature had exhaled deeply and begun breathing once again. A cool breeze crossed our faces as the wind spirit gently caressed the two humans standing in its encircling arms.

"You done?" came the whispered reply.

Somewhat embarrassed, I said that I was.

Pink gums gleamed. Eyes twinkled. And, reaching for my hand, the aged visionary led me along the trail. "Summer finally understand what needed for journey's success. Summer finally realize she only need complete honesty. No hide feelings or words. No hide thoughts under baskets. No push ideals under rocks. Summer gonna do fine with *decisive* honest mind."

Her teaching methods often took the long way around. She could've saved us both a good deal of time and energy, but that wouldn't have made the student face the realities that needed to be confronted. And for that, I loved her.

We turned, hand in hand, and headed back along the pathway. For several moments we basked in our sweet silence, each quietly reaping the rich beauty of one another's friendship.

A timid chipmunk scuttled across the trail. He peeked out at us from between the shiny kinnikinnic leaves, then scampered onto a mossy rock. Standing on little hind legs, forepaws poised to his tiny chest, he watched unblinking as we passed. No-Eyes withdrew a few kernels of corn from her pocket and tossed them in his direction.

"He know all 'bout what be in No-Eyes' pockets," she chirped with glee. "He always scamper on No-Eyes' lap. He usually nose 'round in pocket here," she said, patting the fold of her skirt. "Guess he bein' cautious today 'cause No-Eyes got stranger with her."

I looked back at the wee fellow who was preoccupied with the serious business of inspecting each golden kernel as he comically twirled them in his delicate paws before packing them firmly into the bulging cheek pouches. I smiled with the tenderness I felt for the little nature person.

The old one spoke softly. "Little ones gonna poke 'round in Summer's pockets one day. Summer gonna be able to do that stuff too."

"Oh, but I already have done that," I said, grinning wide. "When I'm alone or when Bill and I are by ourselves in our woods, the little ones come right up and nudge our hands."

No-Eyes raised her brows. "I not be talkin' 'bout *your* woods. No-Eyes be talkin' 'bout *any* woods—all forests, all places even."

"I'd like that. I'd love to be able to have that kind of union with nature wherever I went."

"Maybe Many Heart gonna cover that stuff with Summer. Maybe he gonna teach that stuff. No-Eyes not sure what stuff he gonna do."

My wise friend had cleverly returned us to the subject of my upcoming lessons with the young man and, although a flood of questions rushed through my mind, I respectfully awaited further instructions.

"How Summer gonna heed No-Eyes' words if head be racing like wild stallion? Summer want to know so many things 'bout new teacher, huh?"

I wanted to say that I did, but knowing that the particulars of his personal life were unimportant, I resigned myself to that fact. "I suppose if I needed to know these things he'll tell me himself."

The woman closed her eyes and nodded.

"And," I added, "I also realize that a person's private life is just that—private. One's life details have nothing whatsoever to do with the knowledge one possesses."

"That be right, but maybe he gonna tell some private stuff anyway. No-Eyes not know what he gonna say."

The melodic tune of the stream's song began to reach us as we strolled our way out of the deeper recess of the forest. Birds chirped and twilled among the tree branches. A carefree pair of skunks waddled through the underbrush.

I noted all of nature's beauty as we wandered through the stands of high evergreens. Our weaving path twisted around clustered outcroppings of massive boulders that reminded me of the stone rubble of ancient antediluvian places like Mu or Atlantis. It wove through stands of quaking aspens, their birch-like trunks white in the bright sunlight that reached down to touch them. Butterflies flitted delicately from one fragile wildflower to the next, powdery wings transparent in the golden glow. I thought of stained-glass windows, kaleidoscopes and arcing rainbows seen through a misty mountain rainfall.

"Summer gotta remember not to keep beautiful thoughts hidden from Many Heart. All thoughts gonna be important 'long journey. Summer remember to speak those thoughts out, huh?"

"Yes, I will. I'll try to remember that when I'm with him." That specific thought brought another. "No-Eyes?"

"Mmm."

"If I'll have to voice my thoughts does that mean the Dreamwalker isn't aware of them?" I wasn't sure which answer I was hoping for.

The old one halted and gazed into the thriving forest before turning her head to face me. "Nope. It not mean that. I mean Summer gotta be open—completely honest." She shuffled forward and spoke as we walked. "Many, many lessons be learned by going deeper into thoughts. Maybe many of Summer's thoughts gonna lead to important learning. Sometimes a tail end of a thought lead to long string that need to be followed back to ball of thoughts—its source. See? Some thoughts lead to others that need consideration."

Her answer required no further examination. "No-Eyes," I hesitantly asked, "do you know if we'll be going on any multi-dimensional journeys?"

Tap. Tap. Tap, went the walking stick.

"No-Eyes?"

"That journey stuff be up to Dreamwalker."

"Then he can do that sort of thing."

Her nose wrinkled and the eyes squeezed tight in exasperation. The entire small face scrunched together like a dried apple. "Summer think Dreamwalker level be some *kindergarten*?" She lowered her head, shaking it in disgust. A heavy sigh escaped.

"I didn't mean it like it sounded," I tried.

The woman exploded in flares of flaming reprimands. "Summer gotta *think*! Summer gotta *think* before she wag her tongue! Things *gotta* sound like they meant!" She presented her bent back to me as she ambled off grumbling to herself.

"I'm sorry," I gently apologized after gaining her side.

"Humph," came the typical response.

"I'm supposed to be myself, aren't I? Aren't I supposed to be honest with my questions, reactions and thoughts? How can honesty be pure if I'm always guarding responses?"

The reply was frozen. "Summer s'posed to *already* know to think before speakin'."

Frigid silence. She was right and her icy statement had chilled my confidence. My initial physical encounter with Many Heart had been so relaxed. Perhaps that very easiness had misled me into thinking our future meetings were going to be a soft ride along the Pathway. Perhaps the Dreamwalker wasn't the cupcake I thought he was. To hear the old one tell of it, Many Heart was a stern taskmaster who didn't hold to relating with undisciplined students.

"No-Eyes?"

"Yup?"

"Which Many Heart is most accurate, the Dreamwalker who appeared as the Water Bearer in my dream, or the man I met last week?"

Thin shoulders rose and fell. "Which one you prefer?"

"That's not what I asked. Which one is more representative?"

"Neither," came the obscure reply.

"Then do you mean that both are accurate?"

"You assuming here?"

"No. I'm asking."

Tap. Tap.

Waiting.

Although our moccasined footfalls made no sounds, the striking of her stick on the granite gravel echoed loudly into the forest. It counted out the silent seconds of waiting.

"Summer be right," she finally admitted. "Many Heart be both men. Dreamwalkers can be all stuff to student. Sometimes Dreamwalker be only one, but," she added cautiously, "sometimes he seem many to student."

"You mean depending on the student's viewpoint—his different perspectives."

The visionary simply nodded.

"Are the viewpoints altered in any way?"

"Sometimes."

"By the student or the teacher?"

"Depends."

"On what's important to learn at the time?"

"Depends. Reasons be up to teacher."

I thought on that while the water spirit sang louder, with more sharp clarity. Her soprano voice was vibrant above the soft background of nature's accompanying symphonic players. The hushing of the tall evergreens and the staccato trilling of the winged people orchestrated the mystical masterpiece that no man-made instruments could compare to. It was the hymn of life itself. The choir of nature, pure and unadulterated.

"Summer."

The whispered word shattered the private reverie.

"Yes?"

"Many Heart gonna maybe say stuff Summer not want hear."

"*Maybe* gonna?" I knew very well he would. It was expected.

"There gonna be times Summer feel bad, maybe even get angry."

Our hands touched. I entwined my fingers in hers. "I'd be a pretty dumb student if I didn't anticipate that sort of thing happening. What's he going to talk about?"

"No-Eyes not know that, remember? No-Eyes only know Summer gonna go through many deep emotions 'long journey."

"Will he give any new direction for us? I know you keep telling me that you don't know what he'll talk about, but I think you know some generalities."

"He maybe gonna touch on new stuff."

I thought I sensed a peculiarity pass through her tone—one of hesitancy—perhaps a feeling of fear of how I'd react to his ideas. "Can you give me some hints as to the possibilities this new direction's going to take?"

"Nope."

"That's what I thought."

Eyes twinkled. "Summer always be so curious. Summer always gotta know this, know that. Summer be so funny sometimes."

I grinned at her. "Well," I quipped, "isn't that what this is all about? Isn't this journey all about getting answers?"

"Mmm...some gonna be answers. Some gonna be understanding. Some gonna be light in darkness. But, Summer," she advised, "some questions not *ever* gonna have clear answers—only understanding."

We had reached the forest line. And up on the hillcrest, the sun was slanted on the cabin. No-Eyes crossed her feet and sat down in the cool shadows of the sheltering pines. And, placing her walking stick across her knees, she patted the grassy ground beside her.

I made myself comfortable in the lap of nature and, looking up into the deep blueness of the sky, I felt at peace with myself, with nature and with the Great Spirit. The singing stream tickled my soul. It gave it an incredible fullness of joy, so much so, I smiled with the inner laughter.

My companion giggled.

Grinning, I turned to her. "What're you twittering about?"

"No-Eyes full of happy to see Summer so glad with nature. No-Eyes know stuff, that all," she hinted mysteriously.

"That was a mischievous statement," I playfully insinuated. "Are you going to clarify it or do I stay in the dark about it?"

Silence.

Waiting.

"No-Eyes not mean any thing so special. What so!" she hedged closer. "No-Eyes just know that all Dreamwalkers got hearts that nature can make glad."

I toyed with a long blade of green wild grass. "And does that mean what I think it does?"

"Maybe."

"No-Eyes? Are you saying that I'll succeed after all?"

The old one's gaze was suddenly broken off by a shadow that had crossed the sun. She peered up into the brightness and watched our falcon exit the forest's depths to gracefully sail through his turquoise ocean of sky. White foam lazily wafted on the updrafts of the currents as the bird freely rode on the curling swells of the downdrafts. The peregrine was joining his spirit with that of his brilliant shoreless sea.

"No-Eyes?" I urged again after the bird had glided out of view. "Are you saying I'll succeed? Is that what you foresee?"

"That depends," she softly whispered. "That stuff all depend on choices Summer gonna make 'long journey. There be many, many trails, Summer. Many powerful pathways can be magic—lead to Way."

"You're circling."

My old friend patted my knee. "It be too late for more circles. Hoop's nearly complete now. This time it all be up to Summer to answer own question."

I searched for our falcon—the sky was clear. I gazed through the jade shadows of the woodlands—they were peaceful. I felt the touch of the wind spirit—it was gentle. I listened to the water spirit's lilting song—it was sweet. And then I looked into the twin mirrors of the visionary's black opals—they were alive with truth.

There are many magical Corridors.
There are many powerful Pathways.
Beware those who would claim there is but one.

September

Season of the red Moon of Narrow Trails

Down from the Mountaintop

A true Visionary is not the Leader, but rather the Follower—one who humbly follows the Truth, one who refuses to walk ahead of the Seekers, but rather cherishes walking beside them, among them.

Turquoise. Emerald. Bronze. Copper. My September morning was vibrant with brilliant color. Alive. Nature was teeming with undulating life.

Pine. Spruce. Fir. The clear air was heavy with the fragrance of Nature's pureness. The refreshing scents floated through the cab of the truck and, inhaling deeply, I purified myself with their power.

It was a breezy morning and I allowed the fun-loving wind spirit to play with my hair. As I drove along the isolated roadway, my hair was tossed and lifted about. I felt light of heart and free of spirit. I would like to give nature's attributes full credit for this elated feeling, but that was only half the cause for, truly, I was in this marvelously uplifted mood because I knew that for the next few months I'd be learning from Brian Many Heart. It was he whom I was driving toward on this electrifying morning.

No-Eyes' former off-handed comments regarding Many Heart's physical attributes were absolutely founded in truth. He was indeed striking in appearance, but physiological appearances held no particular draw for me. What attracted me was his knowledge, the depth of it. And I was anxious to communicate with the mind that contained that enlightenment. I was more than eager to glean what I could of his deeper comprehension and heightened awareness. It was this singular anticipation that caused the flutter of the butterfly's wings within my heart. It was this anticipation in conjunction with nature's clear technicolors and crisp scents that sent me sailing along in such a happy mood this bright September morning.

Almost as if I'd given the old pickup its head, it nosed into the turnoff and dipped down into the weed-choked path that ended at the familiar lodgepole pine. It knew it was home. I turned off the engine.

Chirps. Chatterings. Squeals. Caws. Whispering treetops. Singing stream. Yes, I was home again, and my happy heartbeats gave clear evidence that this was so.

I peered up through the dusty windshield at the sun-touched cabin. The door was open. My teacher was probably getting our mutually preferred refreshment ready. The thought of our shared Pepsi affliction brought on a smile of amusement as I left the truck and began my ascent. I raised my face to the strengthening sun. My gaze caught the bright blue color of my new mentor's shirt.

He was blocking the doorway, casually leaning against the jamb. Arms crossed, pearly teeth gleaming behind the broad smile, he raised an arm in greeting.

"Hi," I hollered up to him.

He nodded deeply.

Reaching the worn steps, I commented on the magnificent day. "Great morning, huh?"

He admiringly scanned the sea of sky which had altered its former hue to a brilliant robin's-egg color.

"A day made for God," he reflected with a smile of deep contentment before bringing his eyes back down to me.

I smiled back. "A day made *by* God," I added.

"Absolutely," he declared with a glint in his eyes. "It's a perfect day made for and by God." He then stared intently into my eyes while offering his weathered hand in greeting.

I placed mine in his. It was tenderly held—meaningfully. From anyone else, this prolonged moment of touching would mean something entirely different. But it was clear that my teacher was not only warmly greeting me, he was also deriving sensory information as well. He was perceiving my emotions and attitudes and was about to comment on them.

I beat him to the point. "Yes, I'm anxious to begin," I admitted freely. "I'm excited and honored at the same time."

"I know," he said, releasing my hand. He then turned and entered the cabin.

I followed. "What's on the agenda for today?"

The man was busy in the kitchen and spoke with his back to me. "Agenda? There is no agenda. There is no structure to enlightenment.

We learn as we go. We follow the lead."

"What lead?"

He turned, two cans in hand, and inclined his head toward the door. "Let's enjoy the day. Wouldn't want God to think we're not appreciative."

I grinned.

Seated on the porch steps, my companion popped one of the lids and handed me the chilled drink. We remained silent for a few minutes. I was to learn that there'd be many such silences in the weeks to come—some embarrassingly long.

Many Heart snapped his can open and delighted in the long swig. He wiped his mouth and held up the soda to signal an intended toast.

I touched my rim to his.

"To glorious days and peaceful nights," he said.

"To glorious days and peaceful nights," I repeated.

"So!" he began as he settled comfortably back against the porch post. "You wonder exactly what lead we follow."

I nodded.

"You've already begun it this morning. You see, Summer, we've only just begun talking and already your words have chosen a pathway for us to tread upon."

My frown brought a smile from the teacher. "You don't have the faintest idea of what I'm getting at, do you?"

"Not really. Should I?"

"It's not that evident. It has to do with your reasoning for your excitement. Remember you said you were excited and honored all at the same time?"

"Yes," I answered questioningly.

"The excitement aspect I can understand. The honored part I cannot."

"What's to understand? Fact is, I *am* honored to have been given the high privilege to learn from you. Why, that sort of advanced learning only comes once in a lifetime, if at all. It's a rarity for someone to be offered . . . . "

I stopped short when he began shaking his head. "What's the matter? What'd I say?"

"Given. Offered."

My brows furrowed. I didn't think those were such terribly naughty words. I looked to the man. He was studying the distant forest. It was silent time—thinking time. And when I couldn't justify his claim, I decided to forgo prolonging the gap.

"What's wrong with those words?"

"In themselves, nothing. When you apply them to your present situation of learning, everything."

I still didn't get it and I said as much.

He sighed. "Summer," he said solemnly, "*no* one is ever *given* or *offered* enlightenment. *No* one has it handed to them. There are no handouts here. There are no freebies. You make it sound as though sages are standing in doorways passing out gems of wisdom to anyone who passes by with their hand out."

I was ready to contradict with my usual impetuousness, then I thought better of it by remaining silent. I was glad I did, for his next words would've proved me wrong *and* being a smart mouth.

"Enlightenment is always *earned.* How long had you studied before you met No-Eyes?"

His evidence was irrefutable.

"About twenty years," I admitted with a hangdog expression.

"How many years have you existed within long-suffering?"

"The same."

"You spent time with a visionary?"

"Yes."

"And you were tested by a Dreamwalker who came in the capacity of the Water Bearer?"

I nodded.

"The Dreamwalker gauged your level of preparedness?"

I smiled at the sudden thought of Joe Red Sky in his slumber. "Yes."

My interrogator remained serious. "And how were you judged at that time?"

"I was judged ready."

"So tell me then, what is it that you were *given?* Offered?"

I grinned wide. "The opportunity."

Though he tried, he couldn't fully contain his sudden mirth. A smile forced the corners of his mouth up. His head shook slowly.

"I'm already beginning to see what the old one warned me about. You seem to have a certain clever way about you—a humorous one. It's no wonder she enjoyed working with you so much."

I smiled embarrassingly. "What? What'd I say?"

"You know very well what you did. You altered your entire answer after you'd figured out how your initial one would've been wrong."

"No I didn't. You made me see that I wasn't *given* enlightenment because I actually *earned* it. But then I realized that what I *was* allowed was the opportunity. So naturally my final reply would fit the new realization."

He chuckled. "Even your reasonings come out justifiable."

Deep silence.

"There's more?" he inquired curiously.

My eyes slid to his. "Isn't there? I feel you're not prepared to close the subject."

"You are right, too. Something else you said led us into all of this. You said you felt honored. Remember that?"

Guiltily I admitted to my utterance of the forbidden word— obviously it was another no-no in the context used. And, considering the tone of our former go 'round, I saw the light of my error.

"If the opportunity for this expanded learning was actually one earned, then I shouldn't feel honored, I should feel . . . ." I didn't have the precise word for it. "Rewarded?" I tried.

His lips pursed. "How about 'natural'? It'd be a natural step to take your learning one notch further, wouldn't it? Sort of like advancing grades in school. When one completes one grade, they're naturally moved up to the next higher level—a more complex one because they've earned it—they're ready."

"So how come I don't *feel* so natural?"

"What do you feel?"

"Anxious. Eager. Maybe worried too."

"Worried?"

"Yeah. Worried that maybe I won't pass this grade."

"That's always a possibility," he frowned.

Now why'd he have to go and say that for? I was expecting a more encouraging reply than that. Maybe something like "don't worry about that" or even a simple "you'll do fine" sort of thing. Then I reasoned that if this level of learning was supposed to be so natural, then natural I'd be. I let out my natural honesty.

"I don't like your last comment."

"Why? Because you were heavily within expectation, that's why. You were disappointed because you had expectations as to my reply. Right?"

He had trapped me.

"You tricked me."

"No, I didn't. I was being openly honest. Isn't that what this is all about? Complete honesty? There *is* always the possibility that you don't make the grade, that you don't complete the journey to the end of the pathway. That's ultimately up to you. I believe you know that."

The Pepsi can went up to his lips and he gazed out into the clear Colorado sky. He left me to wriggle out of the trap of my own clumsy making.

This *was* all about open honesty. How could I have expected anything less? Would I want him to placate my desire for success? Would I truly want that sort of childish soothing? Absolutely not! Then why had his answer rattled me so? I could see that I had some intellectual maturing to do. This was the serious stuff. The games were long over with. I would have no more expectations from now on. And, no matter what, I'd be totally honest and, even more importantly, I'd accept the honesty of my teacher with the logical reasoning of an intelligently functioning mind instead of a childish display of impetuous emotions.

Many Heart's voice shattered my contemplation.

"There's another reason you shouldn't feel honored. Perhaps this second reason supersedes the first."

He didn't say more. He waited.

I didn't know what he was driving at.

Waiting.

The silence that hung between us became unbearably heavy. I couldn't stand it any longer.

"Will you tell me? Do I have to come up with the answer by myself?"

The man stared at me. "What do you feel about famous people?"

I thought that was an odd question. "Nothing in particular," I said.

"How would you feel if a movie star or famous singer crossed your path and you met—talked?"

I shrugged. "Then I guess we'd talk."

"You wouldn't be nervous? Thrilled?"

"Should I be?"

Dark eyes glistened. "You tell me."

Grinning, I looked deep into the ebony opals. "I'm no common groupie, if that's what you're getting at. People are people. Movie star or construction worker. Famous singer or grocery clerk, people are all the same to me—they're all equal. I believe you know that," I playfully parried.

His serious countenance softened. "Just as long as you do."

Touche.

"Oh, I do! I never understood what the big ballyhoo was all about. To me, the famous and wealthy deserve no more awe than others who aren't rich or well known."

I paused to sip from the Pepsi can.

"Besides," I added, "it's the common people that make the others famous in the first place. There wouldn't *be* fame without the fans. People are people, that's all."

His eyes deepened in intensity. "And what of the visionaries? How do you feel in *their* company?"

Clever, very clever. I saw his point but remained true to myself. "Honored," I muttered a bit under my breath.

No exterior expression evidenced his reaction. He looked away, stonefaced.

I followed his gaze and watched the wind bend the delicate tips of the pointed firs. I had given the wrong answer and I knew it but, right or wrong, I had to maintain honesty at all costs. Not wishing for more silences to pass between us, I confessed to my realized error.

"That was the wrong answer, wasn't it? Oh, you don't even have to admit it, I already know."

I studied my fingers. "But a true visionary is a long, long way from a famous singer. An enlightened being is a far cry from some tinsel town movie star."

The breeze tossed my hair. I wiped it away from my face.

"It's not *awe* that makes me feel so honored. It's an intense high respect." I rested my case—temporarily.

"Respect for what?" he asked, still gazing up at the trees.

"Respect for the visionary's years of long-suffering and continual perseverance, respect for his patience and fortitude, respect for that which he has endured for the sake of attaining truth and its comprehension."

Silence.

Waiting.

Many Heart leaned forward and rested his elbows on his knees. "Respect is honorable, Summer. The feeling of *being* honored is not."

I tossed that one over. "Explain."

He angled himself to face me. "To say that you are honored is to say that you are unequal."

Down in the ravine, I heard the water spirit's sweet voice. She sang, "Listen . . . listen." And I did.

"Summer, tell me, if you say 'people are people,' then to experience the feeling of *being* honored, you are in essence contradicting yourself—people are not all the same then, they are not equal."

"I see what you mean. When one feels honored because of another's presence, then they are admitting that they are less than the one whose company they're in. They're admitting that the other person is better than they are."

He nodded. "Precisely."

"But I *do* believe an accomplished visionary is better than the student."

He shook his head. "You are confusing your comparisons here. You cannot compare that which is not the same. You cannot compare humanism with knowledge. You can compare knowledge with knowledge or talent with talent, but never can the basic state of being be pitted against thought."

I rested my elbows back against the top step.

"Being, the state of being is equal. It is equal because humanism is created without prejudice. All beings are equal to each other."

"You're getting the idea."

"Maybe not," I groaned with the complexity. "This is getting very finely defined. It's like splitting hairs." I hesitated before attempting to do the required splitting.

I sat up, deeply intent upon the precise wording of the philosophical aspect. "People. People in themselves are equal, therefore, the feeling of *being* honored *by* them is an impossibility. But people's *accomplishments* can be honored." Now I had it all untangled.

"No."

"Which statement was in error?"

"The last."

After some thought, I tried again. "Honor is a false endowment."

"No."

Silence. I listened to the water spirit's sympathetic promptings. She was clearly trying to help me out.

"Self. Self. Of *self*!" she whispered.

Self? What could that possibly mean? I didn't want to verbalize an answer I didn't have an explanation for. What the hell did "self" mean? I was keenly aware of my companion's presence as he patiently waited for my reply. Did he also hear the water spirit's hints? Probably. Oh God, what did it all mean?

Self. Self. To honor self? No, that'd be self-aggrandizement—egotism. For self to *feel* honored? No, that wasn't right either. That'd be just like what we were talking about—trying to avoid.

Honor. Honored. Honoring. Honorable? The lightbulb flashed on and off.

"Self," I said softly.

"Self? That's *it*? You took all that time to come up with one word?"

"Yes," I smiled brightly. "That's the answer."

"Well . . . what about this 'self'? How does it relate to honor?"

"Only the *self* can *experience* honor by performing honorable deeds toward *others*! Only the self can *perform* honorably—but *without* the *acknowledgment* of honor of self."

His grin was all the confirmation I needed.

"It came out a bit jumbled, but I see you have the idea. To feel *self*-honor is egotism. To feel *honored* by others is inferiority. But to *do* honorable deeds without the expectancy of admiration from self or from others is correct. The attribute of being honorable does not necessarily mean one is admired. It must only be applied to honesty and goodness, not adoration."

"So," I concluded, "I do not feel honored being taught by an enlightened individual because, in essence, I am equal—I have the same *capacity* to also become enlightened. But I am grateful to be tutored by an honorable personage. Would that be correct?"

"Close enough," he grinned. "Close enough. Just never forget that all the famous movie stars, singers, or the wealthy are no better than you."

"And I no better than they," I added.

"And you're no better than them—just a little further along the Way."

I pondered that thought."What's grinding your wheels now?" he asked.

"I was just thinking how this very concept could change the world if people really understood it—if only they truly believed in it and lived by it."

"Ah, yes. That is the crux of the whole matter, isn't it. Shame," he sighed, "it's a shame how self-pompous they become. They become untouchables among men."

His last words were more meaningful than he knew. Or perhaps he did know and was intentionally leading into the area of one of my concerns. I thought the latter was more probable, considering his advanced stage of awareness. Either way, I took advantage of his baited lead.

"Many Heart?"

"Hmmm?"

"Could we talk about something that's been a personal concern of mine?"

"That's why there's no structured agenda. Remember? We follow the leads of our conversations. What is it that concerns you?"

"It's about a person who is considered famous."

"Go on."

"Do you know who I mean?"

He nodded sadly.

My heart ached. "Then I don't need to explain."

"It's always good to talk it through."

I sighed and raised my eyes to the cloudless bright sky. (When we spoke of this individual we used his name; for the sake of this individual's privacy, I will not do so here.)

"Many Heart, there's been so many, many times that I've been beaten down throughout life. This man's words reached out from his shining spirit and touched mine. His deep words frequently gave me that needed little push to persevere."

My heart was heavy.

"But that was when he knew himself—when he was in absolute

touch with his spirit."

"Yes, that was long ago," he confirmed.

"What happened to him? How does one shut off that beautiful spirit connection?"

He shrugged. "Doesn't have to happen—not unless one allows it to."

I looked deep into the intense eyes of my new friend. "It's the people around him, isn't it?"

"They've insulated him. They've isolated him so completely that he's become a possession of the few who have gained control."

"How does such a personal travesty happen? How does one lose control over one's own life, lose sight of one's own spirit even? Especially when such a complete reversal of spirit purpose occurs."

"You already answered that."

"Those possessive people around him. They're like human leeches."

"Yes."

"But I still don't understand how someone allows that to happen—unless they've suddenly become blind."

He sighed. "There are many types of blindness, Summer," he explained softly, "when one becomes so wealthy and famous, it's relatively simple for them to become caught up in the world and be deceived by those who are clearly manipulative and those who would claim to be friends. Those alleged friends have only one thing in mind . . . to fill their cup of ego by association."

That wasn't logically satisfactory to my way of thinking.

"I don't agree," I said boldly.

"What you don't agree with is the possibility of it ever happening to *you*. Others aren't so one-minded in their purpose. See, it's easy for some people to be kept so busy, so away from home base, that they need to delegate others to take over for them. They become distanced from what's most important to them and, before they realize what's happened, they've become a total stranger—even to themselves. Suddenly they've lost control of everything—they've become controlled instead."

"And that's how they got so insulated. That's how they get so isolated that even the sincere people can't reach them."

"Absolutely. Nobody can touch him without first having the express approval of his surround of people."

I thought on that aspect. "What are the people afraid of that they feel they have to censor all that comes to him? What do they fear so greatly that makes them this man's personal judge of others?"

"They fear losing their control or their juicy piece of the green pie.

94

They also are fearful that someone will come along and open up their host's eyes and then he'll see the false people around him for what they really are."

I bowed my head. "That's sick. It's almost an act of imprisonment." I felt very sorry for my famous friend who was my equal.

"Yes, it is sick, but such is the way of avaricious men. Also, Summer, they fear one may come along, break through their barrier and bring light back into the man's heart. They fear his spirit will again be free to see clearly as it once was. This is why he's so untouchable now."

A mistiness clouded my vision. "I almost feel it's too late."

"I don't think so."

I looked to my companion.

"One day he'll find himself again. One day he'll find someone who will help him rediscover his beautiful spirit and its purpose. He'll be in control again once his eyes are no longer darkened. Then he'll regain the reins of his purpose and return it to the purity it began with."

"I hope so, Many Heart. I truly hope so because I've been censored from him time after time. Maybe somebody will get through eventually."

He smiled. "Someone will get through, Summer. Someone who's meant to will make it through the barriers."

I knew the Dreamwalker knew what he was talking about. And I hoped that this special someone wouldn't take too long in arriving on the scene. I'd watch and listen for the evidence of his presence.

The arm of Ra had reached around to flood the wooden porch with his light. We were becoming uncomfortably warm in the bright sunlight.

My teacher rose and stretched his lanky limbs. "Want to go inside?"

I shook my head. "How about down there in the treeline?"

He offered his hand to help me up. We descended the hill and sat in the cool shade of the pines. The wildgrass was prickly. I ignored it, for here the birds chirped gaily above us and the woodland entities gave us welcome.

"Summer," the Dreamwalker said, "what we were talking about before, the honor bit, there's something that needs extending with that."

I waited.

"Now you know better, but when you first presented the attitude of being honored by the presence of a visionary—a wise man, you were in the mental possession of presumption. A wise man cannot be idolized. He cannot be placed upon the almighty pedestal, for his wisdom atrophies if he remains remote and distant."

"He *is* different though," I tested.

"How so?"

"His wisdom, his light."

"This is true, but his humility of self and his simplicity of living make him easily assimilated into the mainstream. His attitude of acceptance makes him a peaceful member of society, one who melds pleasingly with those around him."

I smiled. "The simple carpenter."

"Never that exalted, but you got the picture."

The Dreamwalker reached down and placed his fingers around the velvety petals of a wildflower. "Enlightened teachers are a lot like these mountain flowers. They dwell among the coarse grasses of the wilderness. They mutually share of the waters and the sunshine. They complement each other and," he cautioned, "although one species would appear more beautiful than the one existing beside it, who can really deem which is more worthy? The flower or the weeds which grow profusely and retain the soil's moisture for the flower?"

"They need each other," I offered.

"Need? No. The wise man does not *need* others, but isn't he then useless without them? In essence, the visionary who secludes himself is no wise man after all. Understand that he doesn't *need* others but, in order for him to be fruitful, he requires cohabitation with those others."

I revised my former statement. "They're useful to each other."

"Yes. The visionary who sits upon the high mountaintop merely atrophies. His great attained wisdom remains contained within self. And wisdom contained is wisdom grown rancid. It is the *selfless* sharing of it that gives it its shining beauty of eternal light and life."

I felt he was actually saying more than his words let on.

"Are you saying that I too should teach others?"

"No, not at all. Your books are all that is required of you. There are enough physical teachers for those who feel this need. I speak here of visionaries in general."

He glanced into the rich, green forest, then returned his gaze toward No-Eyes' cabin.

"People do not fully understand the visionary. They feel he's odd, some kind of weird creature who dresses in long, tattered robes and owns no material possessions."

"I have the feeling these attitudes are in a timeframe that demands change."

"Yes," he agreed, "this is so. People's perceptions will have dramatic reversals in the near future—it's inevitable."

I watched a black Kaibab squirrel scamper away through the shiny kinnikinnic. "Many Heart?"

"Mmmm."

"Well, what you said about visionaries and the wise ones . . . what about No-Eyes?"

"What about her?"

"It's not resting right with me."

"Go on."

"You know what I'm getting at, don't you?"

"I'd like to hear it from you, Summer."

"The bit about the wise ones interacting with society doesn't fit her. Isn't she on a mountaintop?"

"In a manner of speaking, yes."

"But you said the wise ones' humility of self and their simplicity of living makes them easily assimilated into the mainstream and that they're peaceful members of society. Many Heart, No-Eyes can't tolerate society."

"And now you're concerned about an inconsistency of the original visionary statement."

I frowned. "Not so much the statement, but rather the facts that appear to be in opposition. How are they reconciled?"

"Don't you know?"

I thought on it for a while. Finally my eyes locked on his. "Personality?"

He smiled. "Close. But let's term it 'individualism.' It must be remembered that each individual achieves optimum power at differing levels of operation. Some reach their peak among men while others maintain their perfection in solitude.

"No-Eyes wasn't a recluse who allowed her beautiful knowledge to atrophy while living upon the mountaintop. Yes, she was extremely selective, but she shared it all the same."

My recalling of our more precious times together brought a warm smile.

Many Heart shared the sentiment, then became serious once again. "She chose to remain in the solitude of the mountains because, Summer, we are a base society. When compared to the pure enlighten-ment of a visionary, we are a poor, backward society caught up in eternal conflict. We are a hopelessly warring civilization, always inter-nally fragmenting our personal energies for the simplistic striving of the mundane, all the while, forever dissipating ourselves like so many handfuls of sand cast wantonly out upon the savage sea. And in that act of casting, we have ultimately become self-imposed robots of blind-ness, deafness and ignorance. We have become willing prisoners of the negatives.

"Remember that truth remains obscure before the mind that is congested with the divisions of fragmentary thought and opinions."

A gentle smile curled his lips. "Summer, the poverty and deep solitude of No-Eyes created of her life a powerful benediction to unfragmented truth, clear sight, and pure wisdom.

"It is our living bond with nature that contains and insulates our higher values and spirituality from the contaminating pollutants of worldly superficiality."

I placed my palms down on the soft skin of the Earth Mother. It felt so good.

"Yes," I whispered with a new light of understanding, "I understand her reasons for remaining so. Her heart beats as one with the sweet land. The pure vibrations meld with her own and, in that manner, does she dwell above that which would serve to contaminate her being, her spirit."

A stretch of unspoken thoughts filled a short timeframe before I again had another question.

"Many Heart?"

"Yes?"

"How does the average person recognize the wise one? I know that might sound ignorant, but I'm finding that so many people today need to see a doctoral certificate before they'll take advice or direction from another. They need to hear it from the horse's mouth—an authoritative figure who's supposed to be so full of expertise. What is it about the ordinary-appearing wise ones that makes these doubting Thomases heed them?"

"You've asked more than one question here, but perhaps I can catch them both in one hand. The average individual recognizes the wise one by his serenity and clarity of mind. So too do those same qualities make the doubting Thomases look up and take notice of consideration. To the doubters, many times a few well-chosen words from the visionary is all it takes. And usually those are simple words that strike at the negative core of the doubter."

"And the doubter turns away, doesn't he?"

"Yes. Until such time as he has the courage to face his negative qualities and admits to them. Until then, he is forever entrapped within the self-imprisonment which negates spiritual growth. He stagnates within the delusions of self. Everyone is wrong but him."

How terribly, terribly sad that was. I thought how ugly a thing it was to imprison oneself with delusions. Not to be completely honest and to remain within one's own self-created world where no true trust or sharing was allowed inside.

"There's a lot of people like that," I mused. "I know a few. They only trust themselves. They believe everyone else is out to take some sort of advantage of them. Deep down, they're full of a consuming hate which they cannot understand so they strike out with distrust and warped views."

"This is so, Summer."

"Well," I attempted, "how does one help this sad type of individual?"

His brow rose. "One doesn't. The attempt at assistance would merely be turned back upon the giver. One leaves these narrow-minded people alone. Most of the time, that's exactly where they wish to be anyway—alone with the only one they truly trust—themselves."

"What makes them so distrustful?"

"Most often it is love of self and a deep possessiveness that accompanies this self-love. Also they are insecure and are skeptical of all others who attempt to come close to them or their loved ones. Often they are so insecure they will criticize their loved ones' friends, claiming the friends are trying to take their loved ones away."

"That's sick," I whispered sadly.

"Be that as it may, that's how an insecure mind works. They'll often boast about being wonderful, or they'll make joking claims of being a big man or an independent woman."

"Boasting based on repressed inferiority—a coverup of their true inner feelings—nothing more than a show."

"Yes."

I sighed. "No wonder nobody can help someone as sad as that. They are the real master deceivers. The greatest shams of all time."

"Even so, they are to be greatly pitied, left alone to their self-delusions of aggrandizement and exaggerated self-worth until perhaps one day they become unblind to their true mirrored reflections of self."

"Many Heart, do people like this collect possessions? Especially expensive ones?"

"Almost always. They're out to prove to the entire world just how great or successful they are through their self-attained possessions. These 'things' make them feel big. Secure. These *things* make them feel puffed up with a worth that is as false as their thinking."

"I thought so. Anyway, I'm glad to know I shouldn't attempt to help someone like that. Kind of like trying to handle a rattlesnake."

He grinned at the analogy. "Exactly."

A companionable silence hung between us.

"Many Heart?" I asked softly.

"Hmmm?"

"When does a wise one stop helping others? I mean, when does he draw the line in determining who is worthy of help and who is not?"

"The wise do not judge another's worthiness. In his eyes, *all* are worthy of whatever help he can provide."

"What of the lazy man or the habitual procrastinator? When the visionary perceives these harming negatives, does he still offer aid?"

"Nothing is offered, remember? But if it is actively sought out, yes. Psychological or spiritual help must be sought of the wise one *by* the seeker. The visionary does not walk about *looking* for those to help."

"Because then he would be directly interfering," I stated.

"Yes, an enlightened one never interferes."

The golden sunlight had begun chasing the shadows of the forestline back farther into the woodlands. We were once again in the bright, warming light.

Many Heart rose. "That water spirit is calling to us." He began heading toward the ravine where the watercourse raced through No-Eyes' property.

I hurried after him.

Reaching the willow-bordered banks, we sat down, removed our footwear and cooled our feet in the icy waters.

"This is so nice," I sighed, looking down upon the churning current.

"It'll come," he said confidently.

He had perceived my mental wanderings. "You mean our own land. Yes, I know it'll come. Ten years is a long time to wait. But you know what, Many Heart?"

His voice had a smile in it. "What, Summer?"

I looked up to where the high mountain forest met the deep blue receiving sky.

"I'm content. I really am. Even though we've waited a long time to be settled and the negative side has placed so many barriers in front of us, I know it'll come about when the time is right. And I also know that that piece of mountain that we'll eventually call home will be just perfect."

I paused to enjoy the contentment that the serene surround gave me. "Know what else?"

"What else?"

"I don't care about the money anymore. Remember when I said we needed money to get where we needed to be in the mountains?"

"I remember."

"Well, I don't care about that any more. The caring just isn't there now. It's completely gone. I guess I finally realize that all things that are meant for us will come in their own prescribed time—in their own manner."

"What about that old pickup? It's very old. What about that new four-wheel you'll need?"

I got up and stepped out into the rushing waters. I picked my way back and forth through the chilling entity.

"Nope. Don't care about that either."

I stopped in the stream to look up into the depths of the blue Colorado sky, then I shrugged and smiled into the gentle Dreamwalker's twinkling eyes.

"That ol' pickup's been faithful, it'll do until times change. I know everything'll work out just the way it's meant to."

My friend smiled. "Now you have finally stepped within It." He leaned back onto the wildgrass and stared into the sky.

"What have I finally stepped within?"

"You know," he said.

"I do?"

Silence. His eyes were closed.

Whatever it was that I'd stepped within had to do with my new feeling of contentment. It had everything to do with my confidence that everything was going to work out. It had to do with my sudden unconcern about the needed extra money for a new truck and our Mountain Brotherhood land. This thing I had finally stepped into had taken away all of my former worries and deep concerns.

I sluiced around in the clear stream. And while doing some deep thinking, I scanned the bed for pebbles. The water spirit's song began a new tune that pricked my awareness. She began to whisper.

I listened.

Then I glanced over at the reclining man who looked as though he had fallen asleep with his hands behind his head. His breathing was relaxed and deep.

My thoughts conversed with the water spirit's. Then she began to sing another song of benediction and I was left with wonderings within my own mind. How could I have just now stepped within acceptance when I already had acceptance?

"No you didn't," came the deep voice from the bank.

I looked to the Dreamwalker. I had nearly forgotten about him. He was sitting up with arms outstretched over his knees—watching me.

"I didn't?"

His head went slowly from side to side. "But now you do." He motioned for me to join him on the bank.

I climbed up out of the coldness. The lower legs of my jeans were soaked and I stretched them out to dry in the warm sun. Steam began rising from them. I waited for his explanation.

"Before, you were merely existing on the borderland of acceptance. How do we know that? We know that from the evidence of your continued worries and deep concerns over the money. Summer," he said gently, "when one maintains deep concerns, one is not within acceptance—not within *total* acceptance. You *believed* things would work out, but you still harbored those heavy worries about them. You were almost there, but not quite."

"I see. And now that I feel so free of those concerns, I've crossed through that borderland and into the freeing space of *complete* acceptance."

"Yes. Now you actually realize and believe that all things meant to come will appear when the time is right."

That was a deeply comforting feeling. It was as if a great weight had been lifted. It felt wonderful.

"There's something else," he said, breaking my reverie.

"About what?"

"About what we've just been talking about."

I pulled a thistle and studied its spiny flower. "About being within true acceptance?"

"Yes." He faced me and, placing his hand over mine, he became most serious. His eyes were very black.

"In acceptance one accepts."

That was a strange statement. It appeared to simplistic.

"I know."

"Do you?"

"It's a rather obvious statement, don't you think?"

"But is it?"

I frowned.

"Summer, once one has stepped within complete acceptance as you now have, one accepts that which *comes* to one. Sometimes this acceptance will appear to run counter to your inclinations, but your personal tendencies must not interfere with the acceptance."

I solemnly looked deep into his wise pools. "I have the distinct feeling that you're purposely being evasive. You're being terribly vague. You could say this in clear specifics, couldn't you? You could, but I wouldn't want to hear, would I?"

"No."

"The answer's 'no' because I'll need to gain fuller experience in order to completely understand this new aspect of acceptance when it comes—when the time is right."

He simply nodded.

And the sun glistened upon his ebony hair while the water spirit sang the lilting song of life.

I received the warm offering of the sun. And I was comforted by the song that was sung for the struggling newcomer upon the pathway and her wise Dreamwalker who sat beside her.

Accept changes. For, without them, Man becomes as stagnant as the dying woodland pond, never moving forward, always holding on to that which was—until, one day. . .he too begins dying within.

The Eternal Grandmother

What do you see while you gaze into a high mountain pool?
Do you perceive the reflection of your exquisite Spirit?
What do you feel while you tread the mossy carpet of a
virgin forest?
Do you feel the heartbeat of its enchanted Sacred Ground?
What do you know while you stare in awe-struck wonder at the
dark, stormy skies?
Do you then know the forceful Power of the Great Spirit?
What do you see?
What do you feel?
What do you know?

My new mentor had left me with much to consider. Although I wasn't supposed to feel honored by his presence, I couldn't immediately shed away the skin of inferiority I felt when with him. His stately demeanor was so utterly composed and assured. The high wisdom shone from his gentle eyes and his smooth voice was soft and deliberate. The western clothes he wore were time-worn and simplistic, just as was his easy-going attitude.

He was right about the need for the wise man to come down from the mountaintop to be among the people. He was right about everything we spoke about so far. The only aspect of our last meeting that still remained a mystery was when he spoke about my acceptance of what was to come and how it may conflict with my personal attitudes. Did I require a major rethinking on a certain subject? Would my future present negatives to accept? I could speculate until I was blue in the face. I could hypothesize until I had imagined every sort of fear becoming an actuality. In the end, it wouldn't serve any productive purpose. I accepted his cryptic statement and let it go at that. I'd find out when the time was right.

I don't know precisely when or by what manner my acceptance was precipitated, but when I was beside the stream with Many Heart, my heart was light and my mind no longer harbored any more burdensome fears about where our Mountain Brotherhood land money was coming from. I just no longer retained the concern. I realized that suddenly I was without its worry. And it was a wonderfully free sensation. It was as though I'd finally realized that we'd be taken care of when the time came and I now had total faith in that.

So far, my days with the Dreamwalker were comparable to the many serene days spent with No-Eyes. We were becoming the type of friends who could speak freely with one another without fear of misunderstandings. The teaching and learning had gone smoothly. There were no grave matters to work through nor were there any complexities such as involved spiritual journeys or hidden concepts to decipher. And, looking back over those simplistic lessons, I wondered if I'd be so lucky for them to continue or if they'd suddenly become heavy with multidimensional facets. Time would tell. Time would also tell if I'd succeed to the end of the pathway. We were still merely standing upon its broad threshold. I knew that very soon we'd be firmly treading its main byway and I maintained my initial affirmation of complete honesty. If I failed, it'd be through my own making.

When I recounted my day with Many Heart to Bill, he too pondered over the wise man's intended meaning for my future acceptance, only he thought more optimistically than I had. He considered the possibility that a positive situation might present itself but that I wouldn't want to accept it. We discussed probable reasonings I'd have for reluctance and we came up with humility and shyness, for I am guilty of both. Again, only the hand of time will eventually bear this out.

My week was uneventful and the class date was again upon me. And as I drove the early autumn roads, I had thoughts of unrelated matters. I thought of the names of the roads where Bill did service work. Sundance Circle. Red Feather Lane. Shoshone Road. It was good they were named after the red man's identity. For surely, the land was and is most precious to us.

As I reflected upon the street names, those naturally flowed into the Colorado names for towns and passes. The state was a virtual treasury of names, names that immediately brought crisp images behind the mind's eye. Rabbit Ears Pass. Crested Butte. Telluride. Cripple Creek. Monarch Pass. Lizard Head Pass. Durango. Redstone. Glenwood Springs. Silverton. Even my own Woodland Park brought pure nature images to mind.

I smiled as I mentally reviewed the descriptive names. Colorado certainly was a place bursting with colorful place names that were a joy to roll off the tongue—names that instantly conjured up vivid technicolor images of either pristine natural beauty or tintype frames of the untamed frontier of the old West days or of newly settled mining towns.

Nearly everywhere you went had some fascinating history behind it. One glance at the weathered tombstones scattered within the rusted iron gates of a hillside cemetery verified the fact. Each town could boast of its own renowned boot hill. What intriguing, and maybe even hair-raising, stories the haunting ghosts could tell!

And so trailed my wandering thoughts as I concluded the leisurely drive to No-Eyes' cabin this bright September morn. When I eased the pickup beneath the tall lodgepole's outstretched shadows, I cut the engine and peered through the windshield to look up the hill. The cabin door was shut tight. My teacher was nowhere around. It felt uncanny that he would be inside with the front door shutting out the beautiful day. It wasn't in keeping with my perceived impression of him. I studied the frozen scene.

"Looking for somebody?" came the shocking voice in my ear.

I jumped at the touch of his finger on my shoulder.

"A little jumpy, aren't you?" he grinned with the realization that he'd scared me but good.

I managed to laugh and chastise at the same time. "That was plain mean! That wasn't a very spiritual thing to do."

"Oh, wasn't it?"

"No, not in the least and you know it wasn't," I maintained.

He held up a cautioning finger. "But it was. You sensed I wasn't in the cabin so . . . where would I be then? You should've been immediately aware of my presence near you." He smiled wide. "That way, I couldn't have scared the pants off you."

I teasingly looked down at my lap. "They're still on. Guess you didn't scare me as bad as you thought. Besides, am I going to have to be on guard wondering when and where you're going to suddenly pop out from?"

He was no longer laughing. He was stone-faced. "Perhaps."

I took his gravity to be a warning for future situations. I'd have to be more aware next time, especially since I had no idea when the next time would be. I couldn't be caught so off guard again. I was upset with myself, for I hadn't even stepped out of the truck and already I'd received a gentle but definite reprimand.

Many Heart rapped on the door. "Let's walk."

I watched him turn and head into the woodlands. And as I scurried out of the vehicle, I was glad to know that today's lesson was to be conducted outside instead of within the cabin, and while catching up to the striding Dreamwalker, it struck me that, like myself, he too preferred the outdoor settings.

"I'm sorry," I whispered, coming up beside him.

"Sorry?"

"Yes. I know I should've been more aware back there. I should've sensed your presence so close."

"Then why didn't you?"

Silence. I really hadn't expected him to ask that question, but if I voiced that thought he'd know I'd been in expectation—another no-no for an enlightened person. Seems I not only got off on the wrong foot from the start, I was continuing to remain out of step.

We strolled through the early-morning shadows of No-Eyes' forest. I felt uncomfortable with our extended silence and I slid my eyes to sneak a glance at my companion. He was calm and appeared to be enjoying the woodswalk. I wondered how long he'd wait for my answer.

"I'm in no hurry," came the soft response.

I lowered my head to stare down at our stony trail. He had been in my head. Now there would be no withheld thoughts. There'd be no private sacred ground where I could mentally retreat into. There would be no retreating at all. And, since forward was the only directional option open to me, I dove right in.

"I didn't sense your presence because I wasn't in awareness."

The man walked on without reply.

"I wasn't in awareness because I was too busy concentrating on the closed cabin door and where you might possibly be."

"That should not have taken concentration. Your notice of the closed door should have been subliminally recorded, thereby allowing the sharp awareness to immediately take over."

"I see that now."

"Summer," he began gently but firmly, "you must remember that precious energies are wasted on unnecessary concentration. When energies are applied to concentration needlessly, then other mental aspects are depleted and deprived of those vital energies— other mental aspects such as awareness and sensory perception."

I assured him I understood and that I'd remember to apply the concept next time. But again, I had said the wrong thing.

"There's no *remembering* involved here," he contradicted. "By the time you do the *act* of remembering, valuable seconds will have passed—seconds when the awareness should have been operating at its optimum level. If you spend time remembering what you're supposed to do, then you've already *missed* sensing numerous sensory signals. See?"

"Yes. I see that it required an immediate responsive action. It must be quickly based upon instantaneous instinct."

"Awareness must be a speedy and natural response at all times."

I thought back to the former incident. "But you made no sound before you scared me. You were just suddenly *there*."

"Are you attempting excuses?"

"Not at all," I said, kicking at a stray stone. "I'm just trying to understand this. You talk about being aware of the sensory signals, but there were none."

Many Heart shoved his hands in his pockets. "Weren't there?"

I thought deeper about the infamous incident. I thought back further and remembered the day I had met the old visionary in her woods and how my neck prickled and my scalp crawled with the sudden awareness of her presence—her silent presence. She hadn't made a sound. She merely stood statue-still between the green pines and watched me. I wasn't thinking too well this day with the wise Dream-walker. "I should've sensed your *presence*," I concluded guiltily. "Your presence should've activated my immediate awareness response."

"And why didn't it?"

"Because I had misdirected my energies."

He smiled. "That wasn't so hard, was it?"

Silence. I felt miserably out of sync. I felt just like I needed to return home and begin the drive all over again. My thinking appeared to be a beat or two off the mark and it bothered me.

My companion halted and turned to look into my eyes. His hand came up to lift my downcast chin.

I intentionally averted my eyes.

"Hey," he said. "Why the long face?"

I felt like crying because of my obvious stupidity. I simply shrugged.

"Look, Summer, you're being too hard on yourself. This is what it's all about. This is why you're here—to learn. You can't expect to always be on top of things here."

I sighed as I glanced into the sunrays spearing down through the living forest.

"I don't expect that, but I do expect to be in possession of the simple things that I already know." My palms upturned as I looked hard into his eyes. "I'm screwing up the basics. I'm supposed to be getting some expanded comprehension now and, instead, I'm messing up on the baby stuff."

He laughed. "Com'on," he chuckled, "let's drop this whole thing."

We walked a ways in silence while the thin high mountain air brought us the blended essences of sweet pine and heady spruce. Its clarity served to clear my muddled head and bring about a sharpness of the senses. I breathed deeply as we treaded lightly into the heart of the thriving woodlands. A hallowed sacredness pervaded the gentle scene of innocence.

The slow meter of my footfalls paused ever so perceptively. I had caught the soft sound of ripples. I looked to my teacher.

He whispered. "There's a pond ahead."

How peculiar. In all my walks with No-Eyes, we'd never come across a mountain pond. Then again, she had never led me into this particular region of her forest before either.

The soothing sound of ripples was more distinct now. I eagerly searched the heavily wooded area for the hidden water source.

"Where is it?" asked my astute companion.

I looked for the telltale willows. There were none. I listened for the water spirit's sweet voice. It echoed confusingly between the towering pines. I closed my eyes. The sound had suddenly silenced as if it were playing a clever game of hide and seek.

I opened my eyes wide, smiled at Many Heart and pointed north.

He frowned. "You sure about that?"

I wasn't going to be fooled by his ruse to confuse the issue by attempting to place self-doubts in my mind. I grinned and pulled his hand as I confidently led the way through the dense brush. We picked our way up over a rise and down between an aged stand of thick aspens. Lichen-encrusted boulders were strewn this way and that, and, climbing precariously about on them, we cleared their natural barrier to enter a sun-touched dell centered by the shimmering pool.

My hiking companion beamed. "What was your clue?"

I grinned with glee. "I *smelled* it!"

"That was good," he complimented. "You eliminated the senses that were useless and zeroed in on the singular one that would produce results. That was very good."

I smiled at him and, giving unrestrained rein to my shining spirit, I twirled around in the golden sunlight that filtered down through the evergreens.

"I *love* this place," I sang.

"You look like a dancer in the stage spotlight," he laughed.

My pirouettes slowed to a stop. I stared at my mentor.

"I *feel* like a dancer. I do this a lot when I'm alone in my sacred ground. I look up into the deep blue mountain sky and I celebrate its beautiful holiness. And I sing too!"

He smiled gently. "You don't sing, you chant."

My gaiety softened with his words. I walked to the pond's edge and gazed down into its soul.

"What do you see?" he asked, coming up beside me and making our dual reflections glimmer upon the crystal-clear surface.

"I see the soul of life, bared openly to expose its pure innocence. I see an ageless spirit, exquisite still, enduring for all eternity."

"You don't see yourself?"

"That which exists beyond the obvious is most important. That's what I look for. That's what I see."

"That's a very profound philosophy."

I smiled ever so slightly. "Yes, it is, isn't it? I learned it from No-Eyes." I stared down into the high mountain pond. "She says things that are most beautiful to the ears and spirit. She's a spring of beautiful wisdom."

"That she is all right," came the firm reply. "But she's not the only one with this beautiful personal philosophy."

I cringed and looked at Many Heart. "She's been bad," I teased, "she's told you about my private notebook."

The man feigned guilt. "Don't blame her. She's proud of the way those thoughts come to you." He hesitated before going on. "She'd really like you to make a book of them," he eased in.

"A book of my musings? How ridiculous! Who'd read it?"

He shrugged. "No-Eyes says they're very good. They'd strike people's hearts—make them think. She thinks it'd be good to have colorful photographs correspond with your thoughts and sayings."

I was absolutely flabbergasted. "Boy! She's got it all figured out, doesn't she?"

He chuckled and raised a heavy brow. "She usually does."

A peculiar stillness passed between us.

"Summer?"

"Yeah?"

"She thought of a title."

"Title? To what?"

"That philosophy book of yours."

I snapped back. "I don't have a philosophy book, I've got a beat-up notebook."

"Want to hear it?"

"Do I have a choice?"

"You always have a choice."

I sighed. "What is it?"

"*Through Golden Canyons.*"

Silence.

"She said that your thoughts were like traveling through the golden canyons of your mind. She said that to me, Summer. She expressed how touching it was to see someone so in tune with nature and how, when the mountains whisper, you hear." He paused with his deep sensitivity. "You know how she keeps certain things to herself, but she had no trouble unloading on me about you."

I sat down on the velvety moss. "I'm not a philosopher, Many Heart. I'm just a person who writes what she sees and feels...the mountains just seem to bring out the voice of my spirit."

"And those writings about what it sees and feels will make people think. If you're not a philosopher, then you're a thinker," he reasoned.

"Oh, what's the difference anyway? How'd we get on this crazy subject?"

He smiled. "What you saw in the pond brought us to this crazy subject."

I smoothed a long blade of wildgrass between my fingers.

"Then let's go back to that point and take another trail."

"Fine by me," he agreed.

My hand wavered over the softness of the mossy bank. It caressed the velvety green growth and paused to perceive its gentle heartbeat.

Many Heart's broad, brown hand tenderly settled upon the moss next to mine. "It beats like a sleeper," he whispered.

"Yes. Slow and tranquil."

"Like a baby's," he added.

I looked up at him. "Not quite, Many Heart. I've heard the audio of my baby's heartbeat in my womb. It beats swiftly, just like a rabbit's."

And with that, I do believe my wise Dreamwalker did blush.

I altered the flow of the subject.

"I wish more people could feel the Earth Mother's heartbeat like this."

"Mmmm, that would be good," he said, leaning back against the smooth trunk of an old, old aspen.

"But they're too caught up in their busy lives, aren't they?"

He nodded and gazed up through the gilded boughs. "They do not understand about the Earth Mother's nourishing umbilical which connects them to her. They do not even know about such beautiful ways." His voice was saddened. It was heavy with it.

Silence hung between us.

A log bobbed in the center of the pond water as a lively frog hopped upon it from the shore. I watched the little being's bulging eyes. Then, it effortlessly leaped out of sight into the heavy brush. Butterflies playfully flitted here and there among the cattails. As they alighted, stained-glass wings gracefully rose and fell. The medley of chirping birds and buzzing insects filled the light air. A magpie settled on a high branch and curiously looked down at us.

I wanted to speak with my companion, but also didn't wish to shatter the surround of serenity that we rested within. I leaned forward to peer into his face.

The man shifted his eyes to me and gave a smile that wasn't a smile.

"They can learn," I softly offered.

He sighed.

"They can be made aware of such natural bonds."

My sweet friend looked away before facing me. His eyes were intense.

"And who will be their teacher, Summer? Who will bring about this great wondrous move to enlighten men to their Earth lineage?"

I didn't know the answer to that. I didn't know who could bring mass awareness to the people. Several possibilities wove through my mind, but none appeared adequate.

He raised his brows as if to say, "Well?"

"Well, that's a tall order," I responded honestly. "The bond between man and nature encompasses a lot of comprehensive material. One would have to teach total health, ecology, nature ways, and even some sacred spirit ways."

"This is so." And he stared at me. It was a certain qualified look that I'd seen my aged friend use on me.

I was aghast. "Oh, no you don't. I'm not teaching all that. No way!"

He looked innocently up into the cloudless sky. "Did I say anything about you?"

"You said plenty. Your *look* said it all!"

Then the man pulled up his knees and rested his arms across them. "You could write a book. No-Eyes would help you."

So that was it. The two wise ones had it all neatly figured out. They'd been conniving behind my back. Seems they'd have me writing the rest of my life.

"Don't I have a say in this?" I half teased.

White teeth gleamed behind the broad smile. "Of course. But now you're wondering why she's got all these literary ideas in mind for you."

"That did cross my mind."

"That's simple. You're her only student who writes!"

"Wrong. I'm her only student who collects publisher's rejection slips."

"That really showed a hell of a lot of faith."

"Sorry," I said in a not-so-sorry tone. "Besides, when was I going to be approached about these wondrous written works?"

"Don't sound so excited about them."

"I'm not. Who needs another file cabinet filled with sloppy form letters saying 'Sorry, your proposal doesn't fit our list. . . good luck with another publisher.' "

"Sounds like sour grapes to me."

"Nothing wrong with *your* hearing. So when was I going to be approached with it?"

He shrugged. "That was up to her. That's her baby, not mine."

"Well, I admitted, "to tell you the truth, I think it'd be best if people were informed by a wide variety of teachers. Each one offering their own viewpoints in order to give the public a more broad-scope perspective."

"Absolutely."

I looked at Many Heart. He was grinning.

I sighed. "And I'm just one fish in the teaching sea, right?"

"That's a strange way to put it, but the general idea seems about right."

The brilliance of a mountain bluebird caught my attention. My eyes followed it until it disappeared into the forest depths.

"In the end, though," I mused, "people will be forced to change their ways. They'll have to come into the knowledge of their bond with nature in order to survive."

"Yes," he nodded, "this is so. But if many teachers speak out about this living bond now, the future will be paved, it'll be less strenuous.

I had my doubts.

Now it was his time to peer around. He leaned forward to study my face. "Summer?"

"What?"

"You do not agree?"

"People are stubborn beings. They're resistant to change." I sighed heavily. "I'm wondering if all the books and teachers' words will fall by the wayside. So many think this sort of concept is radical or faddish. People change beliefs like they change clothes. They pick what suits their present mood."

"And what will the present mood be for the future? It'll be an unchanging one of necessity and ingenuity for survival. People won't have the opportunity to change from anything but their basic relationship with nature. No other alternatives will be available then."

"That's *then*," I emphasized. "Right now they don't quite see it like that."

He grinned. "We've come full circle, my friend. They don't see it that way right now because they need to be *shown,* taught."

"That was very clever of you to twist it back around like that," I teased.

He winked. "Takes two for one of No-Eyes' famous verbal circle dances."

Many Heart rose and stretched to the sun that blinked down through the spindly tree needles. He leisurely strolled the sun-speckled earth between the pines and pond. It was an enchanting place of respite and, scanning its boundaries, I could easily envision delicate fairy wings fluttering just beyond my peripheral sights. A fantasy world where gnomes popped their red-capped heads in and out of the bushes surrounding us . . . where a rainbow's end slowly arced up from the rich earth and speared far into the depths of the blue Colorado sky.

I looked over to Many Heart. He was no longer actively walking the bank. He was seated cross-legged. Eyes closed. Palms upturned on knees. Smoke. Mist. A swirling surround of a veiled force—a living force encircled him.

I quickly shut my eyes. I attempted to join the Dreamwalker on his own level of reality.

Respiration slowing. Physical sensory intake diminishing. Physiological heaviness. Psychological lightness. Psychic freedom.

Smoke. Mist. A veiled force wavered before me, undulating with each of its soft breaths.

I moved within its gentle being. I looked around me as the moving softness shifted with my new presence. It pleasingly responded to my movements. I smiled at its exquisite grace and form.

I moved again.

Once more the nebulous entity made a like gesture.

Again and again I moved with my enchanting partner until we were literally dancing. I smiled, then laughed as we twirled and bent together in our shared joy of life. My freed spirit had never felt such total happiness before. We two were within an opalescent world of sublime freedom and my heart rejoiced with the entity's pureness of soul.

Dancing. Freedom. Happiness. Joyful smiles. Warm feelings.

I was one with the entity. We now shared minds and hearts. Our spirits were a resplendent bond. I lost myself to its naturalness. I was no longer separate. I *was* the swirling, pearly entity. I *was* its very soul.

Now the mist twirled with the singular form of the dual energies. A *new* awareness added to its life. It danced and spun. It gracefully drifted and dipped, bowed and extended. It was the epitome of shared love. It celebrated the deep love of all living things. It *was* the life force of all living things. And it knew none else but complete happiness of heart and serenity of spirit.

A distantly perceived sound disturbed the entity's gaiety—its eternal dance of life. The distracting sound pulled the two energies apart. The entity now had a companion once again.

I saw my partner swirl. I was again separate unto myself.

Sounds. More distinctly metered sounds pervaded into the delicate fabric of our private pas de deux. The entity slowed its gay tempo. It slowed, slowed . . . and stopped.

I stood alone. Bewildered, I strained to hear its gentle breath. The rhythmic sounds from without grew louder.

Chants. Chanting.

I opened my eyes.

The Dreamwalker was chanting to the noonday sun that hung like a golden nugget set in the turquoise, autumn sky. His tone was clear. His pitch was low. His voice carried his spirit upon the feather-light wings of song.

Silence enveloped us. The song had concluded. A great stillness engulfed the hidden dell. Even the pond waters held their breath creating a glassy, mirrored surface. And time froze.

Silence.

One piercing chirp. Two. Three. A distant caw. A gentle breeze. Ripples. The man turned. Dark eyes intense on mine.

I held my breath.

He smiled softly and joined me beneath the shade of the aged aspen. My teacher held out his hand to me. It was clasped tightly.

I looked at the wide, brown fist, then back up to him.

"What do you have?" I whispered.

"Something for someone called Summer Rain," he replied with dancing eyes locked intently on mine. "You might even say it's a *special* delivery."

I looked hesitantly away from the magnetic depths of his ebony eyes to the enclosed fingers. The hand turned and the fingers un-curled...slowly.

Azure lights. Scarlet rays. Topaz. Purple spires. Lights speared out from the object in his upturned palm. The crystal breathed.

My eyes were wide as dinner plates. "But...where'd you get this?" I asked in genuine amazement.

He merely smiled. "Does it matter?"

"Well...I guess not."

"Do you ask the giver where his gift came from? How he came by it?"

I stared at the shimmering stone. "No." And, at first shyly looking up at his serene face, I then returned my gaze down to the new object. I made an uncertain movement to touch it.

"May I?" I asked.

"Of course," he nodded with a glint of sparkled pleasure in his twinkling eyes.

My finger rested on the stone.

It vibrated.

Quickly, I snapped back my hand.

The Dreamwalker's face lit up with mirth. "It won't bite!" And, extending his arm, he held it out for me to take. "Here, it's yours."

I simply looked at it. "But it's got powerful medicine. It's *magical*!"

"Yes."

I hesitantly looked back and forth between the man and the

sacred object.

"Go ahead. Take it, Summer."

And I did. I held it securely within my curled fingers and closed my eyes. My palm warmed immediately.

"What do you feel?" my gift-giver inquired.

"Warmth. Physically, I feel its deep warmth.

"What about mentally?"

"Mentally, I get a great age, an age as old as the earth itself." Then I corrected myself. "No. Older."

"Summer," he whispered softly near my ear, "and what do you get spiritually?"

I kept my eyes closed as I tightened and relaxed my grasp on the rough object. More impressions came when my fingers were barely wrapped around it. When it was held loosely, it was as if the stone was freed to express itself and, when I held it firmly, its personality was stifled, confined.

I relaxed my grip and allowed its character to emit freely from it. Impressions came in all sensory forms.

The pungent aroma of freshly cut hay. Crisp high mountain breezes. Blue shadows on new-fallen snow. The echoing of rushing gorge waters. Milky moonglow. Salt sea air. Woodsmoke. Heat waves atop vermilion mesas. Mist. Dancing.

My eyes shot open.

Many Heart was grinning and nodding.

"The . . . the *stone*," I stammered with excitement, "the stone's the *Earth Mother!*"

My teacher laughed. "Not quite. The stone contains not only *Her* essence, but those of one older still—the Eternal *Grandmother* Earth. You could say that it possesses a rare piece of *her* aged spirit."

I looked down at my hand. I slowly uncurled the fingers. What rested inside was beautiful.

"It's enchanting," I whispered with deep reverence. "It's simply magical."

Then I looked hard into my friend's eyes. "And you say it's mine? It's really all *mine*?"

He slowly nodded. "I said it was, didn't I?"

I closed my hand around the precious gift. "Who's it really from, Many Heart?"

"Don't you know?"

"Yes," I answered softly. "I know."

"And do you also know what it's for?"

"My medicine bundle. I'll always treasure it there."

"When and for what purpose will you use it?"

I pondered over that question for a few minutes. And, smiling into the gentle breeze, I answered.

"Right now I haven't the faintest notion, but I will when the time is right. I'll know when and how to use it then."

My teacher appeared satisfied with my response. "Better put it away for now," he advised.

I quickly searched around for a secure place to keep it, but found none. I offered it back to him.

"Don't seem to have a good hiding place. Mind holding it in your shirt pocket until I'm ready to leave?"

He took the stone and gently placed it within his breast pocket. He patted the nubby bulge. "Safe and sound."

I smiled at my friend who had been the Eternal Grandmother's special, mystical courier.

We settled back against the aspens. The breeze tossed my hair as it gained in energy. The pond's ripples soothingly caressed the tall reeds. The bullfrog croaked and the pines whispered.

"Many Heart?" I said, breaking the pureness of the woodland voices.

"Mmmm?"

"I tried to join you before."

"Yes. I know."

"But you weren't there."

His head rested back against the grey birchlike bark. Eyes fixed upon a crawling insect.

"Are you certain of that?"

I doubted. "Not absolutely. No."

"Look here," he said, directing my attention to the rich earth between us. "I've been watching this little bug. Now see? Another has joined it."

I listened to the obvious lesson he began to teach.

"The two are together. Each aware of the other. Yet," he cautioned, "here we sit looking down at the two crawling people who believe they are alone together. Are they truly alone because they do not see us? Because they have no perceptual awareness of us? Or are they indeed part of a more numerous group of living presences? Just because they have not *perceived* us, does this then mean that we are *not* there? That they are alone?"

"Of course not," I grinned.

"Well then?"

"You were observing my journey but your spirit wasn't actually present. That's why I didn't see you."

"Exactly."

"And why weren't you present?"

One brow raised. "I believe you already know why."

"So I could experience my bond with the Earth Mother and the Eternal Grandmother. So I could unite with their joyous freedom... their pure duo spirits."

"You did well, my friend. And you did just fine."

I smiled with the warm glow of the cherished memory. Leaning back against the tree, I closed my eyes to envision the magnificent beauty of the spiritual experience... my dancing union with their Spirit.

Many Heart respectfully allowed my silent time for reverie. He granted me the pleasure of privately reliving the beautiful journey into the tandem souls of nature.

When I returned, my teacher was patiently waiting. "This sure is a great place, isn't it?"

I scanned the peaceful scenery. "There's few that could even come close to comparing. I wonder why No-Eyes never brought me here?"

He squinted over at me. "Don't even try to figure out her reasonings. But I do happen to know that she frequently comes here to chant and offer special prayers."

"She ever bring you here?" I curiously inquired.

"Not me. I don't really think she's brought anyone here to this sacred place of hers."

I worried. "Should we have come here then? Maybe this is *her* sacred ground." I had a sudden sensation that we were trespassing.

My mentor reached over to halt my move to get up.

"Relax, Summer. I said she doesn't ever bring anyone here because she wants to be here *alone*. She never intended such beauty to be ignored and go unvisited by others who'd appreciate it."

I settled back down after his comforting statement. "Many Heart?"

"Yes?"

"Do you know a lot about her? I mean, do you know *all* about her?"

My companion laughed at the question. "Are you serious?"

I had thought I was. My dejected expression answered his question.

"You *are* serious! Summer," he softened, "*nobody* knows all there is to know about that little lady. Why, I bet if, by some strange chance, all her students got together and compared their volumes of notes, we'd still only have a small fragment of that lady's life and vision."

I chuckled at that. "I can believe that, all right. It seems that every time we're together, I get new insights to her. She appears to be a spring of knowledge. It just keeps coming and coming—it just flows forth from her."

"I know what you mean."

I became serious. "One thing that's all too clear, though, is her deep love for the land and its natural inhabitants."

He caught the sudden shift to a heavier mood. "Yes. That's most evident. It's not hard to understand, though. It's the only subject I've seen her get out of control over."

I agreed. "The Earth and her protection are very close to her tender heart. She becomes irate with mankind's stupidity when it comes to ecology and the use of damaging energies."

Many Heart looked at me. "She told you about the Phoenix yet?"

I smiled weakly. "Yes. We spent a long while on that subject."

A deep silence drifted between us.

Thinking about those difficult days with the old visionary when she told me about the rising of the Great Phoenix again and how it was to coincide with the changes for mankind representing the new cycle, I now saw something from a different perspective.

"Many Heart?"

"Mmmm."

"I was just thinking about the weeks when No-Eyes told me about the Phoenix Days and I sort of feel bad that she won't experience the final outcome."

"You mean when the Hoop is complete again?"

"Yes. When the Sacred Tree is whole, thriving straight and strong. She should be here to experience those reversals that would please her spirit."

His smile was tender with sympathetic understanding.

"Oh, but *won't* she be here with us then?"

My brows furrowed. "I don't mean in spirit, Many Heart."

Eyes twinkled. "And neither do I, Summer."

I looked away from the mysterious dark pools of my friend. He had made a cryptic statement that made me wonder about the possible mechanics of his suggested probability.

The golden chariot had traversed its expanse of high sky. The afternoon sun was lowering toward its western destination. The buttery light was churning into altered ranges of auburn and russets as it lengthened through the filtering boughs.

What did the Dreamwalker mean about No-Eyes? In the future, would I see her again in a more youthful form? Would she really want to return when mankind was living the Indian Way . . . the Earthway?

"Wouldn't *you* want to?" came the soft question.

The sudden sound of Many Heart's voice broke my mental wonderings.

"What?" I asked. "What'd you say?"

"I said, wouldn't *you* want to return then?"

"Yes," I smiled. "Yes, I would, especially after I experienced so much of man's negative ways with the Earth Mother. Yes, I'd definitely want to return to share the living in harmony and peace."

"Then why the amazement when you consider the old one doing it?"

I shrugged. "I'm amazed at the thought of perhaps seeing her again—being able to physically touch. I just never figured on that." I became solemn. "I know she'll leave one day and I'm dreading that. I'll miss her terribly."

"People come, people go, Summer. No-Eyes has been doing her work for a long time. She's tired."

"Yes. I can see it in her eyes, hear it in her creaking bones when she moves."

He reached over to pat my knee. "Summer," he soothed, "no matter what her form, I know for a fact that she'll always be with you. I believe you know that."

I managed a weak smile and nodded. "I do know that, but I also know that when the actual time comes, I'll be heartbroken beyond bearing."

"You'll have work to carry on—important spiritual work. She entered your life because she recognized who your old spirit was. She took you under her wing and taught you the beautiful ways. She expects you to be strong and carry on—her love for you, and yours for her, would demand such determined efforts to the work she led you to."

"You make it sound as though I'd drop everything when she finally leaves. I'm not going to do that, Many Heart. I wouldn't do that to my dear old friend."

"I know." Then he paused before speaking again. "Besides, your future work involves spiritual aspects you haven't ever before considered."

Another cryptic statement. This time he wasn't going to get away with it.

"Explain."

Palms upturned. Brows raised. His innocent gesture belied the knowledge hidden behind his sparkling eyes.

I moved threateningly toward him. "You know damned well what future work's ahead of me, don't you!"

His grin was suppressed. "Summer no swear," he teasingly imitated.

My sudden indignation made him laugh.

I countered. "I think Many Heart got one big smart *mouth*!"

And together we laughed over the silliness of the loving imitations of our mutual teacher. Although we got sidetracked, I remained one-minded. My smile faded.

"Many Heart, what future work were you talking about?"

"Your books. Remember you promised her you'd do them?"

He was right, but something about his swift response quickened my alertness. He had left something out.

"The books *and*?"

"Maybe that's not up to me to say, Summer. Maybe the old one wants to reveal that herself. We'll see."

"Does it involve teaching?" I pushed.

His exasperated look said that I was being a bad student by being so insistent. He sighed.

"Teaching only through the extent of your books and by answering the readers' questions directed to the Mountain Brotherhood. The Mountain Brotherhood will be just for correspondence...a spiritual information center."

"Yes, I realize that, but what I was asking was if I'd be required to do any *actual* teaching."

His head shook. "Don't you think you'll be busy enough? Your job isn't to physically teach or lecture or tour the country—nothing like that at all. That much I *can* tell you."

Relief. "That wasn't ever actually spelled out. No-Eyes was always very vague about that aspect."

He smiled with his secret knowledge that remained unspoken. "Well, I have the feeling she's not going to be vague from now on in. You'll know exactly what you're expected to do. There won't be any doubts left in your mind."

It was nothing specific my companion had said, but I suddenly had the sinking feeling that something very important was skirted with deliberate and measured easiness. I had the feeling that I had been instrumental in leading the conversation away from the important subject when I began inquiring about teaching. Now as we sat in peacefulness, I sensed my friend was pleased with how he was spared the specifics of just what my future work entailed. And the moment had passed.

The lowering scarlet orb sent flaming tongues out across the land. Slate shadows crept along the soft carpet of the hidden dell. The wind spirit whispered its evensong and all of nature hushed to its gentle lullaby.

I left Many Heart standing in the orange glow of No-Eyes' porch. I had had a most wonderful day. It had begun out of tune, but by the time I was ready to depart, I realized how harmonious most of the day had been.

I had learned and experienced much this glorious autumn day. I had journeyed into the realm of Nature's heart where I danced in her freedom and became one with the Earth Mother's and the Eternal Grandmother's pure spirits. I had been given the precious sacred medicine of their shimmering essences. And I had gained the knowledge of some important answers.

I reached the tall lodgepole and turned to wave a temporary farewell to the Dreamwalker.

He was smiling. I think he was even laughing.

And as I gazed up into the brilliant orange alpenglow that blanketed the highest mountain peaks, my happy heartbeats told me that his laughter was a very good sign—it was good medicine.

The Light of Dawn pierces my heart and it quickens to the Joy of Life.

The Robe of Dusk descends upon my Spirit and it mellows to the Comfort of Truth.

The Forgotten Ones

The slow-speaking Red Man, his silent brother.
The grinning Indian, his shuffling sister.
Dumb?
Perhaps.
Or perchance a simple but cunning veneer which effectively
conceals their ancient secrets.
Perhaps merely a shield which protects that which they know—
for Enlightenment brightly pulses in the mind behind the eyes of the
humble.

It was the third weekend of September, and an invigorating new scent was in the mountain air. It was the clear fragrance of a high country autumn.

Until now, summer had hung on with a white-fisted death grip. And now, her warm breath was weakening, her energies depleted with the desperation of her struggle for seasonal dominance.

The hint of crisp air, its wintery freshness, bespoke of the stealthy entrance of a new entity—one donned with the regal robe spun of brilliant threads of purified gold, flaming rubies, and burnished copper. The advance of the radiant new entity was powerful—there would be no contest between it and the defending one whose time to abdicate had arrived.

The signs of autumn's official reign were clear and distinct in this little town that comfortably nestled itself in at over eight thousand feet up the mountains. And, while the conceding ruler was forced to retreat down the pass into the lower elevation of Colorado Springs, the highland of Woodland Park prepared to rejoice in its victory celebration in honor of the resplendent new monarch—autumn.

As I drove along the edge of the snaking shelf road, I glanced down at the steep mountainside. The tender tips of the aspens were drowsy. Their lids were heavy with the long exertion of staying awake.

I eased over onto a narrow pull-off and got out to sit beneath the white pines that grew precariously out from cliff's rim. Autumn's sweet breath tenderly found me. It reached out to me to caress my receiving upturned face. I smiled and welcomed her into my world.

The entity softly lifted the ends of my hair and began singing a joyous psalm of celebration. I joined the worship ceremony. I chanted low, extending the hymn out over the high expanse of space above the descending mountainside. I closed my eyes and, like Many Heart, I freed my spirit to ride the feathered wings of song. And riding the praising chants, I worshipped the sublime essence—I gave my humble reverence to the pristine essence of the Great Spirit.

When I opened my eyes and scanned the vast scenic panorama, nature had altered her mood. I sensed an electrifying excitement emanating from her soul. I inhaled deeply. The high, thin air brought an infusion of the pungent spices of autumn. The penetrating scent carried vivid images of shimmering vistas of vibrant colors, transcendental beauty and mystic apparitions—all extraordinary aspects of autumn's classic grandeur—her multifaceted personality. And, as my every minute cell absorbed the inhaled energy, I was filled with autumn's mystical being. I was one with her. I was one with her glorious creator.

The invigorating fragrance wafted through the alpine air and as I looked down onto the tree-blanketed hillsides, I could distinctly feel the tall entities' growing excitement, for the grand time was nearing for them to display their true magnifience of soul. In a few weeks they'd be singing out in a virtual united chorale of celebration, and everyone would be swept up in the gay mood of their magnificent beauty. And today, on this brilliantly crisp mountain morn, I had watched the mystical beginnings of what was to come.

Once back in the pickup, I nosed it onto the narrow ribbon of road and continued uphill toward the nearly hidden turnoff that led down into No-Eyes' valley. Birdsong filled the air with a happy trilling. Small four-leggeds scampered about in the bright early morning sunshine. The mountains were alive with good medicine and I loved being such a vital part of it. I cherished the wondrous light-hearted feelings nature gave my being. And it was this expanded awareness of my heart's welling that engulfed my spirit as I parked beneath the old lodgepole and ran up the rise to the meager cabin perched upon its sunny crest.

Many Heart appeared in the doorway. His smile revealing his own inner happiness, he held up a hand in joyful greeting. "Happy autumn!" he bellowed.

My eyes twinkled. "Isn't it just glorious?" I exclaimed, reaching the top step.

We hugged each other without even thinking about it. It was

merely a loving, companionable expression of our hearts—nothing more, and certainly nothing less. I frequently hugged those I felt spiritually close to—man or woman, made no difference. It was simply an outward expression of companionship, friendship.

In my excitement, I pulled back from the Dreamwalker and began to prattle on about my morning's union with the entity of autumn. I was completely caught up in the experience as I followed him into the shadowed cabin.

He turned and smiled, an expression of complete understanding on his face. His hand rose to rest gently on my shoulder.

"I was expecting you much earlier," he said. "When you didn't show and time became of the essence, I greeted the day alone."

My heart felt like a leaden weight. I hadn't known I was expected to join in his daybreak benediction. I was about to apologize when he interrupted.

He smiled. "But you have done just as good. When I smelled the scent in the air this morning, I figured it'd detain you somewhere along the way. Your private union was a beautiful expression of prayer. Don't worry about not being here."

He didn't pause long enough for me to reply; instead, he glanced over my outerwear and quickly reached for his denim jacket that had been slung over a chair.

"We're going outside again today, but our walking won't be done with our feet."

Uh-oh. That meant a spiritual journey was going to take place this day. Butterflies fluttered wildly within my stomach at the mere thought of it. I stood frozen to the spot.

The Dreamwalker turned. "You coming?"

"I . . . I thought there wasn't going to be any scheduled agenda to this. What's this journey about?"

Stonefaced, he inclined his head to the sunshine and strode out the door.

I quickly rearranged my light serape and scurried after him. By the time I caught up with his long strides, we had reached the crest of No-Eyes' hill. Down below, in the lush ravine, the water spirit sang as she freely rode the sparkling stream waters. Her lilting voice rose up to give us soothing background music.

The solemn teacher was studying the skies. They were a cloudless wash of deep turquoise.

"We will face west," he declared, crossing his legs and gracefully lowering himself down onto the prickly wildgrass.

I did the same. Then, remembering the old visionary's caution about crossing my legs, I stretched them out before me and rested back on my palms.

"Sit up," came the firm command.

"No-Eyes told me not to cross my legs because of . . . ."

"Cross your legs. This journey cannot be taken in that position, else you will fall back, and it cannot be taken lying down either. Cross your legs—like so."

He arranged my legs so that they were not tightly nestled, but were rather in an extended cross. To my surprise, the new position actually felt restful.

My teacher then scooted around in front of me. The rising sun was full on his weathered face.

"I thought we had to face west," I said.

"*You* face west. That is where we are going. I face east because, like the sun, I will lead you to the sunset direction. I would have preferred physically taking you to this place, but since it is too long a drive, we must go by other means. *This* way."

I had a concern. "Many Heart?"

"Yes?"

I scanned the rough ground. "Doesn't the physical body require complete relaxation in order for the spirit to journey?"

"You are within fear, Summer."

I didn't bother replying, because we both knew that. I was fearful I'd fall backwards and maybe hit my head against one of the jagged granite stones that littered the ground.

"Exit fear, Summer."

God, this was a new one—one I didn't have the foggiest idea of the mechanics of.

"Exit the fear," he softly ordered again.

I didn't know how to exit a fear and, instead of pretending that I did, I asked, "How do I do this?"

"Each must discover his own way. There is no set manner for this. You will find your own way out. We cannot go on until you do. I will wait."

I averted my eyes from the intensity of his and attempted to concentrate on exiting fear. I tried for several minutes and failed to produce the desired results, so I consciously broke away from the voluntary effort of concentration.

I listened to the faint but clear strains of the water spirit's song of life. A slicing shadow rent the sunny, golden fabric of the peaceful mountain surround and I squinted up into the lustrous sky. Our resident falcon had soared across his vast domain and I wanted very much to join in his freedom flight.

Watching him, the blinding brightness was far too bright. I closed my eyes, but still I saw the magnificent bird. Feathers glinted iridescently on gracefully outstretched wings. Noble beak held into the high air. Lungs burning with the sting of the thin mountain air. The gentle climb above saw-toothed peaks capped in frosty snow crystals. Up. Upward into the beyond of forever we soared.

The high pause came as we momentarily hung in the sky, seemingly suspended in time—a stop-action frame of intense anticipation. Pounding hearts. Elation.

The tilt. And our eyes were focused on the ground far below. Wings angled back. Then, the breathtaking plunge that drove my heart into the solar plexus while the daredevil dive gained in momentum with lightning speed.

Down. Downward we pitched. Slicing. With such incredible ease did we dash headlong toward earth. Air whistling past our ears, rushing through open nostrils it scorched the delicate airways. It was a searing heat. Desert dry. A lonely heat. One cast up from a land forlorn.

My eyes snapped open.

As before, Many Heart was cross-legged in front of me. But we were now perched atop a high vermilion mesa.

How could this be? Where were we? How did we get to this forsaken land of desolation?

The height frightened me. I tilted ever so slightly to peer over the precarious redstone rim.

My stomach churned. Desert spread out far below us. Desert stretched from horizon to horizon. My breath caught with the expansive sight.

I straightened and shielded my eyes to look up into the wavering heat of the sky. I watched my high flier make his smooth arc of descent as he expertly leveled off and disappeared within the cooler shadow of a terra cotta desert tower.

I was mesmerized when I slid my gaze from my feathered traveler over to the Dreamwalker.

His eyes were bright with awareness. He was calm. Cool.

I was sweating profusely. The light woven serape that had been comfortable for the early autumn weather had suddenly become a suffocating and itchy wrap in the presence of this stifling heat. I squirmed beneath its now cumbersome and oppressing weight.

Many Heart stared. Expressionless, he stared into me. Through me.

I had urgent questions that required immediate answers. I looked hard into my teacher's dark eyes. They were like cool, black mirrors that reflected my own image and that of the searing sun above and behind me. I ignored the blinding disc's image and peered beyond the surface of the glassy orbs.

"How'd we get here?" I whispered.

"Is that so important?" came the gentle response.

"Not as important as where we are."

I skimmed the parched horizon line behind him. "Where are we, Many Heart? What strange place is this?"

"Strange? I think not strange, Summer Rain." He paused to look about the barren scene. "But perhaps 'forgotten' would be a more accurate term to apply."

"Forgotten? But surely," I challenged innocently, "who could ever forget such bleak austerity of nature, such utter starkness?"

"Man. Man has forgotten about such places. And yes," he uttered, glancing about, "it is bleak and stark, but it is this simple austerity which creates its enchanting beauty, is it not so, Summer Rain?"

I didn't doubt his premise, but then again, I didn't exactly resonate well to lands without the high snowy mountains with their rushing snowmelt streams amid lush green pines. I never had to relate to nature's austerity before now. I wasn't at all too sure I could, either. And why wasn't he calling me Summer, like always before? Why did he keep saying "Summer Rain"?

"Because Summer Rain is who you are. Summer Rain *can* relate to this place."

"I'm *Mary* Summer Rain, and how do *you* know I can relate to this forsaken land when *I* do not yet know if I can?"

"It's simple. You will allow your spirit to recognize this place for what it truly represents—for what this location *is*. And," he explained further, "during this precise time frame, the 'Mary' aspect of your name is nowhere around. At this moment you are solely Summer Rain. This you will come to realize."

He was the Dreamwalker. I had no right to contradict his foreknowledge. Or did I? I was the learning student here. And a student never learned quicker than when she questioned her wise instructor. But the real question was, *should* I?

"What is it about this place that I should recognize?"

Aged wisdom shone from his bright eyes. "If you are told, then how can you possibly *know* that you recognized it voluntarily?"

"By your reaction."

"What makes you so certain I'd give this *expected* revealing reaction?"

Silence. My overly swift reply had evidenced my presence in expectation.

He explained further. "It's your *own* reaction we are waiting to recognize. That reaction will evidence your recognition of this place."

I moved on down to my second concern. "Why did you say that I am solely Summer Rain at this moment?"

"Because you are."

I had jumped in and asked the two questions, but had received no enlightening answers. I had the distinct impression that those answers could only be found within myself.

I turned my head and looked out over the burnt orange cliffs of the scorched canyonland, their bright vermilion mesas flamed starkly against the lonesome sapphire sky. I looked out in all directions and saw a mournful burning place, an austere and desolate land struck motionless by the ravages of neverending fevers.

Beads of sweat seeped out of the pores of my forehead. Miniature rivulets coursed down my spine and pasted my Colorado T-shirt to my back. The serape was an unbearable hotpack.

I looked at my friend.

He was enviably dry.

"Why aren't you sweating?" I snapped in irritation.

"Should I be?"

He was not only physically cool. He was also emotionally so.

I lowered my head. Salt stung my eyes. Droplets fell from my face. I was slowly stewing, not only physically from the broiling heat, but also from my rising irritability. I angrily swiped at the frustrating wetness of my dripping face. Frowning and mumbling, I squirmed and mopped at the trickling course between my breasts.

"You're in frustration," came the unnecessary words of wisdom.

"That didn't take a Dreamwalker to perceive!" I snapped back. "Of *course* I'm frustrated! I *hate* being hot. Just *look* at me, for chrissakes! I'm *soaked!*"

"Exit the frustration, Summer Rain," he said calmly.

"*Exit* it? *Change* this horrid *scenery!* Give me back my cool mountain *forest!* Take us beside an icy *stream! Then* I'll exit it real quick!"

His expression remained composed. My outbursts hadn't incited a negative response. He merely stared.

"Exit the frustration."

Where was my escape route this time? Where was my freeing falcon? I sighed and again bravely peered over the dizzying rim. Far below, I could now discern the ragged serrated lines of parched gulches that unmercifully cut jagged scars across the dry countenance of the earth's tender face. God, this place was ugly.

The voice spoke gently, lovingly. "You see before you an aspect of the Eternal Grandmother. You think She's unsightly? Ugly?"

Terrified of the stomach-churning height, I nervously inched back from the edge. A loosened stone pitched downward. I listened to the soft mellowed sounds of his words that painfully struck at my heart.

"Is she nothing more to you than an irritation? A source of physical

131

discomfort and mental frustration? Does Summer Rain not perceive her inner beauty? Her very soul? Does this Summer Rain not *feel?*"

As hot and uncomfortable as I was, his words were painful. They cut deeply. They drew blood from my soul.

I leaned back with my palms behind me. They rested on the burning stone, but I ignored it. I had serious thinking to do.

The torrid air stirred upon my face. Nature's breath was hot, but it was breath all the same, and it appeared to momentarily cool my dampened skin. Then it was gone. The stifling stillness returned, making it seem even hotter than before. I closed my eyes, but still the searing colors remained vividly clear against thin eyelids.

Burnished copper. Vermilion. Umber and bronze. Russet and ocher. They were all there. Not my favorite nature complexion, but striking just the same.

My head burned. I envisioned a bright red sunburn line down the center where my hair was parted. My eyes squinted to a half-opened position and I looked out across the silent canyonscape of badlands where the only high noon movement was the layers of scorching heat wavering across the dusty horizon. An undulating haze. The stuff of which mirages were made of. Maybe this was all a clever mirage. Maybe it wasn't even real.

My mental fantasy was being disturbed by an unknown. My thoughts were being intruded upon by a nebulous something. I concentrated. I strained to listen.

At first I thought I was hearing the blood pounding in my ears, for the metered rhythm identically matched that of the beating pulse I could feel in my palms on the hot stone. I closed my eyes again to shut out the visual stimuli. There *was* a pulsation felt, but it wasn't coming from my heartbeat. And, ignoring my waiting companion, I pulled my arms out in front of me and bent far forward—low, to spread my hands out on the searing surface of the high mesa. The beat was barely discernible, but it was there. Within the stone, it was there.

"Summer Rain does feel."

I didn't move a muscle. "What *is* this?" I whispered reverently.

"Summer Rain knows."

And I smiled down at the stone.

"Yes," I softly admitted, "Summer Rain does know the feel of a noble nation's heartbeat. Summer Rain does recognize this high sacred place."

I was struck with awe as I remembered a distant time when I had visited this very place—this high holy place. And the precious memories surged through the floodgates of my opened mind.

I straightened and stood. Upon that formerly dizzying precipice, I now stood without fear, I now stood to my full height and scanned the eastern region with new eyes. Smiling, I looked out at the bold stance of the redstone monoliths that were as towering headstones marking the passing of eons. Their ominous shadows silently crept across the parched land burning at their feet. Long-forgotten memories speared through my mind to flare in a multitude of enlightenment sparks. And I recognized what wonder my simple feet now stood upon.

Sundials of the Gods. Sacred totems of the ancients.

They stood tall and proud, keeping the watch.

Impregnable. Eternal. Bleak shroud of the pyramid of Collective Wisdom.

In heartwelling recognition, I turned to face the west. The high imposing obelisks of the canyonland were ignited by the flaming torches of Ra. The pitted and craggy complexion of their scarlet faces gave evidence to their endurance—their invulnerability.

Sphinxlike remnants. Testimonials left by the Ancient Ones. Eternal keeps guarding that which has passed before their eyes—guarding that which they know. Protecting that treasure of hidden wisdom that rested below my feet.

I was now in full possession of a new perspective. I now knew that I was the Summer Rain of whom the Dreamwalker spoke. I knew because I remembered. I remembered another woman from a long-ago age who was called Sequanu—Sequanu of the Spirit Clan that guarded the sacred, mystical secrets that dwell within the catacomb depths of this mesa.

My recognition was total. My feelings ran deep—painfully deep, for when I again sat upon the stone, my skin was cool and my mind chilled with awareness of other things that the midday sun could not dispel.

A sharp quiver trembled down my spine when I again scanned the stark surroundings, for this was also a haunted place. It was a haunted place where the wind carries the low moanings of forlorn spirits trapped between dimensions. A place where the very ground vibrates with the measured footfalls of a thousand dancers' feet as they perform the ancient ceremonies. A distant keening became clear and shrill in my ears. Ghostly forms wavered just outside the line of my peripheral vision. I spun around to look, but the sorrowful specters had vanished. This was a special place—a haunting place.

I stared into my teacher's melancholy eyes. "Why here?"

A heavy, black brow raised.

"What better place to speak of the forgotten people than from the Land of the Forgotten?"

He glanced at the redstone mesas that pierced the horizon line behind me. "What better place to speak of a desolate people than within the Land of Desolation? An empty place for an empty people."

His heavy words weighted my sensitive heart. I was now deeply humiliated by my former misconduct, by my absolute rudeness.

"Many Heart," I began hesitantly as I studied my fingers, "about before . . . ."

"No need to hash that over," he said with kindness.

"No. I think there is. At least I feel there is. I'd rest a lot better if we could just talk about it. I behaved terribly and I'm very sorry if I disappointed you."

"I wasn't disappointed. Remember, Summer Rain, one who is never in expectation can never be disappointed or surprised. You reacted honestly, openly, without reserve. That was as it should be."

I smiled with a sigh of admiration for my understanding mentor. "You make my juvenile rantings sound as though they were nothing to be concerned about."

He grinned sheepishly. "Not when I knew they'd eventually wear off with recognition. Not when I knew they'd lead you out of your frustration state and into the one of complete recognition."

I gave him a chastising look. "You do have the advantage."

My teacher merely smiled. I had the feeling he didn't like it whenever I separated us into neat teacher/student categories. I rather believe he preferred us to relate as friends on common ground. I would remember to avoid such future referrals to his enlightened "advantage" over me in the future.

"Still," I finished, "I was rude before and I just want you to know that I apologize for it." I then attempted to elicit some sort of acceptance from him. I playfully gave him a pleading look. "I'm sorry, Many Heart. Forgive me?"

The man visibly softened. He grinned and shook his head.

"You're really something," he laughed. "I can see how easily you twist poor No-Eyes around your little finger."

I was aghast. "I do no such thin . . . ."

He smirked. "Yes, you do, and you know it. Amazing thing is, so does she and she loves it."

I blushed. I smiled. The thought of how the old visionary and I playfully parlayed sent a beat of joy throbbing through my heart.

And several meaningful minutes of deep silence fell upon the two sitting atop the high redstone mesa within the heart of the empty Land of Desolation.

The blazing sun had crested its apex.

My eyes skimmed our sultry surround of isolation.

Baked earth, cracked and thirsty. White heat. Drumbeats. Crimson monuments to time. Ancient gravestones, towering high, reaching up through the heat waves for recognition. Soft chanting. Mastabas, singed in copper brilliance against the cool turquoise sky. Redstone spires, petrified fingers pointing upward to the Way. Breathless air. A land without breath. A spirit land.

"Is that what you think?" came the gentle voice.

I slowly turned from the caustic scenery to face my friend.

"That is what I *believe* because that is what I have perceived. That is what the voices say, what the drums speak, what I feel, here," I said, touching my breast.

"What drumbeats?"

"Those of the spirits that inhabit this withered land. Those of the spirits that surround us even now."

He spoke softly, but intently. "What is it that the spirits say?"

"They lament with a great shrill keening." I paused to listen. "They cannot seem to find rest. They are despairing and heartbroken."

He whispered. "Why?"

I moved my eyes to stare out across the sepia country.

"Because their once-strong backs and hearts were trampled upon. Because they were crushed into the dusty earth under the heels of greed. And because they can no longer locate their precious land—it has been ravaged by the conquerors until it has become unrecognizable."

My eyes blurred. My vision distorted to meld with the wavering heat. I stared at the cloudy horizon and uncaringly let a tear course down my cheek.

Many Heart had appeared beside me. His arms surrounded me and I was pulled to his chest. He stroked my hair while I emptied the well of empathy that had overflowed.

"Why are they still persecuting us?" I sobbed. "Why are they still herding our people around like unhuman cattle?"

"Shhh," he soothed and stroked.

But I couldn't be so easily placated. I stubbornly pulled away. My sorrow and empathy had grown into outrage.

"*We* were here first! The Great Spirit set the Indian race upon *this* land. We're the *true* Americans. Yet the invaders killed us off and decimated our beautiful nation. They *ate* our living heritage. Just because they couldn't understand our worship of the Great Spirit and our holy bond with the Earth Mother, they called us savage pagans! Then they pulled our children from our homes and tried to whitewash their language, culture, and sacred beliefs!"

"Settle down," he cautioned sympathetically.

"No, dammit, I *won't* settle down. I don't have to! Listen, they make such a horror of what Hitler did and still they're so damned blind they don't even realize the same thing happened right here on their *own* soil! But oh no, that just doesn't *count*! Our entire *race* has nearly been erased from this country. We've been killed off and we've been starved. Our people's water is being diverted to big cities—we're being made to thirst because they steal our own waters—they're still *taking*! We've been herded off our fertile lands onto parched and barren prairies and empty canyonlands so *they* can have the best, the most beautiful for their *parks*! Then, and then we're herded *again* because now they want what's *underneath* our lifeless, barren land—they want us out of the way so they can let the big power companies dig up our resources! They build us houses that have no running water, no electricity and then they proudly beat their skinny breasts to proclaim how they've so generously provided homes for us. They...."

"*Summer!*"

"NO! They decry the Ethiopian hunger when thousands of Indians can barely feed their children. They make a great outcry about African apartheid and then turn their eyes away from the *Indian* apartheid that's been going on for decades and still *is*! Right *here* on their own *soil*! Where's the *justice*? The *sanity*? Are we mere animals that do not count in men's eyes? Where are people's minds and ears, eyes and hearts? Where has compassion *gone*? Huh, Many Heart? *Where*?"

The tirade had ended. The scorpions of my heart had spent their poison.

My teacher heavily rose to walk the distance to the mesa's rim. He stood tall as he gazed out across the desolate territory of dashed hopes. He cast his gentle voice out across the fiery emptiness toward the towering gravestones, but it was to me he spoke.

"Your outrage is justified, Summer Rain. Your hurt is as real and as deep as my own."

I looked up at his broad back that broke the plane of blue sky. His hands hung at his sides. Blue-black hair shimmered in the brightness of the sun's flaming torch. Dusty boots were tired, so tired. Heart was heavy, so very heavy.

Perhaps I should've been sorry for giving him the heavy heart. Maybe I should've stopped when he shouted for me to do so. Then again, we shared mutual concerns and the voicing of them often helped ease the pain.

A soft moaning shattered my mental musings. A gentle breeze shifted the loose strands of my hair.

A presence was stirring.

I looked again up to the Dreamwalker. He had his arms extended to the heavens.

The low moaning gained in energy to a chant that sent a cold shiver down my spine. The breeze quickened as dust began to swirl about.

Many Heart chanted his heart out across the blazing land. The wind gusted. My hair whipped about my face. Dust churned about like billowing smoke.

I stared at the man on the high precipice. Heart lunging, I was awestruck by the force of his incredible power. The beat of his mesmerizing chant matched the intensity of the wind. With anyone else, I would've been terrified, but I wasn't with anyone else, I was with the Dreamwalker—my friend.

The bellowing requiem song was nearly indistinguishable now as the wind spirit joined in and howled her shared heartache around the craggy towers of stone and cried shrilly through their eroded, gaping eye sockets. And above it all were the unified voices of the canyon-land's spectral inhabitants who mournfully lamented their wails of deep despair.

Heartbreaking chanting. Whipping, howling winds. Tormented cries. The high emotion swept me up with its powerful force.

I flung my arms out. A great agonizing keening escaped from deep within my soul. And my lament rose on the desolate wings of the wind.

Then. . .silence.

The phantoms whispered. The wind sighed into my ear. Gently it stroked my hair. And then it was gone.

Stillness. Sweet stillness.

I looked up.

Many Heart was watching me. Exhausted, he managed a smile.

I slumped back on my heels and looked out on the stillness that seemed to smolder. I glanced around in all directions. Satisfied, I too smiled.

The Dreamwalker had empowered his energies to call upon the Sacred Way. He had cleared away our combined despair. He had released the land's pent-up desolation and all of us were uplifted with the unburdening.

"Thank you," I whispered.

The man exhaled deeply and came to regain his westerly position across from me. Now the lowering sun shaded his face.

I untangled my legs out from beneath me and loosely crossed them again in front. We stared at one another.

His voice broke the intense moment. "That had to be done before we could go on."

"Was I that out of control?"

"No," he half smiled, "*everyone* was." He momentarily glanced out at the lonely sandstone pinnacles before returning his eyes to mine. "*They* required release. They needed to feel they weren't forgotten. I. . .you and I, simply gave them sympathy, our complete empathy and understanding. We let them know someone cared."

"When will things change?" I asked sadly.

"You heard what the old one said about the Phoenix Days. It may still take a few years but, in the end, it'll change." He smiled. "Our people know that, Summer Rain. They have been aware of what is to come. They've been aware of it for centuries. They're simply biding time."

I thought about the present time the people were enduring. The continued herding. The social cruelty. The blindness of others' hearts.

"It's a humiliating way to bide time."

He shrugged. "But they're prepared. In their hearts they're ready because their minds have known of the old prophecies. They cherish those sacred words and, although they're still being treated inhumanely, they hold onto the beautiful truths of what was foreseen for mankind. They treasure the truths of the spirit. It is those precious spiritual revelations which they survive for. While the rest of the world cherishes material things and seeks the possession of them, the Indian people treasure their spiritual beliefs and private knowledge of their prophecies."

These things I knew. But when he spoke of prophecies, it brought me back to my lessons with No-Eyes when she spoke of the Great Phoenix rising again, particularly when she cryptically mentioned a prophecy when I doubted myself. Now I wondered if my young teacher could or, more accurately, *would* enlighten me on that vague aspect. If I didn't at least ask, I'd never know.

"Many Heart?"

"Yes?"

"When No-Eyes told me about the Phoenix and the rising of our nation again, I had doubts about myself."

"Yes, I know. But now you realize that the quality of Indianism is an absolute based not upon the affecting specifics of biological genes, but rather those high ideals that dwell within the mind that have been nourished from the pure heart. Indianism is a sacred heritage matter, of the spirit alone."

I nodded. "Yes, that concept finally made its way through to me, but I had another question."

"Go on."

"Well. . .she said something I didn't quite understand. At the time I didn't think to ask her to explain and she never really did, but when I doubted myself, she cryptically alluded to some old prophecy. Would you know which one that was? Could you maybe explain it to me?"

"I know which one it was."

"Well?" I urged pleadingly.

"It's one that has to do with things many differing tribes are awaiting. Some have ancient tales which foretell of the entrance of someone other than a fullblood who will bring light into the darkened hearts of men—one who will bridge the delineating gaps between races. Tales of another tribe foretell of the reappearance of a missing piece of sacred object. But No-Eyes foresaw this missing piece as appearing in an altered state. In other words, this awaited piece will actually return in a completely unexpected form."

My interest was greatly sparked. "What altered form will this sacred piece take? Did she say?"

"Her exact words were, 'They await but *one* missing sign—one object. But it has altered. It has splintered into *pieces* of the *One*. It will reappear as *many* pieces *within* the One they await.'"

"That's confusing," I said after pondering the mysterious wisdom.

His eyes twinkled. "Is it?"

"It is to me. Probably if I knew what the One thing was that's missing, I'd feel less confused." I tilted my head at him. "You wouldn't by any chance know what this One missing piece is, would you?"

Intense eyes pierced mine. "A piece of tablet."

Silence.

"You still don't get it, do you?" he said in amused amazement.

I looked past him to the evening home of the sun.

"No. Maybe I'm not supposed to get it." I shrugged. "Maybe it really doesn't even matter."

"Perhaps not," he agreed. "Others will, though."

"I hope so. It'd be a terrible thing lost if they didn't recognize what they were waiting for." I paused to mull it over. "Do you think they'll recognize their sacred piece that will reappear as transformed pieces?"

"I have no doubt."

I was satisfied. I smiled. "Good. That makes my heart glad for them."

My friend gave me a doubting look. "Aren't you in the least curious about all this mystery?"

I raised my brows. "Yes."

He nodded knowingly. "Well?"

"What's this sacred piece, pieces represent to them?"

He shook his head. "That wasn't the question I thought you'd ask."

"Tsk-tsk," I clucked teasingly. "You were bad. You were in expectation."

His palms upturned. "Guilty as charged. But since that's what you asked, that's what I'll answer."

He bent close to me and narrowed his eyes. He whispered. "The awaited tablet pieces will represent the great beginning of the end... the beginning of a great new cycle."

I stared into his slitted eyes. I narrowed my own. "Oh."

He chuckled disbelievingly. He laughed.

I frowned. "Did I miss something?"

"No. No," he laughed, "you did just fine."

I didn't see what was so hilariously funny about what had just passed between us.

"If I did just fine, then why are you laughing and I'm not?"

"You're a joy," he said, easing out of his private mirth.

I shook my head. "I don't know what you're talking about. What'd I do? What'd I say?"

"Nothing. It's nothing," he brushed off with a few casual waves of his hand. "Anyway, what's important here is that when this prophecy is recognized as reality, the Phoenix will be making himself evidenced— the Phoenix Days will have arrived—and the people will be getting ready for their final relocation."

I grinned at his choice of wording. "Don't you mean their final 'distribution'?"

"Exactly. You're exactly right. Just as we've been doing for decades, we'll patiently wait it out. And when the time's right, the new beginning will be upon us and the Hoop will be closed for good. The Sacred Tree will thrive strong... forever."

The brightness in my friend's eyes didn't match mine, for mine had dulled. My reaction wasn't hard to miss.

"What's wrong?" he asked with deep concern in his voice.

"I was just thinking, our people are presently so oppressed that they have nothing to look forward to. Maybe a lot know about the good future in the offing, but I don't think that most do. Most are depressed with how they've been forced to live. They're beaten down with the grabbing and the taking of their lands, resources and basic human rights. Many Heart," I sighed, "they *need* some *hope*... NOW."

The former sparkle returned to the dark eyes. "Yes! Hope! Don't you see?"

I didn't.

"The prophecy! The returned *pieces*!"

"That's all they'll need?"

"Yes!"

I grinned. "And then they'll *know* they'll soon be free?"

"YES!"

And my heart leaped for the peoples' final joy.

Many Heart stood and reached out his hand.

I took it and stood beside him.

"It's time," he said softly, raising his face to the lowering sun.

The golden light of the sun's slanting rays ignited the mesas with licking flames of crimson. Long shadows reached out and stretched their dark limbs far across the cooling ground. The entire canyonland flared up. An inferno of scarlet flames shot into the darkening sky. Red earth. Red obelisks. Red blood. A red nation burned with an eternal fire.

We watched as the blanket of night came to save and preserve the sacred land.

Flames lowered. Embers glowed. They faded and smoldered beneath the cool cover of evening.

Shadows deepened. Their ebony forms shifted in the canyon moonlight. Stars blinked down. Blackness surrounded the silver-tipped stone spires. White gravestones glared like skeletal fingers protruding up from ancient burial grounds. A chilling wind whipped around the standing headstones.

And the night was filled with the haunting strains of anxious specters drumming...chanting...waiting for their time.

I shivered. I looked up into the clear night sky at the high, silvered disc. It was not the cadaverous face that stared blankly down upon a ghostly canyonland. It was the shimmering opaline face of an alpine moon that clearly glimmered down upon a silvery forest.

A mountain breeze lifted my hair. An owl hooted. The stream hummed her lullaby. The milky moonlight illuminated Many Heart's face. He was contemplative.

"How'd we get back?" I questioned gently.

His eyes opened. Twin black pits appeared. "Same way we went."

That told me absolutely nothing. "I flew there on falcon wings," I said.

"Did you?"

"Yes."

"And you also returned on falcon wings?"

Down in the forest, the wind spirit hushed. Down in the ravine, the water spirit giggled.

"I don't *know* how I returned. That's why I asked you."

The man's hands gestured. "Summer, the falcon was merely an aid. Remember you were attempting to exit fear? The falcon simply caught your attention and distracted it. Your consciousness then made its own exit, but the bird did not carry you there."

"Then what did?"

In the high country darkness, I saw his even teeth catch the light. He was smiling.

"There are many trails which lead to many places. Today we

simply chose a less traveled trail—a lesser known one—that of a Dreamwalker."

I had no response. I couldn't request an explanation of such a sacred and secret Way. I was still the stumbling novice who was not yet advanced enough to be privy to such high spiritual matters.

My teacher perceived my thoughts. "Do you wish to know and understand this special pathway?"

I couldn't deny that I did. "Yes, I do, but not by your explaining it to me. I wish very much to know, but only of my own accord. I wish to come naturally into the knowing."

Silence. Through the light of night I couldn't see his reaction.

"Many Heart?"

"Yes?"

"What we were talking about today, I'd like to finish it."

The Dreamwalker bent forward, elbows resting on knees. "Finish?"

"Yes. I want to talk about our image. Oh, not yours and mine specifically, but that of the people."

"Go on," he urged with interest.

I paused to listen to the wind breathing through the high pines and firs.

"Well, I feel bad that people think the Indians are just good-for-nothings and drunks. They think the Indian doesn't *have* to live like he does. They think they're just a lazy race."

"But we know better, don't we?"

"Of course. We know how desperately they need to remain within the circle of their own kind in order to preserve what little remains of their beautiful culture and heritage. We know that when they do attempt to assimilate into the mainstream of society that the friendly melting pot won't let them. But I'm not talking about what we know. I'm talking about what society as a whole *doesn't* know as compared to that which they *think* they know."

"I'm with you," he confirmed, "go on."

I wasn't confident I'd make myself clearly understood.

"Well, that negative image is wrong and it should be changed. Will it change and, if so, how?"

His hands flipped back and forth. "Why is this image so important to you?"

"Because the general public has painted their own. The drunken Indian. The loafer. The dumb, shuffling Indian who hardly speaks. People need to see the truth to the matter—the purpose of the culture, the ancient wisdom, the beautiful spirits within the body. And now they can't see these wondrous qualities because they're sequestered behind and under the desolation of the reservations they've been herded on."

His tone held a hint of caution. "Are you falling into outrage again?"

"Oh, no! Not at all. It's just that the real beauty is masked by the desperate living conditions and oppression. That's just plain fact. And I want to know what'll change that so people can see the Indian race for what it truly is?"

I heard a weighted sigh. "This appears to be very important to you. Summer," he hesitated, "appearances are superficial. I think you know that."

I did. "But. . . ."

"But you persist in maintaining that our people's image must alter in order for mankind to see clearly—to appreciate their true character, purpose and wise spirits."

"Yes! That's it!"

"That's not it. That's entirely wrong," came the correction.

Silence.

"Summer, since the beginning of time, when the red race was placed here on this continent by the Great Spirit, the people have cherished their ancient wisdom and their beautiful spiritual bond with the living Eternal Grandmother. They have deeply respected her. They have always prayed to the supreme power. And so have they treasured such sacredness.

"Today is no different, Summer. Although they have had their lands, their nation, stolen and have suffered through genocide massacres, degradation, relocations, and desolation, their beautiful beliefs remain pure and unaltered. Their ancient wisdom remains guarded and their radiant spirits maintain their luster.

"*Who* needs to change, Summer? *What* requires changing? Our people remain the same within. They are true to themselves, to their heritage and to their spirits. They care not for the superficial outer trappings of men for, within their minds and shining spirits, they remember the ancient words and that is all they require."

"Until the sacred pieces reappear," I added.

"Yes, until the sacred tablets reappear and free men's minds—*all* men's minds."

There was nothing left to say. My teacher had eloquently said it all. There were no more questions coursing through my mind. It rested in the comfort of Many Heart's words. And I was no longer plagued by the unfair image that cruel circumstances had cast upon my beloved people because they awaited the glorious day that would fulfill their age-old prophecy—the reappearance of the mysterious missing pieces would free them. . . and the world.

They waited.

And so did I.

The Indian Soul remains primeval.

Its Core Light retains the pristine clarity of its Messianic heritage. Its ancient secrets remain a cherished sacred treasure which brilliantly shimmers amid the dark vulgarities of ignorant present-day thought.

A Handful
of Magic

Magic lies dormant within the heart of Awareness.
But within complete Understanding and wise Utilization . . .
Magic lives!

I was a bewildering enigma.

Throughout my troubled childhood that was plagued by a father's alcoholism and frequent violence, I oftentimes found serenity within the powerful core of my spirit. Escaping into the safe corner of her small bedroom closet, the frightened youngster closed her ears to the screaming and shouting to listen to a gentle, soothing voice. In that darkened space, she shut her eyes to the upsetting sights to see beautiful visions. The gentle voice and the beautiful visions remained as permanent senses—never to fade, only to grow through natural acceptance, maturity and, later, wisdom.

I'm not that small, hiding child anymore.

As an adult, I was magnetically drawn to the Native American culture. I had vivid dreams of peaceful days living as a fullblood Shoshone. Although I had no physical contact with any Indian friends, my heart ached with excruciating pain and my spirit continually yearned for something I could not touch. A great emptiness filled my spirit until I encountered No-Eyes within her mountain forest. It was her recognition and wisdom, her sympathy and kindness that filled my emptiness and returned my lost identity.

However, coming so late into the knowledge of my rightful heritage, I was a loner. I felt I was neither here nor there. Neither white nor Indian, yet an unprecedented blend of both. My skin prevented assimilation into the red culture, and my spirit prohibited the melding with the white. Always was I delicately weaving between the two... never quite belonging to either.

How does one justify light olive skin without, and an Indian heart and mind, memory and spirit within? In this sojourn, had my Indian spirit missed its mark by entering the wrong vehicle? I agonized over the incongruity of it. I was mismatched, a freak, a bizarre spiritual mystery. I felt I didn't belong in any *earthly* race.

I was a bewildering enigma.

These painful memories and thoughts subliminally wove in and out of my mind when I recalled my day with Many Heart to Bill, for the fact that I was unaware of the prophecy struck hard.

My life companion attempted to smooth it over.

"You remember a lot of them," he reminded compassionately. "You can't be expected to know them all. Besides, No-Eyes told you not to do a lot of historical reading because she wanted you to rely on your carryover spirit to bring it out into the present."

I managed a weak smile. "I know," I said, hoping I'd make his words seem helpful. "I know what she said, but I just wish I understood more of it. Many Heart appeared to think it was humorous that I didn't."

"He wasn't laughing at you, honey," he assured.

"I know he wasn't, but *something* sure tickled his funnybone."

"Well, like everything else, if you were meant to know the full story of this prophecy, you would—somehow you would."

I sighed. "Yeah, I would—but I won't."

"What makes you so sure?"

"Feelings, just strong feelings. I'll probably never know."

As I made my way up into the Pike National Forest that last weekend of September, the conversation that had passed between Bill and me replayed in my head. I thought that perhaps if I read a lot of sociology books relating to the Native American culture, or history and religious books, I would eventually come across mention of the mysterious prophecy No-Eyes and Many Heart alluded to. And, if I did, pehaps I'd also be able to figure out what was so humorous to the Dreamwalker. Should I try?

Crisp autumn air blew into the pickup. I inhaled deeply. And I then knew I'd leave well enough alone. Was it so important, this knowing? If the two visionaries left it be, then so would I. I had enough to do with my hands and head full of new learning. I'd leave the prophecy recognition to those who were patiently awaiting it. I'd leave it to those who knew about it and would cherish its reappearance.

Once the final decision was made, I freed my mind and opened my senses to receive the entity of autumn. It was a perfect mountain morning and I wasted no time in thanking the Great Spirit for sending it my way. Always, I remembered to express my gratitude to the master creator.

As I nosed the truck up and around the narrow mountain road, the spectacular scenery made me think of its counterpart of last weekend. Such sharp contrasts existed within Nature. One facet was vital and fresh, while the other was barren and parched. One aspect was green and blue, while the other was copper and scarlet.

Streams. Deserts. Mountains and chasms. Prairies and rangeland.

All characteristics of the Earth Mother's stark beauty, her ravishing personalities. When the totality of her character was fully comprehended, what a truly magnificent being she was! I thanked God for my awareness and appreciation of that totality.

I passed the pull-off that I had stopped at the weekend before. I continued up around the curving road and pulled into the weedy drive. Here in the high of the high country, the aspens were more excited than in the lower elevations. I could literally feel their intense anticipation for the final dance recital of the year. They were getting ready. Soon they'd don the sequined costumes and quake them in the golden sunlight. Then the entire mountainside would shimmer with the energy of their dance. Today their anticipation ran high.

When I parked the truck and reached for the window crank, I secretly smiled.

"Mornin', Many Heart," I said, rolling up the glass.

Stepping out from behind the wide trunk of the lodgepole, he expressed his satisfaction.

"You wasted no time on concentration this morning. That was good. You remembered?"

A very clever question indeed, but not quite clever enough.

"I don't waste valuable time with remembrance. It was instinct, plain and natural instinct."

He lowered his head, then looked at me squarely. "I wasn't trying to trick you with that. I meant the question honestly."

"And honestly I say I reacted instinctively without remembering what I was supposed to do." A glint of sparring justice sparked from my eyes.

He noticed. "Then you did very well. You naturally applied your learning."

He breathed in the autumn air and extended his arm toward the forest. "Well? Shall we begin?"

I loved how he loved conducting my lessons in the outdoors and I told him just that.

He laughed and said that, in that respect, we were very much alike.

We strolled on.

As I followed his lead through the heavy growth, I wondered if my teacher had a special subject matter planned for the day. Except for last week's journey into the canyonland, it seemed that the lessons were precipitated by our off-handed conversations. My random thoughts or serious concerns most often started a lesson in logic or the revelation of certain wisdom.

"It's almost October," I began.

"So it is," he said, looking up into the sleepy tips of the leaves.

"No-Eyes said she'd probably see me again around the first of November."

"Probably so."

"Well," I hinted, "that means I've only got four more weeks with you."

Silence.

"What I mean is, I've only got four more weeks to finish the path of the Way."

"This is so."

My line of direction wasn't going well. He wasn't responding enough. It felt like a one-sided conversation. I continued to string it out.

"Maybe I'll need more time. Four more weeks isn't very much."

"No, it isn't."

"I might need more time," I repeated.

"Perhaps."

Silence.

We struck out through the woodlands. Many Heart had left the footpath and began to make his own way. I followed, picking my way through the wide bushes.

"Well, how long can you stay here to teach me?" I asked, pushing away the branches that had snapped back on me after his passing.

"As long as it takes."

His brevity was getting to me. "Are you upset today?"

"No."

"Have I done something wrong?"

"You tell me," came the reply that made my heart plunge.

"Was I wrong to tell Bill all about our days?"

"No."

"Should I have understood about that prophecy?"

He waited to answer. "Your full comprehension of it isn't required."

We entered a clearing and now that our follow-the-leader game was over, I came up beside him and looked him squarely in the eyes.

"Tell me what wrong I've done."

"Always speak true, Summer. Speak *direct*."

"I do speak true."

"Do you?"

"Yes, but you haven't been responding true. I've been talking to you ever since I got out of the truck and all I've been getting back from you are one- or two-word responses."

His brow raised. "Perhaps the responses would be more to your liking if the questions and statement made were true."

Silence.

"Summer," he explained gently, "ever since your first statement about October almost being here, I knew what was in your head. I waited and waited for it to come out your mouth, but it never did. Instead, all I heard were stray threads of the main question—the unspoken one, and that's what you received in return—clipped threads of answers."

He was absolutely correct. I had beat about the bush for an answer to a question I was afraid to come right out and ask. I lowered my head. "How am I doing so far?"

A gentle finger nudged up my chin. "Pardon me?"

Eyes locked. "How am I doing so far?"

His head tilted. "I haven't sent you back, have I?"

"No," I said, lowering my gaze.

My chin was lifted more. I looked up again as he spoke. "You're still here, aren't you?"

I grinned. "Yes."

"Well, then, I suppose that counts for something. I suppose that about says it all." He turned to continue our walk.

"Thanks, Many Heart," I said, coming up beside him.

"You just would've saved us a lot of time by coming out direct with your question. You don't have to lay a line of traps to get your prey. Remember that."

"I will."

A few soft moments passed between us before another question came to mind. This time I didn't bother wasting valuable time by baiting traps.

"I have a question about that prophecy business of last week."

"Mmmm."

"Can we talk about that now?"

"Of course."

"Well, how many people believe in it?"

"An entire nation believes in it."

I thought on that.

"Does that adequately answer your question? Are you satisfied?"

"Yes to both."

"So?" he asked, insinuating I had more to say on the subject.

"So that's a lot of people who believe—a lot more than I had thought."

"Ah, so you figured this prophecy was known and shared by only the few. Perhaps you thought only the powerful visionaries and a handful of shamans and medicine people were awaiting this foretold sign."

I smiled sheepishly.

"Summer, an entire *nation* awaits it!"

I exhaled deeply. "That's really beautiful."

"Explain that statement," he directed.

"It's just that I think it's so beautiful to have so many people believing in a prophecy. Well, not just *one,* but the *reality* of them."

"The people of the Indian nation have always believed in the reality of such things. I believe you know that."

"Yes, I do, but living in the mainstream of society shows me how many don't believe. The skeptics are always finding superficial reasons to debunk everything, especially those things that they don't understand, or else they make other excuses for them—technical or scientific excuses."

His voice was soft with understanding. "This is so, Summer, but this too will change in the future."

I shook my head in disgust as I kicked at a stone of granite. "I know it'll change, but right now I can't seem to accept the mentality of a confirmed skeptic when all my life I've lived with paranormal functionings. It's like if *they* haven't experienced it then it simply doesn't exist."

"I know what you're saying and you're right, but what does it really matter? Are you trying to prove a point? Are you trying to convince everyone?"

I chuckled at the ridiculous questions.

"Well?" he continued, "then what's the importance of the skeptic? You're you. You've *lived* with it. You *know* it's real, it's natural. So why concern yourself with those who disbelieve?"

I merely shrugged. "I see your point. I guess I just can't stand ignorance. Their alleged logic makes me think we're back in the Stone Age. It often makes me think I don't belong here in this backward society. I believe this civilization should be so much more advanced and when I look around I continually wonder why I'm here with them. The attitudes and development of this society are far less than they should be . . . I just feel misplaced in it."

"Go on."

"The cutthroat striving for materialism and position is primitive.

The spiritual beliefs aren't where they should be. The overall grasp of universal truths is rudimentary at best. There's too many still caught up on the more debasing aspects of an undeveloped culture...murders, stealth, crime. Some days I can hardly bear the unbelievable reality of it all."

Silence.

Then I grinned wide.

"What?" he said, suddenly smiling.

"Oh, nothing," I said, trying to stifle the silly grin. "I just thought of something I saw in a store."

Now his curiosity was really piqued. "Com'on, share it."

I was embarrassed with the telling. "Well, I saw a T-shirt with a clever saying on it. When I spied it, it really struck home—it was perfect for me because it expressed my own attitude."

"What'd it say?"

"It said, 'Beam me up, Scotty, there's no intelligent life down here.'"

His smile faded.

"I told you it was silly."

"Was it?" came the solemn reply.

Our eyes locked in seriousness. "No."

"You should've gotten that shirt."

A light smile came to me. "Maybe I will, maybe I will."

Another stream sang nearby and we paused to sit on some boulders that were naturally clumped together. We silently listened to the sweet voice that echoed through the high hills.

"Summer," he began, continuing a thread of the former conversation, "I think a good deal of your concern stems from the fakers and the psychic deceivers."

"Possibly," I mused.

"Problem is," he said, going deeper into it, "far too much publicity is given to those fame-seekers. They'd do and say anything to make a quick buck. Their paranormal claims border on the ridiculous, their minds exist in fantasy, so much so they too convince themselves of their own miraculous capabilities."

I sighed with the ugly vulgarity of it. "And they've sullied and shamed the beautiful spirit gifts that are pure and true—the natural ones."

"Yes."

My thoughts sped to the books I was was expected to create—the ones I'd promised the old one I'd do for her.

My astute teacher perceived my concern. "Don't worry," he soothed, "everything'll be fine. It's not like you're going to go about claiming to do miracles or alter shapes with your mind. The big obvious difference will be that you're not selling yourself. You'll simply be the messenger of No-Eyes. You'll be creating a beautiful legacy for her. There's a world of difference between the two."

We allowed the water spirit to carry the conversation while we each scanned our peaceful surroundings. We were taking delight in the innocence of the mountain forest. The sunlight reached down through the tall evergreens and gilded all it touched.

My teacher's voice broke our reverie. "It's funny," he said, "that the ones who are cognizant to the powers of the spirit are most often those who are closest to the earth. Their relationship creates the natural spiritual bond by which the powers are evidenced.

"The Indian people have powers. Nature has powers. All those close to nature believe in the powers because they can feel their touchable reality."

I raised my feet up on a wide boulder. I wrapped my arms around my legs and rested my chin on my knees.

"No-Eyes explained about the future and how it'll affect belief in the paranormal. She said it'd be generally accepted, but that a certain percentage of the people would consider it biologically activated instead of spiritually. I thought that was a step backward for man."

"Sometimes certain backtracking is required in order for actual advancement to occur. There's times that a society travels too far in the wrong direction and they require a retracing of steps in order to discover the right path."

"That's true," I considered. Still, to me, it was another clear evidence of humanity's prehistoric thinking.

"You've listened to a tree?" came the sudden change of subject matter.

I raised my head to gaze into the dense, green forest. I smiled. "Yes," I answered softly.

"What did the tree say?"

"It *said* nothing. It *conveyed*."

Remembering the many times I was compelled to hug the trees, I told my teacher about it.

"I often hug the trees. And when I do, I can feel their lifeforce drumming next to my heart. I feel their living heartbeat. Their blood flow pulses within my ears and I know that we are indeed connected with the bond of life. I feel their happiness, their sadness, their excitement. They convey their helpfulness to man. They celebrate the act of living, sharing, and giving. I appreciate their existence and, because I'm ever grateful for that, I hug them to show my deep appreciation and love for them."

"You've hugged the earth?"

"Yes, for the same reasons. The Earth Mother generously provides for us. Food, medicines, water, nutrients, it's all there and I'm truly grateful. I love her so much."

"And the streams?" he asked with a raised brow.

I blushed. "Them too."

He smiled with his knowledge of my frequently uninhibited habits.

"Don't be embarrassed. Don't ever be. Clothing tends to hamper the total spiritual union. There's nothing wrong in what you occasionally do."

He was intensely serious.

"Maybe if more people touched their beings with the streams and the trees, the earth, there wouldn't be so much pollution and widespread destruction as there is today. They'd realize their precious bond and wouldn't be so ready to dump in their chemicals and garbage. They wouldn't dare take a pocket knife to a tree ever again."

Many Heart slid off his stone perch and offered me his hand.

I climbed down and stretched before continuing our journey.

Again, he chose to stay away from No-Eyes' footpath by blazing his own trail up toward a rise. I walked beside him.

"Has the old one spoken to you of power points?" he asked.

I nodded. "She mentioned the term, but only briefly in passing. We never really got heavily into it."

"Do you know what they are?"

I ducked a low-hanging pine branch. "Don't they have to do with nature's energy centers?"

"Yes, that's half of it. Basically, power points are those geographic regions around the earth which are physically more magnetically intense than others. Great power exudes from these centers and, when one knows how, he can utilize these for beneficial purposes."

"You said that that was the half of it. What's the other?"

"Well? Half of the power points are magnetically induced, while the other half are spiritually manifested."

I followed his premise. "You mean like psychic imprints?"

"No. Those are frozen in time. I'm referring to *live* manifestations."

I tried again. "Spiritual presences of human spirits."

"Or?" he prodded further.

"Or vital nature spirits."

"Yes," he exclaimed, somewhat surprised. "How'd you know?"

I grinned. "I hug trees, remember?"

He had referred to the vital spirit of nature that is ever present within a geographical region that is completely healthy. He referred to those regions which were virgin and untouched by destructive forces such as campers, logging activities, pollution, and acid rain. Virgin areas possessed a vital living spirit which emanated great power that could easily be felt by a sensitive individual.

We had just stepped into such a power point. The ground virtually vibrated with its pure energy force. The very air appeared electrified.

I stepped cautiously, slowly, so that I could feel its current pulse through me.

Many Heart was beside me doing the same thing, and although the acknowledgment of each other's presence was no longer uppermost in our consciousness, we experienced a warming comfort in the companionship of our present sharing. We sat within the active center and journeyed within ourselves to recharge our own energies.

Our place was so magnificent with vibrant life. The trees were greener than I'd seen them in a long time. Their jade and emerald colors nearly jumped out at you. The air was full of exotic mountain spices. The sunlight was radiant as it reflected its warm rays off the forest floor. Happiness existed here in this sacred power place. Contentment thrived here and its serenity filled my heart.

When I opened my eyes, Many Heart was waiting for me. "Feels good, huh?"

"Yes," I smiled contently, "it feels very good."

The teacher looked around the ground, spied a small stone and picked it up. He studied it while turning it over and over in his fingers.

"What'd you find?" I asked, while curiously straining my neck to see.

He stared at me as his fingers slowly uncurled to show what lay upon his palm.

I looked at it. "A stone?"

Without taking his eyes from mine, he whispered, "A piece of magic."

I stared at the piece of quartz-veined granite. "Magic?"

He gazed down at it. "Yes, magic." And he held it out for me to take. "Hold this simple stone and we will talk. We will speak of special centers of the earth. We will speak of this simple stone's magic. We will speak of power."

I took the common stone and closed my fingers around it. It was warmed from the Dreamwalker's hand.

He said, "Feel its heat?"

"I feel its warmth from your palm," I replied honestly.

"Yes, that warmth is also there. It will now be there from the warmth of your own blood. But perhaps you will feel *its* heat also."

If I continued holding the plain stone, how would I distinguish the bodily warmth that emitted from my hand from the stone's own warmth? I would wait and see.

"Summer," he began, "before, when you spoke about your books and the skeptics, what did you really mean to say? What was your *real* concern?"

I squeezed the stone and saw his eyes take note of the action. "Many Heart," I sighed, "until I met No-Eyes, my life had no real spiritual direction. Oh, yes, I had the strong spirit and certain undeniable promptings to guide me along the right path, but she was the one who gave me the strength and final direction."

I kneaded the stone.

"I feel heartsick with the fear that perhaps some people might not be touched by her. She's been so gentle, so wise . . . so old."

"Then you're still concerned over the skeptics."

"Only because their hardness would be like a slap in the face. I don't think I could handle that with much composure."

The teacher frowned. "Not only would such negative reaction be an affront upon No-Eyes herself, it'd be a shameful attack on the Indian people as a whole, on their sacred age-old beliefs. Their very religion would be attacked because that is what No-Eyes represents—the sacred beliefs."

I looked up into the sunrays that danced upon the evergreens' spiny tips.

"She represents that and so much more. No-Eyes represents the Earth and its bounties. She's synonymous with good and right living, ecology and brotherly love among humanity. Her wise words teach of natural health and well-being. Her basic philosophy easily compares to those of our history's greatest deep thinkers. Her bottom line is love of the Great Spirit and all His glorious gifts to mankind."

I sighed. "For a skeptic to doubt No-Eyes' wisdom would be tantamount to criticizing all the beautiful concepts she represents. That'd be a sad and pitiful thing."

"Yes, it would, but don't forget about the changing times that are about due. People will realize how important she is. They'll come to recognize her wisdom as being deeply profound. They'll ultimately come to love her just as much as you and I do."

My eyes widened at the lovely thought. "That's what I hope will come of the books. That's what I wish for most of all. I wish that everyone will come to know about her sweet life, her important purpose and her deep humility."

He grinned. "She sure does like her solitude."

"Yeah," I smiled, "that's because she's not self-seeking in any way. Her power is great and she cherishes it."

"That's because it's a precious gift to her."

I opened my fingers and glanced down at the common fragment of Rocky Mountain ground.

"It's precious to me too, Many Heart."

"I know," he said softly. "That's why you despise the fakers—those who are self-seeking. You cherish your power gifts like a rare gem to be protected, not flaunted. It's personal characteristics like that that'll separate the sheep from the wolves in the future."

I was silent as I thought about my natural spiritual gifts that were compassionately bestowed upon me as a young child. I thought about how beautiful they were—how incredibly private and personal. These thoughts drifted to those who were given such gifts but misused them for personal gain or self-satisfaction.

"Many Heart?"

"Yes, Summer?"

"What makes a spiritually gifted individual go public? What I mean is, what motivates them to sensationalize their gifts?"

"Emotionally weak personalities find the notoriety fills their well of obscurity. They attempt to make others believe that they know all the physical and esoteric answers to life's more mysterious questions and enigmas."

"That's silly, though. *Nobody* knows all the answers. Only *God* can claim such total knowledge and wisdom!"

"This is so, Summer, but if they *claim* these powers, then they see how other weak and lost individuals pay homage to them."

"That's *sick*! Nobody but *God* deserves homage."

He grinned. "This is so, too. But don't forget that homage may be expressed in many forms. It comes in a variety of attractive packages that appear irresistible—one of them being money. People are eager to pay handsomely for the all-knowing advice from a psychic."

I merely shook my head disgustedly. "That's just what I mean. True spiritual gifts are meant to be selflessly *shared*. Many Heart, when I see the high price tags people place on the gaining of enlightenment, I become very despondent. . . . I just want to give up and go home."

"Now I know I'm going to find that T-shirt for you," he humorously interjected before becoming serious again. "But the fact remains that all those who are charging for spiritual information are wrong. . .dead wrong. Summer, there's a big difference between an aware individual who charges for their insights and one who doesn't. Know what that is?"

"Yeah," I grinned, "one's rich and the other's poor as a prairie dog."

"No," he laughed, "one's *enlightened*. The prairie dog's the enlightened one. There's a vast difference between the two because you'll never, *ever* see a spiritually enlightened individual demanding payment for the exercising of their gifts. Just knowing they've been instrumental in helping a fellow man is payment enough for them." He hesitated for a moment. "Now if the grateful recipient wishes to give the enlightened individual something in return, that's fine because the recipient's appreciation is shown by his free will offering. A gift for a gift. But set price tags? Never."

"That's the people's way," I mused. "The people give gifts out of the goodness of their hearts, in appreciation, and never expect anything in return. And they offend the giver if they do *not* accept an offered gift. That would be rude."

"Yes, you've got it."

The nearby stream chanted her hymn to the Great Spirit. She paid simple homage. She gave the only gift she had to offer. And I gratefully accepted it.

"That's a beautiful song," I said, rolling the stone around between my fingers.

"The water spirit's happy today. Maybe she's happy because we've come to give a little company along the way."

"Maybe she's happy because this is such a vital region and it makes her feel good passing through it."

He shrugged. "Who can say? She carries many secrets with her."

My eyes shifted to his. "Yes, many secrets, just like the People have."

He squinted over at me. "You're changing the subject."

"Am I? Don't the Indian people cherish secrets and power? Aren't we discussing power here?"

"Ahhh, but Indian power stems from their umbilical with nature. They have retained their ancient religious beliefs and have not lost sight of the ageless natural laws. Yes, Summer, some of them have great powers through their close ties with nature, for of herself, nature is very powerful. One day renowned doctors will make a great medical breakthrough. Internationally acclaimed scientists will make technological history. The renowned doctors and the acclaimed scientists will discover man's unique bond with the earth's power—power we stupid Indians have been working with for centuries."

I sighed. "And the doctor and scientists will get all the credit."

"Yes. But does it matter? Isn't the universal utilization of something so beautiful the real issue?"

Silence.

"You don't want to admit the injustice of it all, but, Summer, you must understand that this is what the greed for power causes. Those who have the answers, also have the power. The native people have the answers but they do not wish to turn it into selfish power. They do not wish to make a grotesque sideshow out of something so beautiful.

157

They *have* the power and they protect it. They cherish and secret it away from those money-mongers who would misuse it or take negative advantage of it."

He placed both palms in the dirt on either side of him and raised his head to the sun. "This is a good place, Summer. This is a powerful medicine place."

I let my free hand nonchalantly slip down beside me in a like manner. My fingers touched the earth and I spread them out until my palm was flat. The heartbeat was strong.

The Dreamwalker closed his eyes, then looked at me through narrowed slits. "Your land will be like this."

My eyes widened with excitement. "Do you *know* where our land will be? Many Heart, do you *know*?"

His expression remained intense. "Yes."

"*Where!*"

He shook his head. "This I cannot tell, for it must be recognized by *you*. You will know it when you see it because you will *feel* its rightness—its sacred power."

"Can you tell me if it's going to be around Woodland Park?"

"No."

"'No' what? Which?"

"I *can* tell you that and, no, it's nowhere near Woodland Park. I think you already knew that because of your Phoenix Days lessons."

Yes, I had figured that much out from what No-Eyes had foretold, but since I had him on a roll, I didn't want to lose the smooth meter of the questioning, for some of the answers were finally forthcoming. My heart was pounding furiously.

"Is it in Colorado?"

"Yes."

"Which region?"

"High. Very close to the Continental Divide in a range proximity to one of Colorado's highest towns."

I frantically researched my mind. Leadville was one of the highest towns in Colorado. I couldn't take the additional time to mentally dawdle.

"Remote?"

"Fairly."

"Is there water?"

"There is a high river. It rushes year 'round from the high Divide."

My mind raced. "Lots of pines?"

"Pines that are so dense they look like mountain moss from a distance. Autumn aspens that blanket the mountains in carrot and copper. Firs and spruces. Cougars. Bears. Elk and deer. Peace."

I suddenly dropped the stone. It was burning my palm.

The Dreamwalker's eyes flared. Black opals shimmered. "Are your hands so hot?" he wisely inquired.

I felt both my hands. They were neither hot nor cool.

"They feel normal," I said, looking curiously down at the stone that had been quickly tossed out.

He grinned. "Magic."

And magic it was. The earth was full of magic. It was a powerful force full of magical properties. The Indian people knew of these mysterious amenities of the Earth Mother's and they cherished them within their tender, pure hearts. They remained the silent protectors of the Earth's incredible power.

I bent low to the Earth Mother and kissed her sweetnesss. I gently stretched out my arms to scoop up the soil in my hands. I held my prize high. And, letting it sift down through my fingers, the golden sunlight reflected minute bits of glittering mica and pyrite. The falling sands shimmered with their own rich treasure. I curled my fingers around the remaining soil and brought it to my breast. I looked down protectively at it and saw the Earth's very soul. I saw a living, breathing handful of pure magic.

Be not insensitive or numb to nature's many facets for, I say truly, that the tree, the stream . . . the stone are alive with Power!

October

---

*Season of the
silver Moon
of the Dreamwalker*

Shadow of the Specter

That Death be the bitter, barren Winter of Life is but illusion. For, upon crossing Its shimmering white Threshold, do we then perceive Death as the refreshing Spring of Life Eternal.

After I had told Bill about most of my day with Many Heart, I sprang the good news about our land. He was silently pensive and I was concerned.

"What's the matter?" I asked.

"Colorado has more high peaks than any other Rocky Mountain state. Leadville is one of the highest towns in the state, it's over ten thousand feet."

"So was our cabin," I reminded. "Three years living up there never bothered us in the least. In fact, remember how clear the night skies were? And all those wild animals that'd come around? Anyway, Many Heart didn't say we'd be right in Leadville, he just said *near* its range proximity. That could encompass miles and miles of available land."

His eyes brightened. "Get the maps."

We looked over both the state road map and our plastic raised one. When we studied the possibilities, we found that our circle of possibilities was too numerous to pinpoint. There were several year-round rivers that flowed off the Divide that high up—most were on the western side. We hadn't considered moving that far and now began to wonder if we should include the possibility. The remote areas were usually the deadend four-wheel roads that went up the Divide as far as they could go.

I felt disappointed after a thorough look at the maps.

"I should've known he wouldn't give me enough clues," I groaned. "He said it wasn't up to him to tell. I just should've known better."

Bill pulled me to him and rubbed my neck. "I certainly can't blame you for being so excited. Those were the first solid clues we've had." He pulled out one more map. It was full of criss-crossed red marker lines that had traced all the areas we'd journeyed into.

When I saw it again, I was amazed at how many places we'd traveled through looking for our special resting place for the Mountain Brotherhood. The heavily marked roads stood out like a sore thumb . . . but so did the *open* spaces. We honed in on these and, to our surprise, by keeping Many Heart's words in mind, we were able to draw a rectangle that encompassed our possibilities. We looked at each other. Grins crept up our faces as we shared one thought—we'd begin the weekend trips again because now we were vividly pointed in their right direction.

Bill explained our pattern. "Look here," he said, pointing to the red-lined map. "According to what Many Heart said, we've got choices of these two towns on the eastern side of the Divide." He pointed to Buena Vista and then moved his finger up to Leadville. "We've got choices of land between these two."

Then he moved west along the interstate and stopped at Glenwood Springs where he inched south to McClure Pass.

"These are the possibilities on the western side of the Divide," he said, tapping the paper, "these and anything in between going back up into the mountains." As he moved his finger toward the Continental Divide, it casually stopped at Aspen.

"We're not going *there*! I cried.

"No way. I just showed you the directions that would coincide with Many Heart's descriptions . . . . I went too far."

I peered over the map. I pointed. "I want to go here."

He looked. "Marble? Looks pretty far in." Then he said, "We'll look around Buena Vista and the Leadville areas first because those are closest, then we'll take a look around the Roaring Fork Valley into Marble."

"I wonder if there's marble in Marble," I mused.

"Of course there's marble in Marble, just like there's lead in Leadville and silver in Silverton."

"And rabbits on Rabbit Ears Pass and lizards on Lizard Head Pass and crippled donkeys in the creek at Cripple Creek," I played.

"It's getting late," he sighed with a grin. "You're getting punchy."

It was late and tomorrow was to be my first October day with my young teacher. But before I climbed into bed, I took one last look at the worn map. I may have been tired, but I wasn't so weary that I couldn't see the thick red line through Buena Vista and its surroundings. We'd

already been through those regions—all around and through them—
and we never ever felt anything special touch our spirits. That left the
regions north and west. I smiled at the realization that our rectangle of
possibilities had been literally cut in half. We were definitely closing in.

Saturday morning the house was cold when I got up. Frost laced
the window corners. Being as quiet as I could, I built a small fire in the
kitchen woodstove. The house would be toasty warm by the time
everyone else crawled out of bed and the kitchen would be cozy for
breakfast.

As I got ready, the remembered smell of woodsmoke wafted
through the air. The homey aroma gave me a feeling of comfort. From
the bathroom I could hear the crackle and snap as the kindling worked
to feed the logs on top.

Good sounds. Good scents. Good home.

And I left the warm serenity to brave the first really cold autumn
day of the season.

It didn't take long for the old heater to warm the cab of the pickup.
The coziness inside contrasted sharply with the briskness of the
mountain morning. The trees and shrubs had been coated with vanilla
icing. Hoarfrost glistened like powdered crystal in the early sunlight.
Delicate pine needles, silvered and fragile, looked like they'd shatter
with the wind's soft breath. Ice-blue mountain snowcaps against
brilliant lapis lazuli sky. A frozen painting. Mother nature's portrait. Her
ravishing beauty captured upon the eternal canvas of life. It was a
masterpiece that was fluid—ever changing, for when the sun later
gained in strength, the land below would warm and the magical crystal
frosting and silvered icing would disappear. But still, nature would
retain her sublime magnificence. She was an elegant lady.

When I parked the truck, I took a brief moment to look out the
windshield up at my schoolhouse. The forest by the vehicle was a
fantasyland of frost-tipped whiteness while the cabin was a study in
tranquility. Perched atop the clear rise, the meager building was
dwarfed by the overpowering stance of the surrounding mountains. A
trail of smoke snaked lazily up from the crumbling chimney. In the
early light, a rich, buttery glow flickered out from the thinly curtained
windows. I could literally feel the hominess within.

I left the vehicle and raced through the chilled air. Scurrying up
the wooden steps, I reached for the door. It was thoughtfully opened
for me. And, entering the orange glow within, I greeted the handsome doorman.

"Morning," I chirped excitedly. "Thanks for getting the door."

The man warmly smiled. "Good morning. And I got the door so it wouldn't break in your exuberance. I was warned to 'watch that door.'"

I rolled my eyes. "She didn't."

"She did."

I didn't care if the old one had tattled on my frequent over-excitement. Today I was literally bursting with it. My eyes widened.

"Many Heart," I exclaimed, placing my hands on his arms, "isn't it absolutely *supernatural* out there!"

I sprang to the window and pulled back the fragile curtain. "Look, it's just like a crystal fairyland! I love it when it's all sparkly like this."

He came up behind me to peer out. His head touched my cheek. "Want to go out in it?"

I turned to him. "Could we?"

He was open to the idea. "If that's what you want."

I gazed back out the window.

Crackle. Snap. Dancing reflections. Homey warmth . . . beckoning.

Then I looked to the fireplace. "No, it's beautiful to look at, but it'll be burning off before long and it's very cozy in here."

I gently lowered the delicate woven curtain and turned to face the small room. Looking around at the flaring golden aura that undulated over the smoky log walls, I missed the presence that belonged there. In the corner, the old rocker stood motionless. It looked lonely.

"She misses you too," he said softly.

I attempted a smile, but it failed to materialize. I quickly looked away from the frozen chair. I pulled the serape over my head and laid it on the lumpy couch.

"Where do you want to sit?" I asked, trying to get into the lesson.

"Wherever you want. That's not important today."

"What *is* important today?" I said, staring up at him.

"Your understanding," came the deeply solemn reply.

I decided not to question the cryptic response. Instead, I grabbed a pillow from the couch and propped it up against the fireplace stones for my back. Stretching out my legs, I patted the braided rug.

"Sit here," I suggested. "Here I can see the firelight on your face."

My teacher chuckled. "Is that important?"

"Not really, but it helps when I can read people's faces."

He crossed his feet and lowered himself to the worn fabric. "How's this?"

I nodded.

"So," he began, "you preferred the fire over the fairyland. You said it'd burn off soon, but it won't. It'll remain for quite a long time. It's going to be a very grey, chilly day."

"That's all right, we've been outside a lot lately." I glanced around the snug room. "This is real nice."

166

"Heavy clouds are moving in," he said, looking to the window. "It's going to get darker in here. Do you want me to light the lantern?"

My eyes scanned toward the darkened kitchen area where No-Eyes kept the oil lamp. "I don't think so, the firelight's enough."

After several quiet moments passed, Many Heart spoke.

"You two figure it out?"

I grinned. "No. We tried real hard. We pulled out our ragged maps and studied them real good. I know one thing, though."

He smiled. "What's that?"

"I know that we'll be almost on the Divide. We've got it narrowed down."

His head tilted curiously. "Narrowed down to what?"

"The range."

Brows raised. "I see. And which one is that?"

I smiled. "The Sawatch Range."

The man's countenance gave no revealing signals. "Your spirits will know." He remained noncommittal. "At least you have the right national forest."

Another solid clue. I looked intently at him. "Many Heart, you just told me that our land would be in the White River National Forest."

"And why not? You already had the 'general vicinity' narrowed down."

I tried to really pinpoint it. "What county?" There were several that the national forest covered.

He shrugged. Then his black eyes shifted to mine. They were deeply intense as they searched the depths of my own.

"Beneath your feet will be a power point. At your head will the mighty winged person fly. To the east the great water spirit will sing. And in the west, three rivers converge as one."

I stared at him. "I asked a dumb question. I'm sorry I tried pushing it."

"That is your right to ask. I have no right to tell . . . only your spirit has that."

"That's okay. We've never been this close before, so I guess we can pretty well take it from here."

The pitch in the pine logs snapped. Skies darkened. The tiny living room flared with an orange glow.

The Dreamwalker raised a brow. "What're you thinking?" he asked softly.

"The orange light from the fire reminded me of the blazing sunset on the canyonland." I scanned the room. "The moving shadows reminded me of the shadows there."

Eyes narrowing, he inquired, "Which shadows?"

Our eyes met. "Theirs."

Eyes locking, he said, "Want to talk about it? Them?"

I shrugged. "We pretty well covered it."

"Did we?"

"Didn't we?"

"We spoke of *specific* lost spirits. We left many of the underscoring generalities unsaid."

"Is this something I need to know to advance along the path?"

He stared into the fire. The tone of his voice was ominously grave.

"Let's just say that this is something *you* need to know. This is something that requires your absolute comprehension."

"Then we'd better go into it. If there's things I *need* to understand, then we need to go into them." Then his actual former words struck home.

"Why do *I* need to thoroughly comprehend this subject?"

His head slowly turned to square with mine. His eyes were intense with reflections.

"That is for No-Eyes. She will prompt your memory. She will do the preparing. I will simply supply the basic background facts of the matter."

He was being cryptically evasive. "What promptings? Memory of what? *Preparing* for what?"

"Those answers are not for me to give."

I sighed. "I thought my learning on the Dreamwalker path was to enlighten me to these things. Now you say No-Eyes will do that."

"Your present learning comes not from me, Summer. It comes from your own enlightenment within. I can and do bring that about. I bring you to points of realization, but the true enlightenment comes not from me, but from you. I guide you through and am here to help you *expand* your comprehension, but certain areas still remain within the domain of your original teacher. And regarding this singular matter, *she* wishes to be the one to bring you to it."

Silence.

He peered at me. "Summer?"

"Okay, I understand."

My friend leaned forward, elbows on knees. "You were reminded of the lost Indian spirits among the mesas."

"Yes," I whispered.

"And what were your thoughts when this memory stirred?"

"I felt sorry for them."

"That was your *feelings,* what were your *thoughts*?"

"I thought how forlorn they were and that it was a waste for them to still be hanging around the mesas."

"You didn't think they were within their rights?"

I hesitated. "No."

"And your feelings weren't of a frightened nature?"

I examined that. I recalled my emotions at the time I first experienced impressions of the spirits.

"No, I don't remember being frightened really. I think I was more curious than anything. Maybe at first, when I had the initial physical signs of some presence. When my scalp crawled and my neck prickled, those physical warnings always serve to put me on guard and maybe scare me a little because I haven't yet discovered their cause. But after I knew, no, I don't recall being scared at all."

"Then No-Eyes was right," he said without further explanation.

I let the comment pass.

"Summer, we're going to talk about spirits. We're going to talk about spectral manifestations."

I smiled. "Ghosts."

He remained serious. Evidently my layman's term wasn't amusing.

"I'm sorry," I apologized, recognizing the gravity of the subject. "I didn't mean to be flip when you're obviously so serious."

He shrugged. "'Ghosts' is all right, but it's usually a term applied when one is fabricating a scary tale around a campfire."

I was duly corrected.

He wasn't quite finished. "When referring to a spirit whose physical body has died, we still call that a spirit. But when this spirit *remains* within the earthly boundaries, we call that spirit a *wayward* spirit."

I understood. "'Wayward' because the spirit's wandering—it hasn't gone where it should."

"Exactly."

Now that I had gotten back on track, I'd be sure to stay there. I listened intently.

"A spirit becomes wayward for several reasons, all of them having a direct relationship to its former physical life. The underlying cause is always emotion."

"Like deep love," I interjected.

"Explain that statement," he ordered.

"Do I have to?"

"Yes."

I looked away at the old furniture that glowed with the warm firelight. I scanned the familiar room that held the essence of my dear, old friend.

"No-Eyes told me that I was her last student. She said that after she made her final walk into the woods, she'd still live." I paused. "She said she'd always be with me."

His voice bespoke his sensitive heart. "And you think because of her love for you she's going to stay around you and become a wayward spirit."

I nodded.

"Summer," he said tenderly, "No-Eyes is much too advanced for such foolishness."

I looked up at his softened eyes. "You mean she *won't* be with me?"

A gentle smile curved his full lips. "That's not what I said. Summer, haven't you yet realized that she's *through* with the cycle of return? Haven't you guessed her spiritual status?"

My heart pounded.

"Summer, she's all *done* with that. When she said she'd always be *with* you, she meant as an *advisor*. She'll have the *right* to choose that option when she sheds the physical skin."

I sighed in relief. "She doesn't have to do that."

He smiled with understanding. "We all know that. And nobody knows that more than her, but this is what the old one is planning. This is what she wants."

I was concerned for her. "But why?"

Heavy brows raised. "Why? Because she loves you, because you have spiritual work that she wishes to help with, because she sees you'll need help with your book writings, because she cares. Shall I go on?"

My eyes were misting. "No," I whispered.

The Dreamwalker compassionately withdrew his attention to allow me solitude while I thought about all he had said. And when I closed my eyes I wished the old one was with me in this serene room of warm firelight. I wished she was here with me so I could hold her wrinkled hand, touch her time-worn cheek, hug her frail form. I missed her so much my heart ached. If only I could just see her. I missed her sensitivity, her shuffle, her way of speaking.

"Better come back," said the distant voice.

My head jerked up at the man. "I miss her so."

"We've only got three more weeks and we'll be finished." He smiled. "I'll try not to drag it out by being too boring."

I blushed at his words. "Oh, no, please don't say that. You've given me so *much* to *think* about. You're a *wonderful* teacher. I've come to such deep understandings by being with you. You're *never* boring. Why, you're...."

"Okay! Okay! I got the message," he chuckled.

I relaxed. "Well, it's all true. Just the same, it's all true." I paused a second while I gained the courage to speak my heart. "Many Heart, I may miss No-Eyes, but I do love being with you."

I had touched him. His eyes softened. "And I also love being with you, Summer."

I smiled warmly. "Thanks. That meant a lot to me."

He sighed. "Well! I guess we'd better get on with our discussion. You said that love was an emotional cause for a spirit to become wayward, and now you understand why I had you go into it. You held a grave misconception regarding No-Eyes' future intentions."

"Yes. I'm glad you cleared that up. Thank you for taking a heavy concern off my mind."

His palms upturned. "That's what I'm here for. Now," he jumped right in, "emotions, strong emotions such as anger, revenge, hatred, jealousy and such can bind a spirit to the physical realm of reality. Things not yet accomplished also can."

"Unfinished business?"

"Yes. Because the spirit is man's consciousness, his mind, it therefore retains the physical memory and emotions. When the spirit is released upon physiological death and it does not speed toward the light, frequently it pauses too long and the strong emotions gain control; therefore, the spirit hovers about in a wayward manner to take care of unfinished business."

"That's so sad," I said painfully.

"Yes, it is sad, but that doesn't have to be the end of it."

I frowned. "What do you mean?"

"I mean that there isn't a single wayward spirit that can't be helped to find its way back into the light."

I smiled. "Their guides, their advisors."

"No."

His negative reply confused me. "Their advisors can't help them back?"

"Oh, don't get me wrong, a great many can and do. But there's many circumstances when a spirit can't help a wayward spirit."

That didn't make any logical sense to me. "Why? What sort of circumstances?"

"Summer, can the blind lead the blind? Can a drunk rehabilitate another drunk?"

"But you're giving me negatives. An advisor isn't a drunk or blind."

He shook his head. "Doesn't matter. The premise still stands. Listen, sometimes a person can only be helped by an *outsider,* by one who is *different.*"

"All right, I see what you're getting at, but what sort of 'outsider' are you talking about with wayward spirits?"

"Physical, living people."

"People!"

The dancing firelight glanced off his black hair as he bowed his head. When he raised his face, the light played in the dark pools of his eyes. When he spoke again, the voice was calm.

"*Aware* people can do it, Summer."

"But how? Many Heart, I really don't want to appear totally stupid with this, but I don't get it at all. How does an aware person communicate with spirits?"

He merely stared at me. His silence was deafening.

I remembered when, on a journey with No-Eyes, I had spoken with a wayward spirit and had helped her return into the light. I thought about that memorable experience.

"That was *spirit* to *spirit*, Many Heart."

He continued to stare at me. "There are *ways*, Summer. There are *Dreamwalker* ways."

I inwardly shuddered at his ominous tone. Again he had plunged my mind into thought. I voiced them.

"There are ways for a physical being to *talk* to a spirit within *this* plane of reality?"

He nodded with absolute assurance.

I slowly peered up at his serious face. "You're going to *teach* me this way?"

"No."

I exhaled with deep relief.

"*No-Eyes* is."

Silence.

My teacher stared into the snapping flames. He said no more on the subject, as if it were closed.

It wasn't, not by a long shot.

I wasn't going to let this matter slip by like I had others. I was through being led down roads and coming up with dead ends. This road was going to *go* somewhere. I started out composed.

"Explain that statement," I said softly.

Reflections played across the teacher's solemn face. He remained unmoved.

"Many Heart?"

"Yes?"

"I asked you to explain."

"I heard."

"Well?"

"That's up to the old one to do, not me."

I sat up. "Oh, no, I think not. *You* brought it up. *You* explain it."

His eyes slowly closed and opened. "I simply answered your question, that is what I'm here to do. You asked if I would teach you the way and I said no."

"But you *baited* me, you had to *extend* it by saying that *No-Eyes* would teach me. And now I'm asking you *why* I need to learn this."

"No-Eyes will explain that to you." He was so exasperatingly cool.

I stood. "That's not acceptable."

Silence.

I bent over to talk down to him. "You said that this lesson had to do with a way for aware people to help wayward spirits. You said it was a *Dreamwalker* way?"

"Yes, a Dreamwalker way."

"Well, who's the Dreamwalker here? If this high learning is a Dreamwalker technicality then let the *Dreamwalker* teach it!"

"She *will*," came the whispered response.

I froze. I literally felt the blood drain from my face.

"No-Eyes is a *Dreamwalker*?"

"Yes."

I was confused. "Then . . . why you?"

"Perspectives, Summer. I shed a different light on things. I give male balance to the way you have been walking."

I knelt beside him. "Many Heart, how long have I been on the path of the way? How long have I been on the trail of the Dreamwalker?"

His head slowly turned to mine. We were literally face to face. We were both intent. His eyes were like huge black marbles.

"You placed your feet upon the path of the Dreamwalker the day you first stepped into No-Eyes's woods."

I slumped back on my heels. My eyes shifted over to the licking flames.

"Does that really surprise you so much?" he asked.

I didn't know. I felt surprised and yet I didn't. I was in a mental limbo. I was numb.

His voice was firm, yet gentle. "The path of the Way is long. The trail of the Dreamwalker is difficult and complex. It progresses gradually with advancing steps, each of deeper enlightenment than the one preceding it. The novice Walker goes slowly, gaining in comprehension as the progression advances. You have been steadily progressing."

The red embers shot up from the logs like shooting stars.

"And now that I've come so far, things are getting more complex. Now I'm to those things that are the most spiritually difficult."

"The difficulty depends on the learner. What you have now approached is not the threshold of greater *difficulties*, but that of greater *complexities* of the sacred guarded knowledge. And No-Eyes wishes to be the one to bring you into the circle which will then close behind you. *She* brought you onto the path, *she* will be the one to close it."

I turned my head to him. "Why am I just now finding out that she's a Dreamwalker? Why hasn't she ever mentioned it before?"

"That is her way. This is how it must be with her."

The crackling fire broke the heavy silence that hung between us as I thought of the old one's deep humility.

"Summer?" he said.

"Yes?"

"Dreamwalkers don't wear signs. They don't go about advertising who they are. But when we are through with our days together you will know when you see one on the street, in the marketplace, or anywhere you go. Recognition is not given to each other, that is the way."

"Many Heart?"

"Mmmm."

"Are all of No-Eyes' former students Dreamwalkers?"

"Does it matter?"

I lowered my head and fumbled with a frayed thread of the worn rug. "It's not important for me to know, I just wondered, that's all."

"Only three."

I looked up at him. "What designates that decision?"

"What the old one sees within the student's heart and spirit the first day she looks into their soul. Many had the mind for it, but only three had the rest."

The light from the windows was murky. The autumn day remained heavily overcast. I had no conception of the passing of time, nor did I care. Inside, I was surrounded with the homey warmth of my old friend's dwelling. It was comforting and peaceful.

The dark shadows quivered up and down the old log walls as the firelight danced about the small room. The soft orange glow muted the harshness of the old one's austere furnishings. The broken rocker seemed to move back and forth as the fire's reflections animated its looming shadow. This was a good medicine place. It was a place of the heart.

"Summer?"

My attention was awakened. "Yes?"

"We need to finish."

"Okay," I acknowledged, plumping up the worn pillow and resting against the warm stones again. "But before we go on, I want to apologize for my ignorant outburst before. I didn't understand about No-Eyes."

"Don't be sorry, just learn from your mistakes and move forward. We'll do that now."

The man shifted his long-held position by stretching out on his side and, leaning on his elbow with head in hand, he smiled.

"Can you see my face?"

I grinned. "Yes."

"So, when an enlightened person learns how to help a wayward spirit, they must utilize that sacred knowledge to the fullest."

"Do you?" I cut in.

"If the occasion arises, yes. Let me explain something here, Summer. Spiritual knowledge cannot be hidden nor can it be allowed to atrophy because of voluntary neglect. There are many, many spiritual ways by which an enlightened person can give aid. This aid is broad in scope. It encompasses all aspects of spirituality, humanistic help, and the sharing of higher knowledge.

"In essence, the Dreamwalker is a spiritual jack-of-all-trades, if you will. He helps wherever aid is needed, wherever he perceives that he can be of use. Helping people along the way, giving support or knowledge or working with a wayward spirit are all aspects of his life."

"I see," I said. "But do you go around *looking* for these lost spirits?"

My friend laughed. "Not usually. People who know me come with information about certain unusual occurrences or strange manifestations. It's my spiritual obligation to try to free those poor souls and show them the way they need to go."

I thought that over. "If I complete the path, will that also be *my* obligation?"

"That's for No-Eyes to determine."

I tilted my head. "Many Heart, will I too be obligated to do this?"

He sighed. "If you complete your path, yes. Our Indian beliefs run deep and sacred. The spirit is that aspect of man that is most important. The final destination of that spirit is most important. A spirit must not tarry within the earthly bonds, but must speed to a higher domain. The guiding of those lost and confused spirits is frequently left to those who know the complex mechanics of such things."

He made it sound so natural. The act of helping a spirit out of its earthly bond was beautiful work.

"That's a beautiful thing to do," I said.

He shrugged. "In the end, it is. It's often a very moving and touching thing to see." He paused. "But getting the lost spirit where it should be—convincing it—is often serious business."

"Isn't it always serious business?"

Brows furrowed. "What I'm referring to is its frequently *dangerous* side. Spirits are pure energy, Summer. Don't *ever* forget that. They have free access to incredible powers at their disposal. They possess great control over their energies and the energies of nature. They can be unbelievably cunning and deceiving. Depending on the circumstances which bond them here, they can be docile or violent. *Never* trust them. That is rule number one. Always be on guard. Always expect the unexpected in their presence. Always be prepared for a violent attack."

He was scaring me. "I don't want to do this. You made it sound like a beautiful thing to do, but now you sound like it's going to be some kind of nightmare."

"It *is* a beautiful thing to do. It's just also frequently a dangerous thing in the performance of it."

I repeated softly, "I don't want to do this, Many Heart."

Silence.

Now when I looked again at the dancing shadows, they weren't happy, they were lurking grotesquely. My eyes shifted to the blackened corners of the room. My weak heart drummed with the new thought of crouching specters.

"Your imagination is very active," he lightly chuckled.

I looked to him. "No it's not. You made everything vividly clear, that's all."

"I did?" came the innocent response.

"Yes, you did. You made it vividly clear that I don't want anything to do with this dangerous spiritual job."

"You can't pick and choose," he informed very matter-of-factly.

"Oh, can't I? I'll do everything else. I'll write the books, I'll answer letters, and help people in any way I possibly can, but this violent spirit business isn't for me."

"Why not?"

My eyes rounded like new moons. "Because the entire idea scares me to death. Why, if I ever came across a mean spirit I'd faint!"

He tried to control his mirth. "No you wouldn't."

"Yes I would! I'd faint dead away. And it's *not* funny!"

He forced a straight face. "But, Summer, once you have the knowledge and a little experience...."

"Oh, no. First off, I'm not going to *let* No-Eyes *give* me the knowledge and as for the experience, well...if I don't *have* the knowledge, I won't be *getting* any experience."

"But, Summer, you *already* have experience."

"With *spirits*?"

He nodded confidently.

I was incredulous. "Whatever gave you that idea?"

"Your past."

"The time with No-Eyes?" I laughed.

"No, this was way before that, when you were only this high," he said, raising his hand a little above the floor.

I smirked. "Oh, brother, have *you* got the wrong person. You'd better recheck your information."

"Is that your final decision?"

"You bet it is!"

"Seriously? You're serious?" he asked in disbelief.

"I've never been more serious in my entire life. There's no way I'm going around confronting violent specters who want nothing more than to be left alone."

"Even if No-Eyes can convince you otherwise?"

"She won't."

"Even if she prompts your memory about those spirit manifestations of your past, your childhood?"

"There's no prompting to be done because there *weren't* any spirits in my past. I told you, you've got your *facts* confused . . . you've got the wrong person!"

"Suit yourself," he concluded.

Silence.

The firelight waned and the shadows deepened as they snuck about the room. I looked to the windows at the grey day that was getting greyer.

Many Heart rose to stoke the embers and replenish the wood supply. "Maybe you'll change your mind later on," he maintained.

Deep silence.

"Perhaps No-Eyes will be able to open your eyes to make you see the totality of your true obligations—make you see what's in your past."

I stared ahead at the shadows that had suddenly jumped to life as the fire flared. They gyrated before me. I whispered low. "I'm not changing my mind."

Slowly his head turned and eyes bored into mine. "You actually *refuse* to help lost souls?"

He had tried to make me feel ashamed. It didn't work.

"There's others who know how to help them. Let *them* do it."

He replaced the scorched poker and again sat cross-legged before me.

"That's not *apathy* coming from Summer Rain, is it?"

"No, but the weak can't help the weak."

"Ohhh," he crooned sarcastically, "so now you're weak, are you?"

"Many Heart," I blurted angrily, "some people are cut out for certain work that others aren't. I'm just not cut out for this certain work!"

"And how do you know this?"

"I know because it scares me to death, that's why."

He softened. "You'd get over that. It doesn't take but a couple of encounters to shed that. After a few, you quickly learn to exit the fear. Besides, you'll be busy working on convincing the spirit to leave instead of thinking about what you feel."

"Is that so," I snapped.

"Yes, this is so. You'll see," he added.

I shook my head. "I'm afraid I *won't* see. I'll *never* see because I'm *not* going to do that."

"You're *stubborn!*" he shot back at me.

His sudden sharpness was the first display of impatience I'd seen coming from him. It hurt, but right then I didn't care.

"I'd better go, we're not getting anywhere," I said, rising from my spot.

"Running away, are we?"

Pulling the woven serape over my head, I uncaringly muttered, "We? I don't know about *you,* but I don't see the logic in prolonging an impossible impasse."

Unmoving, he remained in his position and stared intently into the bright blaze before him. His words were soft, but chillingly cold.

"You've just jeopardized everything."

I purposely slammed the door behind me and strode out into the dreary autumn afternoon. The cold dampness struck my face to slap some sense into me. I stopped midway down the hill and turned to look up at the warm place of the heart.

Oh God, what *had* I done?

The Wise Man does not claim to plant seeds, for the Seeds are already there.

The Wise Man perceives the Seeds and merely attempts to nourish Them into Fruition.

Distant
Echoes

Reverberating through the corridors of my mind, distant sounds reach out and cry to be heard. And I harken to the echoes that enkindle clear visions of ancient memories long locked away within the golden treasury of my mind.

If anyone had seen me driving down the mountain roads that led away from the cabin that dreary afternoon, they would've thought they'd seen a woman who had certifiably lost her last remaining marble, for I mumbled and talked to myself the entire way.

I animatedly discussed and argued with my invisible passenger. I was angry, hurt, and scared. I was angry at Many Heart's presumptuous attitude. I was hurt because of our argument, and I was scared as hell that I'd blown the chance to complete the Dreamwalker path.

Was I supposed to blindly do everything I was told? Was I supposed to be led by the nose and forced to perform spiritual work I wasn't yet prepared to do? Didn't I have the right to personal input? Didn't I have a free will to choose my own work? And did a Dream-walker *have* to help the wayward spirits? Nobody told me about *that* when I first stepped into No-Eyes' woods that day!

Oh, dear God, this was such heavy business. Why couldn't I just have been a store clerk with nothing more important to think about than punching in the right keys? Who would want to have to worry about the destructive forces of an angry spirit? Who would want to put themselves in such malevolent circumstances? Me—*I* was supposed to want to do this high spiritual thing! Well, I certainly had news for them!

My anger was flaming when I walked through the door and Bill immediately pushed me right back out.

"Let's go for a walk," he suggested. "Maybe you'll cool off."

Good idea.

My high energy level was ready to explode. A walk would alleviate the building pressure. And after I had hurriedly recounted the day's events, I felt much lighter.

Bill took some time to ponder the story. His deeply analytical mind weighed each opponent's logic and reasonings for their particular responses.

"It's logical," he finally judged.

I was almost afraid to ask. "What's logical?"

"It's logical that an individual as enlightened and as spiritually trained as a Dreamwalker would be involved in such work. It's logical that these spirit clearings would be naturally encompassed within their realm of work."

I sighed. "Oh God."

He squeezed my hand. "No, listen, honey. It's fact that the spirit is most important because that is the living force which always survives physical death. The spirit *must* go directly to the Source, otherwise it wanders about in confusion. It stands to reason that someone who has the ability should help them."

"I know that. But why should I be expected to get in on this work? I don't know anything about dealing face-to-face with spirits."

"You're expected to get in on this because evidently that's part of what Dreamwalkers do. And," he cautioned, "you don't know anything about the mechanics of it because you refused to accept the idea of No-Eyes' future teachings on it."

Silence.

Why was he always right? Why was he always the anchor that weighted down my erroneous rationalizations? Yet, as always, the logic from his steel-trap mind stood unchallengeable.

"Then, was I wrong to get so upset?"

He shrugged. "Those were your true responses at the time. You're supposed to be free to react honestly and openly. I'd have to say that, initially, you were within your rights."

"Initially. You had to put that in, didn't you? You obviously think that after my 'initial' response, I should've calmed down enough to hear him out more and then maybe I'd have seen the light that'd change my mind."

"Perhaps. Since you didn't stay, we'll never know."

"Then I *was* wrong," I decided sadly.

"You should've stayed."

We walked down the dirt roads that criss-crossed our neighborhood. The dampness of the day had kept the dust out of the atmosphere and, although the skies were still murky, the evergreens were vibrant with new freshness. I inhaled deeply of the pine fragrance that filled the air.

"Do you think I actually blew it?" I asked, nearly cringing to hear the reply.

My life companion smiled warmly. "I think you blew today. As far as the path goes, no, I don't think one argument could actually do that. The path of the Way isn't some superficial class. You've already spent almost two years on it. Think of all the heated arguments you've had with No-Eyes—a Dreamwalker. Did she chase you away or shut you out after those?"

"No," I hesitantly admitted.

"It's clear that a Dreamwalker has a fine mind and great understanding. They're patient, tolerant, and sympathetic. I hardly think Many Heart is going to expel you for one display of contest. In fact," he added with a bit of humor, "he probably admires your gutsiness."

My eyes narrowed with my frown. "Nahhh," I crooned half-disbelievingly.

He smiled wide. "Yeah. Why, I bet he's chuckling over your rampage right now. I bet whenever he thinks about it he's going to smile at the thought."

"Really?" I chirped with the rise of new hope.

"Your occasional tirades often ended with No-Eyes laughing. Why not Many Heart?"

"I don't know," I groaned. "His final words were pretty grim. You should've heard the coldness in his voice."

Bill conceded the point. "I think he was serious, all right. I think he meant it to be a serious warning to make you realize your impulsiveness—that you should've reconsidered going through with the final act of actually walking out on him. I don't think he meant it the grave way you think."

"I don't know," I worried. "I sure hope not."

His voice was gentle, yet stern. "You're going to have to tone down your impulsive responses, you know. You have to control them better."

"I know," I agreed. "I've done a lot better since being with No-Eyes. I'll work harder on that."

"You're going to have to work on it until it becomes natural. You're going to have to be able to mask your explosive responses the way the old one said to."

He was right . . . again.

The entire experience embarrassed me. I was ashamed of my behavior and I felt sheepish. "Do you think he'll bring it up next week?"

"That wouldn't be in keeping with their way. He'll most likely ignore it and act like it never happened."

"Why? Why wouldn't he bring it up?"

"Could *you* forget it?"

I cringed. "No way!"

"Then I'm sure he too knows you'll remember it. Why should he need to remind you? He won't say anything unless *you* give out hints of reference to it."

His point was clear.

"I'm going to be terribly embarrassed when I see him again next weekend," I confessed.

"I'm sure he'll sense that, but I don't think he'll give attention to it. Just go ahead as normally as you can and concentrate on the new lesson."

And that's just what I intended to do. I'd swallow my pride and carry on by giving the Dreamwalker my fullest attention.

By the time the following weekend rolled into the present, my shame wasn't as acute. It had faded into mild feelings of remorse that subliminally remained to remind me of my serious offense.

When I headed the truck out of Woodland Park, the glorious scenery evaporated all residual negatives from my consciousness. Nature compassionately healed my heart wounds.

Sun-touched earth. Bronze and gold. Orange and scarlet. Quaking coins. Shimmering rubies. Jade and jasper. Emerald needles. Gossamer viridescence. Thriving life. Celebration.

My heart thundered with the intense beauty before my wondering eyes. My spirit swelled to join in with the heartbeat of nature. Everywhere I looked, I saw and felt the shining embodiment of God.

The brilliant autumn mountainsides glimmered in this, their regal prime of life. They gave undeniable testimony to their returning spirits. In autumn they exposed their pure souls to give credence to the eternal life of all living things. They bared their magnificent cores and created an exquisite symphony of benediction to their glorious creator.

My heart was feather-light when I hurriedly parked the old truck beneath the sheltering lodgepole. My spirit was soaring high as I took the steps two at a time and stormed the fragile pine door.

"Many Heart!" I called excitedly.

The cabin was dark. It was empty.

My heart sank.

Dear God, no. Please don't make it be so.

Quickly I checked through the shadowed emptiness. My teacher was nowhere around. Oh, my God. I *had* blown it.

Numbly, I stood in the center of the tiny room and wondered

what I should do next.

"*Sum-mer! Sum-mer?*"

My head pricked. My heart pounded and I ran onto the porch.

Many Heart was far down by the stream...waving up to me. "I'm down here! *Com'on!*"

I nervously laughed away the mistiness that had begun to sting my eyes. "I'm coming!" I shouted back.

He hadn't left me after all. Maybe I hadn't blown it.

I raced down the hillside toward the waiting man. The stream giggled behind him. Golden cottonwoods showered down their breeze-tossed raiments. I nearly slid down the last few feet. Breathlessly, I regained my footing and came to land before him.

"I was so scared to find the cabin empty. I thought you'd gone."

He was grinning. "Where would I go?"

"Away! I thought you left for good!"

His arms came up in question. "But we've more to do. We're not finished. We've got two more weeks yet."

My impulsiveness exploded. I hugged him. "Oh, thank God, I was so scared I'd blown it when you weren't there. Don't ever scare me like that again."

Strong arms came around to encircle and reassure the frightened student. Then he gently nudged me away to hold me at arm's length. His expression was soft.

"I never meant to scare you, Summer. I just thought that since it's such a beautiful autumn day, we'd spend it here under the cotton-woods. I heard your truck door close, but by the time I got to where I could call to you, you were already inside the cabin."

I sighed with deep relief. "Well, I'm just glad everything's all right."

I strolled over to the water's edge and looked up into the clear sky. "It's a gorgeous day today." And, turning to the broad trees, I added, "Soon they'll be bare again."

He too glanced up into the goldness. "By the way they're falling, I'd say by next week, especially if this breeze keeps up." He chose a grassy spot, sat down, and patted the ground. "Com'on, sit down here and we'll watch the transition."

I sat beside him. We were both facing the rushing stream.

"Life goes on," he commented.

"Yes, if these trees are any proof. I guess that's a general law of nature. Changes, always constantly changing and altering, but still the same underneath—within."

"No-Eyes say that?" he asked.

"No, that one was mine."

He winked teasingly. "Hope you're still writing those down."

I grinned. "Yes, I'm still writing them down."

A leaf fell at my feet. I picked it up and twirled it between my fingers.

"Penny for your thoughts," he said.

"Oh, I was just thinking how the tree's spirit changes its outward appearance all the time. Each year it alters itself. First it's a baby green, next it's deep jade, then it's bright gold and finally it's bare until spring again. And all the while the outward transformations are taking place, the same life force lives within—the same unaltered spirit."

"Just like you," came the odd statement.

I looked at him with a wry smile. "Me, why me?"

"You just explained the carryover soul concept."

I reviewed my wording. "Guess I did at that."

"I think that'd be a good subject for today," he said, snapping off a thistle.

"Whatever you say, although No-Eyes went into it already."

"I know that," he admitted, "but until you're comfortable with it, it needs going into again and again."

The wind hushed through the trees and rustled down the leaves. The ones that fell over the stream were quickly whisked away with the rush of water.

"Tell me about it," he suggested.

"It was during the middle of the Phoenix Days lessons when she brought it up. She seemed anxious to get it out. It was as if she was afraid she'd leave me before she got to explain it. Anyway, she told me that She-Who-Sees was actually me." I lowered my head. "I overreacted and got upset with her."

"You've been known to do that," he smiled without condescension or any hint of reprimand.

I blushed anyway. "Yes, well, *that* time I stayed to the finish and, in the end, I had it reconciled."

"I'm curious," he said. "I heard about your vision quest—about the time you spiritually reviewed the Book of Records. Didn't you see all your former names at that time?"

Now it was my turn to do the smiling. "I know exactly what you're getting at. You're wondering why I didn't put two an' two together when I saw the name of She-Who-Sees, the name that used to be mine."

He nodded with interest.

I glanced across the stream into the forest beyond.

"No-Eyes never brought that up, but I thought of it later on. After reviewing that aspect of the quest, I remembered that when I initially saw the name, I thought it was an ancestral listing. The real truth to the matter didn't dawn on me until *after* No-Eyes told me who I'd been.

That was when the real significance of it came to me."

I looked at him. "Does that satisfy your curiosity?"

"Yes." He leaned forward with great seriousness. "Your spirit has been knocking at the door of your consciousness since you were a small child. It has been trying to get through the new veneer."

I thought of different instances as he spoke.

"Although you weren't raised in the native way, your heart always followed that which it yearned for—that which it remembered. Your spirit remained true and pure through the outward alterations. It remained strong with its intended purpose. She-Who-Sees clearly sits here beside me today, just as Summer Rain does."

"It's incredible, yet it's not," I reflected. "It's unbelievable, yet it's believable because it's *happened to me. I am* just like these cotton-woods," I mused, looking up into their sunlit brightness. "I'm *just* like them. Their outer appearance has altered over the centuries and through the seasons, but the living core remains the same, the spirit remains that of She-Who-Sees and Sequanu. I could go back further with more names, but those two are the ones that are so strong now. Those are the two that retain memory today. It is *their* sweet voices that I remember most."

"Beautiful memories, Summer."

"Yes," I thought, "but ugly and frightening ones too. Of course those are the ones I try not to dwell on . . . they happened long ago."

My friend's tone was sympathetic. "Are you sorry you have a carryover soul? You sound as though you sometimes are."

"Oh, I'm not really sorry, but considering the beautiful and peaceful ways of Indian life that Sequanu experienced long before the coming of the white man and then the ugly and deeply sorrowful memories of She-Who-Sees, it's often difficult for Summer Rain to contain certain emotions that come from those vivid spirit memories. Summer Rain still lives in a backward time of bigotry and apartheid toward her people. Summer Rain lives the prolonged injustice."

He reached for my hand. His rested upon mine.

"But Summer Rain will live to see it come full circle. As Sequanu and She-Who-Sees, Summer Rain retains their history. As Summer Rain, Sequanu and She-Who-Sees will experience the final justice that comes full circle into peace once again. It is only right. It is spirit justice carried out within physical reality."

I understood the concept, but remained uneasy.

He sensed the unsettled mood.

"It's hard to deal with, right?" he correctly targeted.

I simply hung my head and nodded.

"If it's any solace," he said gently, "I understand. You feel like you're living on a fence. You feel caught between worlds. The past of centuries remains fresh within your mind while you physically are confined living in today's reality. You experience vivid flashbacks. They carry strong emotions with them—they carry the intense emotions of the times, the events. You now have to deal with those."

"Yes, it's like I'm eight hundred years old. That's how far the memories go back. The dreams all my life have been filled with old, old memories that have crossed the barrier. Sometimes just a certain sound or scent will bring on total recall of some event long buried within my memory—when my consciousness was once of Sequanu or She-Who-Sees. It can't be denied that the fact exists. After No-Eyes explained it, I finally had a valid reason for their cause. Sometimes I feel good that Sequanu and She-Who-Sees will live through me to see it all turn out well."

"Sometimes?"

"Yes, because other times I feel so mismatched, a bewildering mystery; a walking, talking freak of nature that belongs neither here nor there. I know we discussed this before, but still I walk in an eternal limbo . . . forever alone."

"Dreamwalkers are always alone."

"That's not what I meant. Dreamwalkers *choose* their state of being. I was *born* to it. Besides," I reminded, "I'm not a Dreamwalker."

Silence.

The sound of the wind was sweet. It brought to me the homey fragrance of cedar, sweetgrass, and sage. Scents I loved drifted before me while the water spirit sang her song of love. I saw specters of Indian children laughing in the stream. Memories. Eight-hundred-year-old memories, fresh as yesterday.

"Summer?"

I jerked to the sharp sound that rent my reverie. I looked to my fullblood companion.

"Smell that?" he said with dancing eyes.

I sniffed the crisp autumn air. "Woodsmoke."

"Your favorite. Know why?"

The golden trees rustled above me. "Woodsmoke takes me back to the better times, the serene times of when I was Sequanu."

"Yes," he whispered. "Those restful times bring peace into your heart. They comfort your spirit. This is why the smell of woodsmoke is your favorite scent."

"I love cedar and sage too. I have bouquets of sage hanging from the rafters of our house. I burn cedar just for the wonderful smell and its powerful cleansing qualities."

He inquired further, farther back. "And the frankincense

186

and myrrh?"

"That too I love, but from a far more distant spirit time. I burn those when I'm alone because they're too pungent for Bill."

He smiled. "See how the distant echoes came through the memory? They're heard, they prompt the spirit and the mind reacts to them. You're fortunate you know why. Many people have no real idea why they prefer this or love that so much. Their inclinations have no viable causal basis."

I allowed that to be absorbed. Were they really not better off not remembering?

The clear sky was a vibrant blue—so typical of the high mountains of Colorado that I dearly loved—the same mountains I'd lived within for so many centuries.

"Why the memory at all, Many Heart? I mean, what's the purpose of the phenomenon?"

"The carryover soul phenomenon?"

"Yes. Physically speaking, it causes great confusion until it is understood and rationally accepted. Spiritually, I don't quite understand its purpose."

"The carryover soul is most evident in those individuals who have returned for a specific purpose. Always these are for the eventual beautification, advancement, or awakening process. When the past memories *enhance* those purposes, then they are carried over through the spirit's present memory."

"What did you mean by beautification?"

"Cultural enhancement such as great musicians who have much to contribute. Child prodigies are prime examples of these. Their advanced talent has been carried over in the memories of their young minds. Even though they are little more than babes, their spirits and the corresponding memories of ability are the same as that of the masterful talents they once achieved in a former sojourn. These young masters can be found within fields of the arts, science, and philosophy."

"Young geniuses are products of carryover souls."

"Absolutely. Yours is of a race. Yours carried over because of its purpose at this extremely important time."

I hinted for clarification. "Purpose being?"

Silence.

"Is this something the old one has to tell?"

"No," he replied kindly. "You've had spiritual promptings all your life. You've had inclinations and urges that you couldn't understand. You moved to the Rocky Mountains because that is the regional location your spirit yearned for...remembered...resonated with."

"Because it lived there centuries before—twice before."

"Exactly. So, after you've been patiently acting on those unexplainable impressions and inclinations, you've ended up in No-Eyes' woods and, ultimately, with me."

"Which hopefully will bring me to the end of the path of the Way so I can...what?"

He smiled. "So you can do what you came here to do. So you can fulfill your spirit's whole purpose."

"Which is...."

"To revolutionize how enlightenment is brought to the masses—to bring *free* enlightenment in the manner of the ancient masters. Heightened awareness. Preparedness for what is to befall mankind during the Phoenix Days. Hope for our people. The closing of the circle."

I sighed with the heaviness. "That's a pretty tall order. My spirit has grand ideas that don't quite coincide with mine."

"Your spirit *is* the mind, Summer."

"I know, but maybe my *conscious* mind is a little simpler than the subconscious. The spirit is the superconscious and I'm just little ole me down here trying very hard to make sense out of what it wants to accomplish....I'm trying very hard to reconcile the two."

He chuckled. "That was very good. You described it about right. When your consciousness is in absolute touch with the superconsciousness then you're right on track—then you're doing what the spirit is here to do....you're a Dreamwalker."

"Do Dreamwalkers ever question the spirit's work?"

His perception of my not-so-subtle question was clear. "Never."

My heart sank. "Guess I've got a long way to go, huh."

"Two more lessons."

"Guess I'm not going to make it in time, huh."

"That's not for me to judge."

"But you just said I only have two more lessons with you."

He looked at me with wise eyes.

"That's true, you do. No-Eyes is the one to finalize your journey. Whether you complete it is up to her. I take you up *to* the circle—she takes you *into* the circle. If you've passed, she'll close it. If you don't, she will leave an opening."

I hesitated before asking the next question. "What do you think she'll do?"

"Summer," he said gently, "there are yet grave things for you to conquer. You have done well with me, but last week hurt you. You will have to overcome that one obstacle before your circle will be closed."

"Will No-Eyes attempt to convince me of my error?"

"Of course."

"And will she?"

Silence.

I peered up into his eyes. "Many Heart? I know you can see this. Will she?"

"It's not for me to say, Summer. You must use your free will to decide when the time comes. Her wise promptings will have to stir your memory enough for your complete acceptance. I can only tell you the probability I see, but your will does the eventual future deciding."

"What's the present probability then?"

Hesitation.

"Please? This is so very important to me."

Mental considerations were taking place. It was visibly clear that the Dreamwalker was weighing the pros and cons of voicing the revelation I requested.

Doe eyes glistened with hope as they looked into the man's.

Finally he sighed. "You're very difficult to work with, you know."

He was softening.

I frowned. "I know. No-Eyes is always reminding me of that fact." Then I glanced away—hurtfully.

He watched me and laughed. "Ohhh, *yes*! Yes. It looks as though you'll find your way to be convinced of your obligations!"

I squealed with unbridled delight and went to hug him.

He quickly raised his hands. "No need to get all mushy. Just remember that probabilities are always altering outcomes. It's not carved in stone yet."

"Oh, I know, I know."

I thought about the grave subject matter of last week. Still, she was going to have to be at her ultimate best to change my mind because, as of right now, I still felt the same. The old one was going to have to pull a miracle out of her calico pocket for this one to come off. But, knowing her cleverness and deep wisdom, I believed she could and would.

Birdsong filled the air and I looked to the sky.

"Searching for the falcon?" he asked.

"No," I said contentedly, "I don't think I want to fly away today."

"Your head full of woodsmoke?" he grinned.

I laughed. "Yeah, maybe."

He chuckled. "She doesn't like it when you do that."

"How well I know."

"But she does understand. She, more than anyone, understands. She *wants* you to remember, but she also wants you to be able to clearly separate the realities."

"I do. I just like remembering the truly beautiful aspects. I suppose I get a little too into them at the wrong times, though."

"That'll straighten out, Summer, that'll straighten out with spiritual maturity. Things like that come with time, experience and acceptance—a lot of it."

"I'm working on it."

The falcon appeared. He effortlessly glided through his cerulean sea of sky.

"Oh, look!" I pointed. "There he is!"

The Dreamwalker raised his head to the burnished sky, and together we watched our feathered friend rejoice in his total freedom as he so effortlessly rode the mountain currents that swiftly carried him into the far beyond. When the graceful winged being had sailed from sight, I sighed. "How magnificent he is."

"Yes, but he too is not without care."

I rested back in the prickly autumn grass. The heavy woven serape offered a cushion between me and the weedy ground. The sky was brilliant. I forced my eyes into its magnetic depths.

"Every being has cares, Many Heart. And although our falcon up there may have his, he is safe within his accepted order. There's a grand design to nature—an order established from the causal beginning. It's an order nature hasn't ever resisted or tampered with."

"You're suddenly very solemn," he perceived.

I snuggled my hands behind my neck. "Why doesn't man take more lessons from nature's living example?"

The teacher reclined on his side. His face was very near mine.

"Because man supposes that *he's* superior."

I inhaled the mountain's essence and slowly released my own.

"Must men always resist the prescribed order of things?"

"Summer," he hinted gently, "you're leading into something."

"Yes, I suppose I am."

Silence.

I had become melancholy with the deep pleasures of listening to the restful waters and gazing up into the serenity of the clear sky.

The wise one didn't want me to lose it. "Talk about it, Summer."

I turned my head to gaze deeply into his strong eyes. And, looking back up at the sky's brightness, I thought that maybe he was right, maybe I should talk about it—again, for there were still things yet unsaid, unresolved.

"I once cursed the old one," I began softly. "I didn't mean it, but she was unmercifully needling me into admitting to a very sensitive and deeply embarrassing moment."

My companion didn't say anything. He wanted me to carry it alone for a while.

"I'll never forget that day in her cabin. I'll never forget how upset she got me."

I paused for a few minutes.

"She made me verbally voice that I'd broken out crying among a large crowd of people. She did it so she could explain my deep feelings—so I'd fully understand them."

"And did you?"

"Yes."

"But?" he added, realizing there was a lot more behind my response.

"But although I understood, the terrible pain of it still hasn't lessened—it still hurts very much."

I had inadvertently clouded the issue and my companion spoke.

"The pain from cursing No-Eyes or the pain that created the tears?"

"No-Eyes and I resolved the altercation between us. I mean the pain that made me cry in the crowd . . . it's still there."

"Let's go into it then, Summer. Let's talk it through."

The vibrant yellow leaves of the sleepy cottonwoods contrasted so sharply with the turquoise sky, it nearly ached my eyes. It was so incredibly beautiful.

I watched the treetops sway in the gentle breeze.

"When I was among the people, a great sadness washed over me. It flooded like a deluge and weighted my heart with a terrible heaviness. I could see their intricately made costumes and their smiles as they sold their crafts, but I also saw what was beneath all that exterior. My spirit reached out and touched their pained souls. I saw listless eyes and unshed tears. I saw crying behind the broad smiles. I saw empty hearts.

"Many Heart, they were brave people who were desperately trying to grasp onto the threads of what was. They were bravely making an attempt to retain the beautiful pure heritage."

"And?" he whispered.

The trees blurred. "And some spectators laughed. They snickered during the beautiful ceremonial dance. I saw it, Many Heart, I really saw that."

"What would you have our people do?"

"Hide it."

"Hide what?"

"Their ceremonies. Keep it all sacred. Keep the dances private. They need to move away from displaying themselves. They need to protect the ceremonial aspects of our heritage. It's not a sideshow. It's not funny."

"Who said it was?"

"The eyes of those few spectators did. They acted like a circus had come to town."

Silence.

"Know what else?"

"What?"

"At nightfall, when the people were drumming and chanting around their campfires, I overheard someone on the street say that 'Those injuns are drunk again, better go get our guns.'" Then I hesitated. "Many Heart?"

"Yes, Summer."

"I *heard* those drums. I listened to the chanting. And it was so moving. There was so much heart in it...but to others, it was just a damned carnival come to town. We can't allow that, Many Heart, we can't tolerate such travesties with something so sacred and rare."

"Get to the point," he tenderly urged.

I blinked away the smudged sky. "A few of the younger Indians were embarrassed."

Deep silence.

My voice was barely audible. "Their heritage visibly shamed them."

He spoke softly. "These are confusing times. This is not uncommon in this day and age. But were you certain you saw this *there*?"

"There was no doubt. There were just a few, but the few soon become the many. It's got to change. It's just got to."

"What did *you* feel?" he asked, getting to the real bottom line.

I turned my head to stare into his onyx eyes. "Do you really want to know?"

His head nodded. Sunlight glinted off the ebony thickness of his hair. "Tell me."

Our eyes were solidly locked. My voice was barely above a whisper.

"When the ceremonial dances were going on, and after I noticed the few in the audience who snickered...."

"Go on, Summer."

"I...I felt Sequanu very strong. I felt compelled to walk into the center of the arena. I felt the intense urge to just slowly walk into the center of it and begin speaking."

"About what?"

The recalled memory of Sequanu's powerful influence sent a chill up my spine. "About our noble beginnings...the real beginnings. About who we *really* are. I desperately wanted to sit down with them and remind them of their precious and sacred purpose. Sequanu wished with all her heart to speak of beautiful remembered ways. She had soul-stirring things to tell...and She-Who-Sees desired to speak of changes and prophecies. She had soul-revealing things to utter. And

Summer Rain yearned to speak of the Phoenix Days. Summer Rain yearned in her heart to speak of hope."

Silence.

"But Summer Rain couldn't," I whispered. "There were sneering spectators in the stands. So...she turned and walked away with a bleeding heart. There was nothing left to do but hide her pain."

"It's going to change, Summer. It'll all change soon."

"It hurt so bad. It just hurt so bad."

"I know," he soothed. "I know."

I closed my eyes. "I feel so alone, Many Heart. I'm all alone."

"Why do you feel this way?"

I envisioned how I felt. I made the sensation visual for him.

"There's some frequent images that come to me when I feel this certain loneliness. I'm walking through a reservation, but nobody sees me. Some older ones seem to sense my passing presence, but no one actually sights me.

"I'm holding something, but I never actually see what it is. I walk through the entire reservation and then I'm standing alone atop a redstone mesa. I set my precious bundle down and tearfully chant to the flaming sunset."

Silence.

I didn't wait for an explanation because I hadn't really expected one.

"Anyway, these images come whenever I'm feeling especially alone."

"The images are not for an outsider to explain, Summer. One day you yourself will come into the understanding of them." He hesitated before going on. "And perhaps even then you will not be within full acceptance of their meaning."

"All I know is how I feel right now. When I'm feeling this great aloneness, I seem to think that the time for hope has been surpassed. I think that it's too late for everything and I feel like I'm walking a road that is no road, a path that has no visible substance, a trail that exists in no one reality. I feel I'm in a great limbo, an in-between world that spans all worlds. It's like I'm a fish out of water and I'm slowly dying.

"Many Heart, I can't express this grave feeling other than to say that I don't feel I belong here with this civilization....it's so primitive I can hardly bear it."

Silence.

And I had said all there was to say....there was nothing left.

"Summer, it's not rare for a Dreamwalker to feel these things. You *aren't* alone with them."

"You're forgetting one thing—I'm not a Dreamwalker."

The teacher sat up to gaze down at me. His tawny face was dark against the blue background of sky.

"Your carryover soul has much to do with these feelings. Not *all* of them, but most. Your spirit knows things that you yet do not. Your mind requires more comprehension and your heart more acceptance of these unchangeable things that are to be...and that have been so long, long ago."

I slowly shook my head. "You're speaking in circles," I sighed. "I hear your words, but they're not getting through."

"That's okay," he comforted. "Perhaps the time for understanding has not yet arrived. It will come when you are prepared for its acceptance. Things are not always what they seem. The murky ultimately becomes clear; the nebulous, defined."

I didn't respond, but would keep his words close to my heart.

We remained within a velvet silence for a long while before I softly whispered to the sky.

"I don't belong here."

The barely audible comment nearly blended in with the strains of the stream's lilting voice and the wind's sympathetic breath.

My companion turned. "Why?" he whispered.

I looked into the solemn eyes that had such depth.

"It wasn't really a statement...more of a private final conviction."

"And I wasn't really supposed to hear it."

"Not really."

"Are you sure?"

"No."

The Dreamwalker rested back into the bank grass. "I'm going to tell you something, Summer, and you don't have to say a word when I'm done. Just listen."

I made no sound.

"Long ago, the chosen wise ones from all civilizations prepared for the coming of the age of ignorance they foresaw entering. To carry out this massive task, they had to gather together all the precious articles of the sacred wisdom. They did this. They compiled papyri, tablets, artifacts, and scrolls. A wealth of treasure accompanied the articles of truth, and upon each continent, the wise ones of each race hid the sacred knowledge deep within the Earth Mother."

Sphinx　　　　　　　　*Mesa*　　　　　　　　*Pyramid*

Vivid frames of visions speared before my mind as the man spoke.

"These various wise ones were assisted in their monumental task by civilizations far beyond earth's. And they too added their own artifacts to the hidden caches."

194

The visions continued to flow unhampered.

"On this continent, the task was delegated to those of the Spirit Clan. They labored in tandem with the higher civilizations. And together did they create a complex catacomb...within a pyramid... beneath a towering mesa."

And I again saw the mesa that towered so forlornly within the Land of the Forgotten.

"The wise ones of the Spirit Clan kept secret the sacred hidden chambers beneath the burning place above. Through the centuries did this Clan dedicate itself to its preservation and total protection.

"Today several of this holy Clan have returned, but they are finding it nearly unbearable to coexist with those of the backward society that dwells upon the land—they feel they do not belong...but they do...more now than ever before."

It was a while before I found my voice.

"So you too feel the great aloneness. *You* are one of those, aren't you, Many Heart."

And when he turned his eyes to mine, no answer was necessary.

After allowing his narrative to warmly settle within my receiving heart, I realized that I needed much more time than a simple two more weeks together. I needed *months* more—I *wanted* months more.

"Can we have more time together?" I asked.

"The remaining time will be enough," he informed, softening the reply.

I didn't agree, but then who was I to contradict? "I haven't done well, have I?"

"What makes you think that?"

"Because it took me so long to reconcile my feelings of not belonging, because I've got so much more comprehending to do. There's so much that still eludes me and two more weeks just aren't going to do it."

"I told you, Summer. There are some things that only time can clarify. You don't *need* total comprehension for No-Eyes to close the circle behind you."

That made me feel somewhat better. "What is this circle you keep mentioning?"

He was very serious. "When you're at the threshold—when you're ready, No-Eyes will create a mystical atmosphere for you to walk within."

"What does this do?"

His eyes narrowed. "She has great power. You have seen some of it but never does she show all of it. She will work intently and, when it's completed, it will emit very strong medicine. She knows ancient, sacred ways...ways of the Spirit Clan."

"What ancient, sacred ways?"

His head tilted slightly. A brow raised. His voice came low and soft. "Think back, Summer."

He leaned forward and mysteriously whispered.

"Sequanu knows."

Through the awakened Spirit, the Eternal Mind suddenly shudders—it trembles and...it remembers.

Into the Smoke

One autumn daybreak, while reverently performing my solitary Sacred Rite of Benediction, I raised the Pipe to the eastern horizon just as the sun's first long rays stretched out over the distant mountain ridge.

The golden beams touched the Pipe . . . then my heart.

I looked up beyond the upheld Pipe and saw not the fiery sun, but a brilliant Bird of Light that was superimposed over the shining orb.

The magnificent Bird majestically unfolded its iridescent feathers—gracefully, they unfurled. They raised slowly. Royally, the massive wingspan reached out to touch both east and west horizons.

And the the Winged Being softly whispered out across the vast expanse of land. It breathed powerful words into my listening Spirit—words that etched deeply into my Soul.

"I live!" it mystically echoed. "Quetzalcoatl LIVES!"

Wedgewood sky. Skeletal aspens. Rustling leaves strewn across the deserted mountain road. Bitter changes. Chilling wind.

Many Heart was right. All week the wind spirit blew hard through the high country. It stripped away the golden garments of the joyful aspens, leaving only their chalky spines. The wide cottonwoods were blown bare, leaving their heads in a Medusa-like tangle of twisted branch twigs. Only the stately evergreens remained untouched, but their spirits braced for the bitterness that was soon to be.

As I made my trip out to No-Eyes' cabin, I thought how quickly the autumn color disappeared this year. I could remember other autumn seasons when it seemed the celebration went on for weeks and weeks. I remembered this because, out of all of nature's wondrous seasons, I loved autumn best and Bill and I would pleasure in taking long mountain hikes together. We'd sit in a remote forest and join in the celebration of color. But this year was different. It had come and gone within the flick of a squirrel's tail. And if it wasn't for my lessons with the Dreamwalker, I'd have thought I had been shortchanged.

I leisurely drove through the mountains that the season had so quickly opened up. Glancing through the deep woods along the roadside, I could now see farther into its heart. Naked aspens bravely stood in defense of their spirits. They were prepared for the icy breath of winter.

Ahead three elk nibbled. Heads bent low until the warning of my approach was given. Noses darted up into the wind. Sprinting deeper into the forest, their evasive zig-zag movements pleased me. "Better practice those," I whispered to my little friends. And the thought of the hunting season weighted my heart. It seemed that reality had many things I had to accept. Life was full of acceptance of those things we had no control over.

Gunmetal clouds began to blanket the sky with an ashen canopy. The mood of the woodlands became stark. Impressions came flooding in.

Tall teepees clustered amid nature's austere season. Smoke trailing up out of the smoke holes and hanging low in the icy air. Tethered horses, their breath wafting about their muzzles. Huddled, blanket-wrapped figures scurrying to and fro from one warm house to another. Purple mountains capped in white. Blue ice-encrusted ponds. Cold without. Serene and warm within.

The aged lodgepole welcomed us. The familiar landmark signalled the end of one journey and the beginning of another. I got out and breathed deeply. Crisp air caressed my senses. The fresh fragrance of the pine and spruce blend was as sweet as the earth after a rainfall. Although the vibrant colors were now gone, the delectable scents remained as pungent as ever.

Woodsmoke. It trailed up from out of the cabin. A warming fire was radiating the place with tranquility. I envisioned its interior as that of the teepees of my earlier vision. Warm orange glow, tender and sweet upon the contented faces of those within. I smiled with the peaceful thought and walked up the slope to join the friend I knew would be waiting inside.

When I opened the door, it was just as I had visualized it. The fire flames crackled sharply in the quietness. A gentle peacefulness permeated the small room.

Many Heart was in the tiny kitchen. He nodded. "Sort of a grey day out there. Too bad all the trees are nearly bare already."

"Yeah," I readily agreed, dropping the heavy serape onto the couch. "Its starkness is a statement, though."

"Its starkness makes more than one statement. Any one in particular you're singling out?" He had been making some hot tea and he came around with a steaming cup in each hand.

Taking the one he offered, I sat on the braid rug in front of the blaze.

"Oh," I smiled, "just that *all* of nature's faces have magical aspects. They're all mystical doors to me. I can take off through any one of them."

I glanced down at the cup of dark liquid. Pieces were beginning to settle to the bottom. I eyed him suspiciously.

"You haven't fixed me a 'No-Eyes' Special,' have you?"

He gritted his teeth with the insinuation. "She doesn't do that sort of thing."

I gave him a look of doubt. "Then what'd I drink before I met with Joe Red Sky? It wasn't Pepsi."

He shrugged. "I couldn't say for sure, but it wasn't any strong drug. It most likely was just a good relaxant—she really doesn't use any sort of drugs with her students. She doesn't believe in it. She refuses to journey in that manner."

He nodded toward my cup. "Go ahead, it's just a natural blend of mine."

Again I peered questioningly down into the mug.

"Want to switch?" he asked, offering me his. "I don't use that stuff either, but if it'll ease your mind, you can have mine."

"No," I said just before bringing the rim to my lips, "I believe you." Then, sipping on the hot drink, I praised its light flavor. "It's very good."

He nodded his appreciation of the compliment. "If you thought about it," he said, referring to my former experience with No-Eyes, "if she had given you a drug that day, her after drink couldn't have sharpened your senses so quickly."

"You're right. I never considered that."

"It's your job now to consider all facets of a situation."

"Is that a reprimand?"

"No, just a simple fact."

"I'll remember that simple fact."

My teacher was staring at me. His intensity made me somewhat uncomfortable.

"Is something the matter?" I asked.

"Should there be?"

"Then stop staring at me."

His expression remained solemn, but he turned his face toward the firelight.

"I'm sorry if I made you self-conscious. I was lost in thought."

I peered around at him. "Penny for your thoughts."

Dark eyes momentarily shifted to mine before returning to the firelight.

"I was thinking how nice this is here with you. You're very comfortable to be around."

I looked away into the shadows, then back to him. "Many Heart?"

"Mmmm."

"Do you mind if I ask you a question—a personal one?"

The man hesitated. "Go ahead."

"Do you have somebody? I mean, somebody special like a girlfriend or maybe a wife somewhere?"

Silence.

I had overstepped our friendship. "I'm sorry, you don't have to answer that."

His hand came up. "No. That's all right. No offense taken. I did have someone once, but things didn't work out. I suppose Dream-walkers are difficult to live with."

He looked at me.

"You're one of the rare fortunate ones who has someone who believes in you and is aware. You've got companionship along the way. Be good to him, Summer."

I felt sorry for my lonely friend. "I know what I've got," I assured. "I'm good to him."

My friend's mood was contagious. I felt a great sadness for him, but also one for myself.

"I don't know what I'd do if I was ever without him. He's been my anchor through all of this. He's always been at my side to offer support, protection, and love. We're like one person."

"That's so, but don't forget how supportive and loving you've been when he needed those same things. A matched relationship is equal sharing."

I wanted to turn the subject away from myself and back to him. "Do you have *any*one?"

"Oh, there's been a few here and there; however, nobody really special. I guess I move around too much for a solid, meaningful relationship."

"Couldn't you settle down in one location?"

He laughed at that. "What're you trying to do here, fix my love life?"

I blushed and looked down into the cup. Then I grinned at him. "Just trying to help."

My friend was grateful. "Well, I appreciate your concern, but I'm doing all right in that area. If that was a real problem," he chuckled lightly, "the old one or Red Sky would've had me fixed up long ago—or at least they'd still be trying."

He'd insinuated that No-Eyes had played matchmaker and I thought that was funny. I could easily envision her bringing 'round suitable girls for my friend. I grinned at the vivid picture of it.

Many Heart's eyes widened. "Oh! So you think that's funny, do you?"

I snickered behind my hand. "Yes. I can just see her having all kinds of girls here for you to meet."

He smiled wide. "Well," he finally admitted, "you're not far off.

Actually, she did try that a time or two."

I couldn't believe it. I laughed. "Oh no! What happened?"

"The girl was so afraid of me she never spoke a word the entire time No-Eyes shoved us together. This girl just mumbled and nodded whenever I asked her a question or tried to talk with her."

It was funny but, at the same time, it wasn't. I listened as he told me more about how many times the visionary had different "ladies" here for him.

"Did she finally give up?"

"She finally did because she got too disgusted with me," he said. "Yeah, she finally said that I was too picky."

"I can just see her saying that."

"Trouble was," he admitted, "she gave no attention to physical appearances. A man's got to like what he sees, at least a little bit, before he gets any serious thoughts about a lifelong commitment. But no, not her."

"Poor Many Heart," I crooned a bit too sympathetically.

His back straightened and the proud chin jutted out.

"Many Heart's not so poor."

I thought that I had bruised his tender manly ego. "I'm sure you've got someone very special somewhere."

He softened and eyed me suspiciously. "You think you injured my ego, don't you? Well, my friend, Dreamwalkers don't have egos. And as for any sort of manly machoism, well, that was shed long, long ago. I do have someone who understands my situation, but then again," he shrugged, "I too am a loner."

I had no adequate response to the statement that sobered our joy-ful moments. Our attention was turned to the fire while it blazed in the ancient stone fireplace. The snapping sounds were loud within the small cabin and the erratic shadows flickered wildly against the log walls.

The Dreamwalker reached down into his pocket and quickly threw something into the blaze. Vivid colors shot up the flue. Sparkles filled the hearth. Grey smoke billowed blue.

We watched.

The smoke curled back upon itself. It snaked. It twisted around with a pulsing life of its own. The fire hissed. Smoke swirled.

I slid my eyes to the solemn Dreamwalker.

His face concentrated on the eerie movements behind the hearth. Obsidian eyes watchful with high anticipation. Black glass orbs, intense with strong medicine. Hair like raven wings, lustrous with firelight. His power was a touchable presence. It caught my very breath to watch it. My heart drummed as I looked back to the bright flames.

Curling cobalt. Bending azure. Stretching indigo.

The colors were altering, becoming separated with distinctive outlines. The former murky nebulance was undulating into isolated forms. I watched in utter fascination as the images faded. They appeared to withdraw into the now solid indigo color.

I looked over to my companion.

He watched. He pointed to the smoke.

Slowly, my head turned to give the smoke my concentrated attention.

Out of the dark indigo background emerged a wavering bright powder blue smoke that shimmered. It rippled with energy.

I watched the pulsing swirl alter to a pure white color. It pulled into itself and formed an enormous white buffalo that raced and surged headlong across its windswept prairie. It halted suddenly, sliding, hooves dug into rising dust. It reared. High, it reared to expand itself into a tall and slender woman in white. Her mouth was moving. No sound emitted.

Caught up in the powerful intensity of the apparition, I leaned forward, straining to hear words that only the soul could discern.

The sensuous bow mouth moved. The large pleading eyes glistened with shed moisture. Slender arms raised. Delicate fingers extended out, then curled gracefully as the arms folded to her breast. Hair billowed to narrow hips. It billowed out across her face, around her form. She vanished.

The dark indigo smoke paused its heartbeat before pulsating again. I watched as the light-colored veil gathered unto itself once again. The undefined halo pulled and consolidated its density. It effortlessly labored to make its new transformation.

Right and left extensions stretched far out wide and lifted gracefully in a royal upswing of wings. The majestic feathered creature softly rippled the massive wings. It held a stance of waiting. It waited in absolute readiness. Then it fluttered. Smoke swirled around it like dust before a descending helicopter. It too retreated back into the main body of the undulating shroud.

Other living images rose up and out to present themselves before us. Each, in turn, represented breathing symbols of truth. They were spiritual representatives pulsating with messages of power. Ominously, they manifested and vanished back into the indigo source that undulated with Many Heart's magic. Each symbol white as the one preceding it—white with the mantle of truth.

A shimmering medicine pipe that expanded and narrowed with each of its sacred breaths. Encircling smoke rose gently from its engraved bowl. A rotating hoop, full of hanging eagle feathers, turned slowly around a starry universe. A tree, strong and tall, grew before my eyes. It grew and blossomed fruitfully until it encompassed the whole of the earth at its roots. A tablet emerged out of the indigo source. A tablet that broke in half as its evanescence separated. . .half hovered while its replica scattered into fragments of smoke—the missing and long-awaited pieces.

I intently concentrated on the emerging, then vanishing symbols. My enrapt eyes watched and my uplifted spirit listened to the spirit voices that were so sweet and clear. The voices were individually distinct, each speaking of the past, the future. Changes. Hope and eternal peace.

As`the indigo lightened, and the licking orange flames sent up their natural grey smoke once again, the magic slowly dissipated. The flames were again just flames. The smoke, merely smoke. But the atmosphere in the small cabin room was electrified.

I turned to my silent companion.

His eyes were closed. His hands were clenched into a knuckle-whitening fist. He was still within power.

I sat statue-still. I didn't dare move a muscle for fear of shattering his fragile state. I didn't blink an eyelid. My breathing was controlled so as not to disturb the gentle man of good medicine. My thoughts were on the undulating symbols. I knew what each had represented. I understood their individual messages, but not the Dreamwalker's reasoning for bringing them so visibly into the cabin. I would wait for his explanation for that when he returned. Meanwhile, I scanned the interior of my cozy home-away-from-home.

Everywhere I looked, I saw my sweet visionary. Her threadbare furnishings, her frayed rug. The wall cupboards so full of rich botanicals and private mixtures. The woodburning cookstove and pine-branch chairs. The rocker. God, I missed her.

A subliminal movement caught my eye. I looked down to my young teacher's hands—they were now relaxed. And, peering up into his serene face, I saw that his eyes were soft. A smile lifted the corners of his mouth. Firelight danced in eyes that came to settle upon mine.

"That was beautiful," I whispered.

He glanced back to the flames. "The mystical entities bring that beauty. Their aura of peace is what makes the rare beauty you saw there."

"But *you* brought them here," I said.

The Dreamwalker smiled at his confused student.

"No, Summer, I did not bring them here. They are independent entities. They are not subjugated to a medicine person's power to summons. The mystical entities appear only through their own wills."

"But after you threw that stuff into the flames, they began

appearing."

One palm upturned, then the other. "I merely set up the condition—the right one. *They* choose to appear or not. *They* make that prime distinction and ultimate decision."

I looked down at his wide hands. "What did you throw into the fire?"

"You liked that stuff?" he asked with a suppressed grin.

"Don't tease me," I smiled back. "I just wanted to know what that stuff was."

He leaned nearer to me and widened his black eyes. "Magic, Summer. It's pure magic!"

I chuckled and waved my hand at him. "No, go on, it's not." Then I sobered. "Is it?"

His laughter filled the room. It echoed into the darkened corners.

I frowned. "You're making fun of me." And I exaggeratedly emulated hurtfulness by bending my head low.

The uproarious laughter stopped. His hand gently touched my chin to raise it. His eyes were full of deep concern, then they twinkled brightly when he saw my feigned pout.

"You're terrible!" he bellowed playfully. "You should've gone to Hollywood and been an actress."

I flashed a Cheshire smile. "Serves you right," I snapped in fun, "you were laughing at me."

"No I wasn't," he softened. "I'd never do that to you."

"Then why'd you say that stuff was pure magic?"

"Because it *is*! Its substances are natural enough, but when properly combined, they *create* the right magical base. They create the *foundation* for the mystical occurrences to build on."

"I see. So what are these 'natural' substances?"

"Oh," he hedged, "a little ground rock, various flaked minerals, some powdered seeds, grains of this and that."

I squinted sarcastically. "I suppose that answer is intended to satisfy me."

He grinned. "No, but No-Eyes wants to go into this kind of thing with you. She's the one to thoroughly explain compounds."

"'Compounds?' Meaning more than one?"

"Yes, different mixtures for different purposes," he clarified, getting up to place fresh logs on the waning fire.

"Many Heart?" I called to his back.

"Yes?"

"What was the purpose for the entities' appearances?"

He pulled out a couple of smaller logs from the stockpile and held them aloft like trophies. "How's this? Applewood!"

I nodded pleasingly. "Mmmm!" I loved the fragrance of its burning wood. "Red Sky must've brought that for her." Then I frowned with a new restraining thought. "Maybe we should save them for No-Eyes."

"Nahhh," he muttered amusingly, "she doesn't care for them."

I was surprised. "Then why does he bring them?"

He strategically positioned the logs and returned to sit on the floor. "She doesn't want to hurt his feelings."

I just shook my head. That was so typical of her sensitivity.

The thick fruit branches soon caught with the surging rage of flames and a new scent drifted through the room. I repeated my former question.

"So, what was the purpose of the entities' appearances?"

"Solace."

Silence.

"Summer, they came out of compassionate concern for our frequent feelings of aloneness. They appeared as companions-in-hand as we tread the lonely path of the Way. They appeared to assure us that we're never alone in our purpose, for *our* purpose is also *their* pathway to man—their ultimate recognition."

My teacher had started out simple enough, but simplicity soon drifted into deep complexity. My brows furrowed.

"*Our* purpose is *their* pathway? Pathway *to* what? *From* what?"

"WHO! *Who*, Summer. From WHO! From the Forebearer, through hope to peace."

I tossed my hair back from my face. "We're talking about *mystical* entities here," I reminded, trying to untangle the mess.

He simply nodded. "That's right."

I hesitated out of innocent uncertainty. "I don't get it. *Who's* a Forebearer?"

Silence. Thick silence. A single brow rose.

I stared at his questioning countenance. "I'm really sorry, Many Heart, I must be totally addle-brained today, but I'm not making any connections between this stuff."

Shoulders rose and fell indifferently. "Then your time's not right yet."

I thought that response was a little too clipped. "Then why can't you explain it so I do understand?"

He was visibly sympathetic. "Because, Summer, if you haven't already made the proper connections, then you're not to the right point of acceptance yet—you'd resist."

"Resist what?"

"What's meant to *be*. What's meant to *come*."

I didn't care for the hard finality that crept into his ominous tone. I left it be.

"Thank you for setting up the condition. I was fascinated by the mystical beings. Thanks for the opportunity to see them. I'm grateful for their comfort."

He reconciled to my sudden change of subject matter and clutched onto the threads of my new one.

"You're very welcome, Summer. Yet you don't need my magical compound for those beautiful entity sights."

I knew what he was talking about. "Yes, I know that, but I don't talk about those."

His voice was gentle with sensitivity. "You don't talk about those with *others,* you mean."

I bowed my head. This time the gesture was not feigned.

"Summer, I'm not *anyone*."

"I know that. I know you'd understand."

He bent forward, elbows on knees. Face close to mine.

"I *also* hear them. I see and I am open to their wisdom. Summer, nature is full of mysteries, mystical occurrences and unexplainable enigmas. We, as Dreamwalkers, do not resist that which comes so naturally to those who are open to receive such communications. We are too in tune. We simply know of their existence and gently do we accept their tender reality."

I slowly raised my head to gaze into his soft eyes. I saw there undulating reflections cast by the living fire. I saw within the lustrous black glass reflected images of the Great Winged Being, a Woman, a Sacred Tree. I saw them all, and, looking out, They saw me.

I am never alone.

Within the woodland depths where lances of shimmering sunrays spear down through the jade and emerald greenery, my hearing perceives the hushed rush of air from Its brilliant, miniature wings as they silently rise and fall.

I turn not to the delicate Entity that softly alights upon my receiving shoulder, for the gentle breath that whispers Its ageless Wisdom does breathe exquisite visions behind my eyes. The Butterfly Being is always and ever a truly welcomed and frequent companion along the woodland wayside.

I am never alone.

Within the ebony forest shadows of the deep alpine night, there is never Darkness surrounding me, for existing within the velvety Black-

ness, like dancing fireflies, the living Lights come to flicker about me. Always there are companions.

I am never alone.

Night of the Dreamwalker

I have sailed the turbulent, savage Seas.
I have drifted the stifling, glassy Doldrums.
I have had my sails billow full to dock alongside both Shores.
And now, now I am content, for now I sail the Tranquil Sea—the
Sea Without Shores.

The weekdays rushed by with the blurring speed of a shooting star. It was now late Friday evening and the girls were in bed. Bill and I sat in the living room, talking. He expressed concerns over the books I'd promised the visionary I'd do.

"You're going to have to be awfully careful," he warned. "People are going to misconstrue a lot of things. They're going to take things out of context and zero in on them like a shark to blood."

I hadn't given it much thought before this because the actual writing of them hadn't begun yet. I considered his premise.

"Can't I just tell it like it is?"

He gave me a dubious look. "Nobody would believe it. To the unaware, it'd be too incredible."

I disagreed. "Oh, come on. There's thousands of people who have paranormal functioning. There's thousands who've had spiritual experiences, not to mention the ones who just plain believe in them. There's all kinds of aware people out there."

He frowned. "There's also all kinds of wackos."

"What does that mean?"

"I just mean that a heck of a lot of people will want to scream 'witch' or something stupid like that. People can be unbelievably ignorant when it comes to the real basic spiritual realities. They right away think your abilities come from the devil or something evil."

My mouth dropped a mile. "That's the most ridiculous thing I've ever heard! Spiritual abilities are *God*-given—they're precious and beautiful!"

"I know that and you know that, but the self-righteous religious fanatics don't quite see the real truth to the matter. Look," he emphasized, "I'm just saying that you're going to have to be real careful when you write them, that's all."

I was shocked at his thinking. Surely, even the fanatics knew of God's beautiful spirit gifts...or did they? I couldn't see how anyone believing in God couldn't also understand His precious gifts of talents because they so naturally went hand-in-hand.

"I can't compromise the truth," I said. "I won't purposely cut corners or smooth over the rough spots. I can't make it out to be anything less than it is."

He shook his head. "You'll be asking for it then. The general public just doesn't understand the paranormal. And what about the Indian way?"

"What about it?" I asked defensively.

"You're not going to include the journeys you've had with No-Eyes, are you? And Joe Red Sky, how're you going to explain your meeting with him?"

Instead of the pot boiling over, I remained surprisingly cool.

"Yes, I'm going to write about my journeys with No-Eyes and Many Heart. I won't write about all of them, just the main ones. And I'll explain about Joe Red Sky by going through the whole thing again, only on paper this time. The Indian way is sacred. It's been saturated with deep spirituality and ancient prophecies for centuries. The Indian way has preserved the sacredness of mysticism and natural powers since long before the ignorant Anglos showed up on the scene.

"The ignorance or narrow-mindedness of people can't ever negate that which has been proven over and over again for centuries. I'm going to write it all down just the way it happened."

He couldn't convince me otherwise. "Well, for heaven's sake then, watch your wording, watch your choice of words. One wrong choice could give people an entirely off-the-track impression." His premise was a valid one.

"I'll watch the wording, but I'm still not altering what was said," I promised with a contingency. "The books will be no good at all if I change things just to save face. They've got to be as accurate as possible...as near as I can remember everything."

He knew in his heart I was right; otherwise, the books would have no purpose. He knew that because of my promise to the visionary, I wouldn't dare to alter the events because of the skeptics' reactions. He knew I'd never compromise the truth for any of them.

And I knew that, although I was going to expose my soul to all the world, I'd do it with a chin held high.

We retired to bed that night with opposing emotions. His were those of concern for the one he deeply loved. Mine were those of a peacefulness in the anticipation of carrying out a promise to a gentle, old woman. I was also filled with mixed emotions regarding tomorrow—my final day with the Dreamwalker. I had come to love him.

It was a deep platonic sort of loving, for his warm companionship and easy way were a comfort. His wisdom and understanding were intense, and I'd learned a great deal of comprehension from being in his warm company.

Then again, my heart yearned for the old one. I didn't really know if this last day was anticipated or dreaded. Either way, I'd lose one friend and regain another. And I fell asleep dearly wishing I could keep them both.

Golden rays slanted in through the woven slats of the bedroom blinds. I watched the scattered dust motes that lazily floated in the morning light.

Today was the day. Today was my final day with the Dreamwalker. How had I done? I didn't dwell on that aspect because, however I had done, it was too late for changes now. I couldn't retract our heated argument. I couldn't unslam the door. However I'd done was now a finality. No apologies. No excuses. I'd accept the decree knowing I'd honestly done my best.

I turned my head to gaze at my slumbering partner. He was far away.

I sighed and thought about our conversation the night before. Yes, I had an obligation to simply tell it like it is and I knew I could count on my sleeping mate to stand tall beside me. I'd never have to physically go it alone. And I gently kissed him.

The light in the room brightened. It was well past the time to get ready. I quietly slipped from the bed and, gathering up my clothes, I left the peaceful sleeper.

It came while I was dressing. It stealthily crept into my stomach and stayed there. Nerves quivered. Butterflies fluttered. My hands trembled.

What was I so nervous about? Was it because, after today, I'd never see Many Heart again? Was it because today I might learn of how I'd really done? I couldn't pinpoint the cause for my physical reactions to the psychic forewarning.

I pulled out of the drive and as I glanced toward the wood slab-covered house, I wondered how I'd feel when I returned to it in the late afternoon. I wondered if I'd feel any different. One thing I did know for sure, and that was my deep appreciation for the warm Indian summer day.

It had been depressingly grey all week which, in itself, was an unusual occurrence for Colorado. Now I was happy that the skies were once again such a clear and vivid blue. As I looked up into it, I smiled, for it was like setting lonely eyes on a long-lost friend.

I nosed the pickup out onto the highway. Today I wasn't in any hurry, and I drove leisurely so as to prolong the finality that was a mere few hours away.

How would we say farewell? Could I even begin to show him how grateful I was for all his patient efforts on my behalf? Maybe I should've brought him some little parting gift. Hadn't he given me a wondrous gift? The rough crystal was safely protected inside my medicine bundle.

I envisioned the different parting scenarios that could take place. My stomach churned. Oh, how I hated final farewells. Would we hug or just shake hands? Would he have a special rite to perform? What would we talk about today, knowing it was to be our last together?

The lodgepole loomed before me. My heart thundered to see it. How had I gotten here so soon? I didn't even remember driving the distance. I shoved the gearshift in PARK and sat to compose myself.

The stomach churnings continued. The heart fluttering persisted with a vengeance. I rested my arms up on the steering wheel and stared up at the place on the hill.

My scalp crawled. Damn! What was it? I'd never know if I remained frozen to the truck all day.

I left the pickup and stood before it. I studied the little cabin for one last minute before slowly taking my time in ascending the sloping rise.

Head down, I watched my dusty moccasins take one slow step after another. They advanced in slow motion. One step. Two. Three and four. I was agonizingly prolonging the parting that was now inevitable.

With that sudden realization, I halted. And looking up again toward my destination, I reasoned that I really should be hurrying so we'd ultimately have more valued time together. We'd make our remaining hours golden.

Now I inhaled a deep breath of the high mountain air and broke into a run. I raced up the hill and stormed through the door.

"Summer gonna break that door yet!" came the unexpected cackle.

I froze.

"Don't break that *door!*"

"NO-EYES!" And with streaming tears, I ran to my frail friend.

Her gums gleamed pink with her wide, welcoming smile. Sightless eyes brimming, her arms outstretched for me. We hugged and I cried like a baby. The churnings and flutterings were gone; they were replaced by the thundering sound of a drumming heart. And time stood still.

I wanted to hug the daylights out of her. I was so happy, so excited to see her again.

"No-Eyes gonna get *crushed,*" she mumbled into my smothering serape.

I pulled away and smoothed down the white hair that I had mussed. I tenderly combed it down with my fingers.

The old one wiped her eyes with my wrap.

"No-Eyes say she not gonna do this dumb cryin' stuff when she see Summer again. No-Eyes say she be too old for silly stuff like that."

"Crying's not silly, No-Eyes. It's an honest and tender way to show deep feelings." I gently wiped her cheek. "It shows how much one cares."

"Guess No-Eyes care plenty." She reached up to feel my eyes. "Guess Summer do too."

I smiled warmly. "Yes, I care very much."

And that was the end of the silliness, for she shot her hand out to point at the two full cups on the wooden table.

"Tea's all cold now," she barked.

She didn't fool me, though. She was just trying to harden herself so she could break away from the incredibly sensitive moment.

"Now No-Eyes gotta brew up more," she bitterly complained.

It was music to my ears. The complaining and the barking, the cackled reprimands about the door were simply beautiful music to my ears.

I helped her reheat the water. We sat on the pine branch chairs in the kitchen.

"By the way," I began, "where's Many Heart?"

Wispy white brows arced. "He not here."

I could see that. "Where is he?"

"He gone. He say Summer be all done."

Silence.

Head cocked. "What the matter?"

"Well. . .I thought this was to be our last day together. He never insinuated that there was a sudden change in plans."

"Summer sorry for that sudden change?"

I wasn't sorry as much as being worried. "I'm sorry we didn't get to say goodbye. I'm worried that something went wrong."

The old one clucked her tongue. "Tsk-tsk. That Many Heart, he never say goodbye—he be Dreamwalker. And what make Summer think some stuff be wrong anyway?"

"Because we never finished."

She leaned over the table to me. Eyes squinted.

"Who *say* Summer not be *finished?*"

I took the double-meaning word at its worst. "Am I 'finished,' No-Eyes?"

Silence. The visionary closed her eyes, rested back in the chair and drank her tea. She understood my meaning.

The silence was killing me. I spoke softly. "No-Eyes?"

"Mmmm?"

"Am I finished?"

"Yup."

My heart plunged.

"Summer be all *finished* with Many Heart. . . but she got ways to *go* with No-Eyes."

My heart soared. If this heart-stopping strain kept up for much longer, I was certain to go into ventricular fibrillation.

I sighed with relief. "Don't *scare* me like that, No-Eyes. My heart can't take it."

An elfin grin of mischievousness crept up the corners of her mouth. "Summer deserve that," she chided, "Summer deserve to be scared for thinkin' so wrong."

"How was I to know?" I groaned.

A bony finger tapped her thin chest. "Here," she whispered, "in here Summer always know."

"But I didn't," I confessed.

"Blah!" she spat. "That cause Summer to mess up true feelings with bad worries in head. Summer block out that true stuff."

I stood rightly corrected. I had worried far too much. "You're right," I sighed. "That's exactly what I did."

The old one suddenly trembled.

"Are you cold?"

"We gonna go sit in sun now."

She rose from the chair and picked up her blanket shawl from the rocker. We resumed our discussion out in the warming sunlight that bathed the weathered porch.

She raised her pixie face to the sun and heavily sighed.

"This be so, so good. It be late for such goodness."

"Yes," I agreed, "we've got Indian summer for a few days before the real cold blows in."

The woman was deeply pensive. I wondered if she was considering how many wintercounts were left to her.

The seasonal respite brought a scent of warmness to the air. It was a good scent that made the body feel warm inside, especially after the week-long stretch of chilled air and pallid skies. My wrap hung heavily on my shoulders; still, it was just enough covering for the lateness of the season.

I cast my sights out toward the surrounding woodlands and caught the passing movement of a mountain bluebird. It quickly disappeared into the forest depths just as my aged companion began to speak.

The old one spoke tenderly of many things that Indian summer day. She delved deeply into past-life experiences that I'd draw on to give me faith in the present. We discussed several of my more recent dreams and I listened intently while she wisely explained their more subtle meanings. We spoke of the present despondency and apathetic state of our people and I sat in fascination while she unraveled the mystical side of the events which were to lead to our dramatic changes and rebirth as a strong nation again. The simplistic ignorance of the skeptics was gone into. The spiritual powers of the Way—the sacred Way, were clearly examined. Magic—true magic of nature's natural laws was covered. Natural phenomena and the paranormal gifts of the Great Spirit were fully discussed.

We had traversed a great deal of meaningful ground that lazy afternoon of the Indian summer. By the time the subject matters drew to a close, the sun had lowered behind the western ridges. Dusk was upon us.

"We gonna go get some hot tea now," the old one informed as she rose from the splintered porch and straightened her creaking back bones.

I glanced at the alpenglow spreading over the mountainside.

"It's getting late, No-Eyes."

The times that I had tarried until evening hours were infrequent. The times that I had stayed late into the night were even more of a rarity. And I hadn't informed the family that this was my intention this night.

When No-Eyes heard my comment, she casually waved it away.

"He gonna know Summer be okay. He not gonna worry 'bout Summer this night."

I had known her long enough to believe her. I smiled. "Let's go get that tea."

Inside, the cabin was darkening at an incredibly swift rate. I lit the oil lantern on the kitchen table. The soft glow scattered the darkness into the corners. It reflected upon the old one's time-etched face and compassionately softened the pain-filled crevices. She appeared more youthful.

Our silence was a loving thing. It felt so warm and right sitting with her here like this. I loved the special way the wick flame flickered within the ebony pools of her eyes. Blackboard eyes…full of wisdom that was written within, stared at me from across the table.

In the two years I'd been with her, I hadn't even begun to tap her deep well of wisdom. I was the struggling fledgling who had just recently come into the amazing knowledge that it could fly. I was still the baby bird with fluff on its wings.

"Summer gonna fly off one day," came the whispered softness. "Summer gonna leave No-Eyes' nest to fly high. All alone she gonna do this. Nobody ever gonna be able to clip Summer's wings."

I looked over at her. I had the inclination to contest her words, to have her explain them and expand on them, but I thought better of it. Instead, I remained silent.

The old one suddenly scraped back her chair across the pine floor.

"We gonna go somewheres now," she announced.

I got up and placed the cups on the counter. "Where are we going?"

"Out there," she mumbled, inclining her head to the blackness that filled the windows.

Although the day had been blessedly warm and lovely, the Indian summer had come late in the season. November was only hours away and the mountain evening would be breathing a winter's breath. With this in mind, I searched around the cabin for her heavier serape. I found it hanging in the crude bathroom.

"Better put this on," I said, placing it in her hands.

She lifted the woven fabric over her shoulders, popped her head through the opening and dropped the woolen weight.

"There," she cackled, "Summer happy now?"

"No, not quite," I smiled, seeing she had the wrap on backward. "You need a slight adjustment." Then I proceeded to make it right.

The old one fussed at me. "Who gonna see No-Eyes but owls an' ferrets? *They* gonna know old woman got blanket on all backwards?"

"Maybe," I kidded, "they're pretty smart little wise guys," I said, smoothing down the fabric. "There, you look real nice and cozy in there."

"Humph," came the grumble as she grabbed up her hiking stick from behind the door and strode out into the chilling night air.

I let her pass after realizing that I probably wouldn't be returning to the cabin with her, and I went into the kitchen to blow out the lantern—she wouldn't be needing it.

"What you *doing* in there?" she shouted from the blackness of night.

"I'm coming. I'm coming," I said, closing the door gently so I wouldn't break it.

When I came up beside her, she had her nose into the night breeze. "Gonna rain tomorrow."

I gazed up into the starry heavens. Not a cloud was visible. The air was dry.

"You sure about that?" I asked as we began walking away.

"Yup, No-Eyes be sure."

"There's no haze around the moon," I hinted. "It's clear."

The visionary didn't take her eyes off the moonlit ground.

"I no care. Tomorrow it gonna rain, it gonna rain hard too!"

We carefully descended the weedy hillside that was covered in the tall dead growth of the season. It was rocky in spots and our footing had to be well placed. Sharp rocks and moccasins were an uncomfortable union. Finally, reaching the soft earth of the forest floor, we entered the silvery woodlands. We walked a ways before I realized that No-Eyes had missed the trailhead to her footpath.

"We passed the trail," I informed, stopping to peer around in the moonlit shadows.

The woman shuffled on.

"No-Eyes?"

Shuffle. Shuffle. Tap-tap went the staff. The old one was deep in thought.

I scampered up to her and peered around into her face. She closed her eyes. Then they opened, only to gently close again. Onward she trudged.

Should I tell her again?

"Summer," came a raspy whisper.

"I'm here."

"Summer gonna do them books?"

"Of course," I assured, still worrying over the missed course.

The woman said nothing while veering off through a stand of spectral aspens. Heavy brush pulled at my legs. I'd never been this way before and wondered if the visionary had. Was she simply wandering through her woods?

"You gotta accept stuff," she stated.

"What sort of stuff, No-Eyes?" I asked, pushing a branch away from my face.

"Some peoples gonna react funny to them books, Summer. Peoples gonna think all kinds of stuff Summer not agree with." She expertly ducked a low-hanging branch that I hadn't seen. "Some gonna get funny ideas."

Strains of Bill's former concerns played through my mind.

"Like what?"

We were ascending a rise in the forest. Our pace quickened.

"Like stuff peoples think Summer need to do. They gonna think Summer need to talk an' talk much. They think Summer need to go here, go there."

We crested the rise.

"Summer, remember your work be the books an' letters. That all Summer s'posed to do. Later, there gonna be other kind of work, but that not be for peoples. That other work gonna be more important than peoples even...it gonna be for them lost spirits."

I sniffed the air. I was going to comment on the new scent, but she wasn't finished. We went deeper into the night woods.

"Peoples gonna say Summer be so alone. They gonna set Summer way apart an' try to make you be somethin' you not be. They gonna say much stuff. Some gonna say Summer be some great somebody who they been wait'n for." She paused. "Some peoples gonna be right...some gonna be wrong."

"Well? Which is which?"

"That not gonna matter. That right an' wrong stuff that peoples say not gonna matter to Summer. It not gonna be important 'cause you be too busy with purpose of spirit."

There it was again. I stopped beneath a sheltering pine to test the air.

My companion halted and turned to solemnly peer up at me.

I looked into her eyes.

The rising moon inched out behind the towering treetops. Silver light flooded down.

"We're not just idly meandering around, are we," I said with a thundering heart.

She made no reply. She simply turned and shuffled forward.

In the quietness of the high mountain forest, I heard the gentle rippling. I smelled the water of the pond that was centered in the dell of her private sacred ground. And my heart raced along with my soaring spirit.

Ahead, the wise one had stopped. When I came up beside her, I could see what she had been looking into. The pond shimmered with the magical touch of silvery moonlight. It appeared like a mystical bowl of swirling mercury. The surround of protective evergreens stood as sentinels that guarded the high holy place and its sacred mystical aura.

I stared in awestruck wonder at how the essence of night had transformed the area into a visual power point. Its vibrating force rippled through my receiving senses.

No-Eyes looked deep into my eyes.

"Summer's own land gonna feel like this," she whispered.

I stared into her black obsidian orbs that had trapped a stray moonbeam. It reflected pinpoints of translucent light...her eyes literally glowed. And, for just a magical moment, she was one of the mystical beings that had appeared in Many Heart's powerful smoke.

The beam passed on. No-Eyes returned unto herself. She stepped toward the mercurial waters.

I followed.

Magic was afoot.

The woman of vision stood beside the shimmering moonlit pond. Slowly, ceremoniously raising her arms up to the heavenly canopy above, her chin lifted proudly. She whispered to the sky. And silvered light speared down to anoint her long, free-flowing tresses.

Then, lowering her arms, they outstretched to pause on a level plane with the water's glimmering surface. She gazed out across its prismatic glass. Again she whispered a prayer before lowering her eyes to peer intently into its depths. Her voice was low, almost chanting.

"Hear me, Ancient Ones. Listen to the words of No-Eyes. Here stands Summer Rain...one of your blood...last who come from the Spirit Clan. Welcome this one as your sister. She is Spirit Woman."

The aged visionary's eyes shifted to meet mine. They were exceptionally clear. Her voice was soft, loving...yet gravely solemn.

"Come beside me, Summer. Come. Look into the sacred waters. Come see your new reflection. There," she mysteriously whispered, pointing down over the shimmering surface that mirrored the moon, "look with a new and clear sight. See what Summer Rain has *become*. Look to your *true* heritage."

With a wildly pounding heart, I hesitantly looked into the aged visionary's wizened eyes. They were wide orbs reflecting lights of ageless wisdom. They twinkled and danced, yet they clearly bespoke an irreversible finality—a deep seriousness more grave than I had ever seen.

I softly stepped up beside her stately form and immediately felt the electrified aura pulsate with unbridled power. She had created the mystical surround Many Heart had spoken of.

Slowly did I turn my head and lower my eyes to gaze into the swirling phosphorescent waters that were made mercurial by silvered moonbeams and her consummate magic.

Slowly did I observe the undulating symbols and perceive their exquisite meanings.

And, slowly did the mystical aura close in behind me, forever encircling me, forever remaining a living reminder of who I am...and what is to be.

Within the still waters of the high mountain pool, I gaze down into the clear reflection that is mirrored upon its obsidian moonlit surface.

I see there a pulsing universe, vast and wide. I see many such universes, for containing boundaries are nonexistent. A slowly rotating Medicine Wheel, its symbols most exquisite, mystically turns...its core a vibrant blue and green living earth.

A regal Thunderbird. Flaming Mesas. Crystal streams coursing through verdant woodlands. Multicolored prisms of snow-capped mountain peaks.

I see there within the midnight pool, an aged woman whose time-etched lines trail outward from clear eyes that have scanned the eons of time.

A brilliant blue Stone. Whispering pines. Ancient Tablets.

I see wondrous secrets, magic, and power that still must remain unspoken—remaining cherished within the tender heart. And I perceive bitter future sorrows that must be bravely shouldered.

A running Buffalo. A smoking Pipe. A beckoning Woman.

Sequestered articles of ancient Wisdom. A hidden Pyramid.

Within the still waters of the high mountain pool, I gaze down into the clear reflection that is mirrored upon its obsidian moonlit surface. And, woven within the shimmering multiple exposure of images...I see myself.

I have come full Circle. For me, the Hoop is closed.

For I have seen and touched the Four Directions and greatly did I suffer through many wintercounts at each wondrous Point.

The Four Directions are within me, for when I look within and when I look without, I perceive the resplendent beauty of the great living Medicine Wheel.

Some say I am alone. They believe I am an island—solitary, solidly anchored amid the savage sea of mankind. They say I am the bright beacon that pierces the grey opaqueness that fogs their lives.

But I don't know about all they say, for I make no such claims.

I simply walk in the beauty that abounds upon the sweet Earth Mother. I merely listen to that which is voiced on the gentle wind, to the wisdom nature does whisper. And I offer my simple prayers and have acceptance of all that is.

I pray that I may tread gently through this life. I pray that my worn and tattered moccasins have left soft footprints across the paths of many. And I pray that my fellow travelers do not strive to follow my trailing imprints, but rather that they glance down now and then along the way and simply take note of my passing.

I don't know about all they say, for I say that I am simply me...just me.